The Fall of the
House of Windsor

The Fall of the
House of Windsor

NIGEL BLUNDELL
AND
SUSAN BLACKHALL

CONTEMPORARY
BOOKS
CHICAGO

Cover design by Graeme Andrew

Published by Contemporary Books, Inc.
180 North Michigan Avenue, Chicago, Illinois 60601
Manufactured in the United States of America
International Standard Book Number: 0-8092-3770-9

This book is dedicated to true friends –

and all those who dared to speak the truth.

CONTENTS

The Fall of the
House of Windsor

Introduction

Elizabeth Alexandra Mary, Her Majesty Queen Elizabeth II, by the grace of God, of the United Kingdom of Great Britain and Northern Ireland, and of her other realms and territories Queen, Head of the Commonwealth, Defender of the Faith ... and also, as it happens, probably the wealthiest woman on earth. Trained from childhood to be heir to the throne she has been a queen for almost four decades. From the evidence offered by opinion polls among her subjects she is probably the most popular monarch in history. By any standard, her reign has been a personal success story for this unique woman who, apart from being head of the Church of England, is at the same time national ruler, international figurehead, business empress, proficient politician, supreme diplomat and dynastic matriarch. Should we be surprised, then, if it were all about to end?

Despite rearing a large and proliferating family; despite raising the best-trained, most caring heir to her throne; despite being blessed with a future queen bearing the best-known face on this planet; despite unimaginable wealth, power, prestige and majesty the dynasty is even now doomed.

That such is the case *should* be no surprise. The institution of monarchy is increasingly regarded as a dinosaur in this modern world. It survives in its truest form only among pockets of less-developed societies. Among most so-called First World nations, monarchy endures only as a veneer, part of the panoply of state, a constitutional device, a face on a postage stamp.

Yet, uniquely in the United Kingdom of Great Britain and Northern Ireland, it has retained a prestige as profound as it is mysterious. It is a prestige forged by the formidable character of Queen Elizabeth herself. Her rock-solid belief in the institution she represents has enabled it to withstand assault better than any other recent monarchy. It has survived through a mixture of affection and pragmatism, awe and apathy. It can survive anything ... except ridicule and contempt.

Today, the stinging barbs of ridicule and the slow cancer of contempt are being directed at the Royal Family by a far-from-fawning public and press. The old pomp and circumstance have become pantomime. The idols have stepped from their pedestals. So long protected by the Queen from damaging controversy, the Royal Family is now embroiled in it. Scandal dogs the House of Windsor and, tragically, scandal is one thing it cannot surmount. The result may be the previously unthinkable. As the broadcasting pundit, historian and author Ludovic Kennedy said on television after a scandal-ridden start to 1992: 'The monarchy's days are really over. The Queen will ensure it survives as long as she does, but after that I fear the worst.'

*   *   *

When she came to the throne, the Queen inherited royal standards and a lifestyle that had changed little since the beginning of this century. She soon proved that she was as great a traditionalist as her forebears. Like her father, King George VI, and her grandfather, King George V, she has adhered to the old adage of Victorian historian Walter

Bagehot, that 'You should never allow too much daylight in upon the magic of the monarchy'. Both Bagehot and Her Majesty have regularly been proved right. Throughout the early years of the Queen's reign she was able to shield most of the misdeeds of her growing family from public gaze. Times have changed, however, and allowing the new breed of royals to reveal human frailty has shaken a prestigious dynasty that was once believed to be unshakeable.

Some still regard the Royal Family as part of a rich tradition, jealously guarded by its people and much envied by other countries. Others see it simply as a family company, destined to pass into the hands of royal offspring for the rest of time. The British monarchy is undoubtedly a very big business, with the Queen not only as chairperson but also a very active 'hands-on' chief executive. There are lesser executives and honorary 'board members' aplenty. The big difference between the monarchy and the world of business, however, is that there is no formal training to become a member of Royalty Incorporated, and in the case of those commoners who have married into the Royal Family, recent years have shown that training to be sadly needed. The acceptance of those with anything but royal blood flowing through their veins must now be seen as a clumsy attempt at opening an élite club to those who could never meet the membership requirements.

Today's younger royals enjoy a freedom as never before. This means that the older, established ones have had to come to terms with modern living and all the threats that presents to the very fabric of what the royals, their servants and their courtiers call simply 'the Firm'. Sometimes that fabric is rent asunder; by weakness, exploitation, sex, greed or gargantuan errors of judgement, all traits, it was hoped, that had been quashed with the abdication of Edward VIII.

To the Queen's great chagrin, everything she had worked to achieve throughout her reign began to collapse around her ears as the younger royals turned the 'daredevil eighties' into the 'damning nineties'. Day by day she learned from the press how her children had been disporting themselves. In the language of the tabloids, her son, Prince 'Randy Andy' Andrew, had romped with a porn-star mistress before marrying his raunchy new wife. Her foppish youngest son, Edward, had tearfully fled his royal regiment before being accused of homosexual tendencies. 'Sensible' daughter Anne was cheated on by her husband for the delights of a one-night stand.

Worse, Charles's suitability as the future king came into question. He was increasingly portrayed as a man who, while showing public concern for the environment, was cold, distant and bullying in private. Many believed he had even become prematurely senile. Meanwhile, his wife, Diana, became the focus of the most shocking revelations to rock the Royal Family since the abdication crisis of the thirties. Far from being destined to share the throne with her husband, she grew unable to bear sharing even a few minutes alone with him. Driven to seek psychiatric help, Diana is said to have attempted suicide several times. Not only was the marriage of the heir and his wife exposed as a sham but the entire image of the royals as a united family was also revealed as a hypocritical façade. The myth that has sustained the Royal Family for centuries was suddenly but irretrievably shattered.

Taking the saga of the modern Royal Family out of the language of the popular press does nothing to sanitise their behaviour. In the 1990s, critics of the monarchy say it has passed its sell-by date. With the stinging plot lines of divorce, jet-set lives, displays of smug wealth and sometimes downright bad taste, the Royal Family has unwittingly transformed itself into a second-rate soap opera. Package the events of the last few years and one ends up with a long-running series that is sometimes hard to consider credible.

*   *   *

It did not seem destined to be so as the new Elizabethan Age began in 1952. King George VI, shy, sometimes uninspired, but popular with his people, died in his sleep at Sandringham at the age of 56. Two days later, on 8 February, Princess Elizabeth returned with Philip from a tour of Kenya and was proclaimed queen. The nation, as the cliché goes, rejoiced. Such clichés were to be the order of the day as post-war Britain forgot the recent gloom and celebrated the accession to the throne of their beautiful new monarch. As plans went ahead for her coronation at Westminster Abbey on 2 June 1953, the symbolic importance of Elizabeth's accession was best summed up by BBC commentator Richard Dimbleby, whose devotion to the Royal Family was often mistaken for sycophancy. In a contemporary broadcast, he told the world: 'The monarchy has long since become our way of life. For us it means justice, respect for the rights of the individual and freedom. The freedom flourishes best, it seems, where there is a monarchy, where there is at the head of affairs one person willing to sacrifice herself entirely to the good of her people.'

The awesome responsibility for maintaining this all-embracing institution rested on very young, very frail and very inexperienced shoulders. With the death of her father, his place as adviser and wise counsellor was immediately filled by the Buckingham Palace courtiers who rather too accurately refer to themselves as 'the Firm'.

The trouble is that 'the Firm' is an élite club of courtiers (almost all of them from Eton public school) who have totally blocked the Queen from the realities of the modern world. Her Majesty's crippling shyness, inherited from her grandmother, Queen Mary, has done nothing to prevent her from cutting herself off from her people. At the same time, she lacks the confidence to impose herself on the 'toadies, stuffed shirts and jobs-worth bureaucrats' at Buckingham Palace, as one senior establishment figure referred to them. The problem is that the Queen relies heavily on her court, comprised as it is of people with very little idea of what goes on in the outside world. Royal observer and genealogist Hugh Massingberd once described them as 'a pretty uninspiring and unimaginative crew', adding that the Queen and her family 'have shown an uncanny knack of befriending the least attractive elements of the upper classes'.

There's nothing new about such criticism of the Royal

Family. In 1957, the late Malcolm Muggeridge wrote an article in the *Saturday Evening Post* which caused a furore at the time. It posed the question: 'Does England Really Need a Queen?' Voicing the then-unspeakable, he criticised the monarchy for being snobbish, obsolete and disadvantageous. Nowadays such an attack would pass almost unnoticed but in 1957 Muggeridge received a barrage of letters containing vituperative abuse, obscene threats and even human excrement.

No similarly electric debate was elicited again for 23 years. Then, on 10 February 1991, *The Sunday Times* devoted its leader column to a fierce criticism of the Royal Family for their lack of support of the nation at a time of crisis. The Gulf War threatened to engulf the globe, and *The Sunday Times* attacked members of the Royal Family for taking Caribbean holidays, playing golf and partying during a period of national upheaval. The younger royals were accused of leading a frivolous, insensitive lifestyle and pocketing their Civil List allowances without giving anything in return.

The effect of this opinion in such an august organ was volcanic. The rest of the press waded in and caused Buckingham Palace to go on the defensive for the first time in history.

The Royal Family has been in trouble ever since. Once the wound was opened, the sore could only spread. It would be unfair to say that the empress had been seen to have no clothes, but certainly her slip was showing. The glamour began to wither. As Sir Max Beerbohm observed, in a wry comment on regal behaviour: 'Royalty, not ever being brought into contact with the realities of life, remain young far longer than others.' Young and innocent? Or young and ignorant?

*   *   *

In 1953, the newly crowned Queen Elizabeth inherited a dynasty that was already creaking. She could have scaled it down; she could have entered the 'modern age', like the fading royal families of most of Europe. By doing so she would have sealed her own fate. Instead, she did just the opposite. She seemed to be heeding historian Walter Bagehot who, in 1867, wrote about the English constitution: 'There are arguments for not having a court, and there are arguments for having a splendid court, but there are no arguments for having a mean court. It is better to spend a million in dazzling when you want to dazzle than three-quarters of a million trying to dazzle and yet not dazzling.'

In short, the Queen had decided to put on a show... and no one can put on a show like the British. When the Queen embarked on plans for her exorbitantly expensive 1953 coronation, she was not being a spendthrift; she was wisely investing in the future of the monarchy.

It seems now as if every royal ceremony is steeped in tradition but this is just not so. Until this century the British monarchy did not require pageantry to exalt itself in the public perception. It was only as its real power waned that it was decided a little pomp-and-pageantry pantomime would not come amiss with the sentimental British masses.

Weeks of organisation now go into ensuring that the State Opening of Parliament runs smoothly, yet many years ago the presence of a king or queen often caused hostility. Queen Victoria hardly bothered with the ceremony at all and it was only later revived by Edward VII. Today the question must still be posed as to whether the State Opening of Parliament is outdated and an unnecessarily costly spectacle. As Anthony Jay asks in his book *Elizabeth R*: 'Is it worth all the time, trouble and rehearsal? That depends on whether you believe symbols and rituals have a place in our lives today. If you do not, the spectacle of so many sober citizens putting on fancy dress to take part in a pointless and protracted charade must look exceptionally absurd.'

The Trooping the Colour ceremony is another annual regal event and, with the horse-loving Queen, a particular favourite. Although initially established as the sovereign's birthday parade in the eighteenth century, no monarch bothered to attend it regularly until Edward VII. The current ceremony was invented in 1914 by George V who wanted an impressive stage for himself. He set the scene for the modern habit of riding down London's Mall from Buckingham Palace, accompanied by massed bands.

George V also reintroduced the Maundy Thursday service, although for 200 years no reigning sovereign attended. The present monarch takes it seriously, but observers cannot help but be amused by the carrying of a herbal nosegay and white linen towels, introduced fairly recently for no apparent reason apart from the supposedly malodorous and insanitary nature of the sovereign's more humble subjects.

All these ceremonies are very pretty to watch but they are also very expensive. Of course, it is the British taxpayer who must stump up for them all. Nowadays there are clear indications that many of her subjects feel royalty is an outdated luxury for which ordinary people have to pay too high a price. Royalty may need its palace, its jewels, banquets and state occasions to preserve its glamour and mystique but an increasing number of people are openly saying that they think the cost of keeping the royals in the manner to which they have become accustomed is money that could be better spent elsewhere.

It is often argued that the Royal Family, if nothing else, boosts tourism and trade. Yet when the British Tourist Authority, way back in the royal-loving early eighties, asked visitors why they had put Britain on their itineraries, only 12 per cent mentioned royalty, Buckingham Palace or the Changing of the Guard. Royalty ranked ninth behind such pleasures as 'general sightseeing' and 'scenic countryside'. The Queen herself has travelled widely in a bid to 'do her bit' for Britain. She has visited more than 50 foreign heads of state during her reign and over 60 have visited her. She has made over 100 Commonwealth visits but what is the actual value of such hard graft on the part of the monarch? In Edgar Wilson's book *The Myth of British Monarchy*, he reports that the gross value of exports from the United Kingdom to eight countries actually dropped after visits from royals! 'The less involvement there is with British royalty the better the prospects for Britain's export trade,' he concluded.

So what service does the Royal Family provide for its

money? Is shaking a few hands really a day's work? Is the £53.5 million that it cost in 1992 to keep 'the Firm' in business an awesome waste of taxpayers' money? Most recent opinion polls have shown that the average British subject believes that it is indeed a waste. In particular, there has been a crescendo of criticism about the monarchy's tax-free status. For the Queen really is the world's most famous tax-dodger. At the same time as she can afford to give gifts such as the £5 million Berkshire home built for the Duke and Duchess of York, she can also beg Her Majesty's Government for regular, multi-million increases in the Civil List allowances for herself and her large, freeloading family.

Even that great pro-royalist Sir John Junor was prompted to write: 'I find it quite baffling that she should seem to be so firmly personally opposed to paying income tax on her purely personal income. Not income tax on the money voted to her by Parliament for the upkeep of the monarchy. Not tax on her personal possessions, her palaces, her paintings, her jewels. But tax only on the investment income she receives from her stocks and shares. What possible objection can she have to that?'

Twice during her reign Parliament has looked at the question of the Queen's finances and decided she should pay no income tax. Whenever the question is raised, Buckingham Palace conveniently leaks stories that the Queen is not as rich as the rest of the world believes. However, as Sir John told his readers in the *Mail on Sunday*, it does not matter whether she is worth £1,000 million or £100 million, it is all a matter of principle. He added: 'What can she possibly want the money for? After all, she can't take it with her and her descendants seem to have quite enough already. Can Her Majesty really still be saving up for a rainy day? The day, perhaps, the Revolution comes?'

He was not being flippant. In his definitive book *Crown and People*, Philip Ziegler said that in former decades any suggestion that Britain might abandon its centuries-old tradition of monarchy in favour of a republic was considered to be merely the raving of cranks and extremists. Ziegler believes that the most important single way of discovering what the British really think of the monarchy is the Mass Observation Archive at the University of Sussex, in which, since 1937, the views and comments of the man and woman in the street have been recorded. His finding is that the Royal Family is actually irrelevant to nine-tenths of the events that disturb or upset the British people. He says the upsurge of rejoicing at times like the Queen's Silver Jubilee might spring from genuine enthusiasm for the monarch herself; but many think it is also an excuse to enjoy a good party and shed a few sentimental tears.

If, as seems clear, there is a growing force in Britain in favour of a republic, just how important is the Crown to the man and woman in the street? In these liberal days, more and more people are debating whether it is right for a democracy to be presided over by a person who is never elected, does not reach office by examination or selection and who can never be legally removed or replaced.

A source extremely close to the senior royals told the

authors that they recognise that the British public is no longer 'infatuated' with the Royal Family. It is a long-overdue indication of the recognition of their fallibility, but it is far too late to save their reputation and public esteem.

According to royal biographer Anthony Jay, there are ten members of the family 'whose behaviour can affect the popularity of the monarchy equally for good or bad, and possibly a further 20 whose power to tarnish the image is greater than their power to burnish it. How are they expected to discharge this responsibility?'

At the head of the list of those 'top ten' royals would obviously be the Queen herself. After her, presumably, would come Prince Philip and then close family, including their children. Any appraisal of Prince Philip, Duke of Edinburgh, should first take account of the two very different faces of this extraordinary man.

*   *   *

No one can ever say that Prince Philip is not an achiever. By the early eighties he was undertaking no fewer than 300 engagements a year and spending up to six months overseas. His principal cause is the World Wide Fund For Nature, which he knocked into shape as a military-styled charitable force after taking over the reins from his friend Prince Bernhard of the Netherlands. Strange, many say, that he can equate his animal conservation activities with his favourite sports of hunting and shooting but after he and his chums have slaughtered a few thousand birds on the grouse moors, he rides the storm of criticism with a typically imperious sneer. If the World Wide Fund is his favourite cause, then the Duke of Edinburgh Award Scheme is his absolute passion. Founded in 1956, the scheme fosters the qualities of self-discipline, enterprise and perseverance which Philip himself most admires. Run in more than 2,500 schools and about 7,000 youth clubs, it has provided awards to about a million youngsters in the United Kingdom and another quarter of a million worldwide.

By any standards it is a remarkable achievement, perhaps only matched by the quiet but solid support he has given to the Queen as her consort over the years. In the early days of their marriage, Buckingham Palace was filled with love and laughter. Older staff still remember the night Philip chased his screaming wife down a corridor wearing a pair of joke false teeth. He stood by her as she made her first television broadcast, and when she 'dried up' he passed her a jocular note which instantly overcame her shyness. As the years rolled by, however, some of his jokes became less amusing to Her Majesty. During a visit to China Philip deeply angered and embarrassed her when he told a group of Scottish exchange students that they would turn 'slitty- eyed' if they stayed in the country too long. The remark boiled over into an international incident and the Queen, in the words of one aide, 'blew her top with him'. He certainly appeared chastened for the rest of the visit.

Although the Duke can be notoriously difficult at times, the Queen remains steadfastly loyal to him. Royal biographer Robert Lacey once observed: 'She does not pity herself as a woman married to a boor. Quite simply, she is still in love with her husband and he with her. If it is no longer the wild passion of youth, one of its principal components over the years has become mutual respect. They talk and listen to each other more than most other people who have been together as long.' Nowadays the Duke is still at the Queen's side as a consort but, like many long-married couples, lives a separate life in private. They have their own quarters and sleep in separate rooms, a fact that surprised some of the Queen's more naive subjects when details of the royal bedroom break-in by Michael Fagan were reported.

Philip has not always been the epitome of good manners. His irascible nature has meant that his career as consort is littered with embarrassing faux pas. He is a bit of a bully, sometimes to great effect, as in his charitable work, but on other occasions causing great harm, as within his own family. Then there are Philip's legendary liaisons, both while as a young Naval officer and throughout his marriage. Just how much of a womaniser he was can be judged by the startling evidence of a Russian spy.

Yevgeny Ivanov was a top Soviet undercover agent in London who, in 1961, seduced beautiful teenager Christine Keeler. (To maintain historical balance, it should be stated that the Russian later claimed that Keeler did the seducing.) The only problem about the couple's lustful afternoon in a friend's flat was that Christine Keeler was at that time also mistress to the British government's Secretary of State for War, John Profumo. Ivanov's fling unleashed one of the most spectacular scandals of the twentieth century. Many years later, however, with the collapse of Communism and the crumbling of the USSR, Ivanov revealed new aspects of the Profumo debacle, suggesting just how perilously close to the Royal Family the scandal had reached. In 1992 he wrote a book, *The Naked Spy*, in which he observed: 'A military spy should welcome information from any source, including the reigning house, although the difficulties of infiltrating it appeared to be insurmountable. But we seamen are an obstinate breed. The more difficult the task, the more stubbornly we attack it ... In Britain I laid my hands on information [about] the Royal Family. It is kept in the GRU archives ready to be used at any moment.'

The information that Ivanov gave in his book – and a great deal more that he revealed outside it – largely concerns one of the principal players in the Keeler spy plot: Stephen Ward, link-man, fixer, procurer, talented osteopath, society artist and close friend of Prince Philip.

In 1961, the year that Ivanov bedded Keeler, his friend Ward was commissioned to draw certain members of the Royal Family, in particular to do portraits of the Duke of Edinburgh, Princess Magaret and Anthony Armstrong Jones. 'You know, Eugene,' Ward told Ivanov, 'this commission was not quite unexpected. Prince Philip and I are friends of long standing. We have known each other for fifteen years, ever since I returned from India and started practising in London.' The Russian set about meeting all three sitters personally, later boasting: 'I had compromising material on each of them, as well as on Queen Elizabeth.'

In the case of Prince Philip, the spy succeeded in meeting his royal quarry at a dinner of the Royal Geographic Society. The Duke was less than revelatory and Ivanov gloomily related his impressions of the encounter to Stephen Ward.

Ivanov recorded Ward's observations thus: 'The Duke of Edinburgh and Philip Mountbatten are two different people. I remember him before he married Her Majesty the Queen and I know him as he is now. I can compare these two persons. You talked with a statesman who tried to appear wise and cautious. The thing is that for many years he lived by different rules, easily and without concern. Now he has to pay for the mistakes of his youth. That is why the Duke of Edinburgh tries to dominate Philip Mountbatten. He probably managed it at the dinner at the Royal Geographic Society.'

The Russian pressed Ward for anecdotes about the Duke's indiscretions in his days as plain Philip Mount-batten. The artist brought out an album of photographs with, as Ivanov put it, 'quite a few nude males and females in them'. The spy had seen the album before but on this occasion Ward gave him a conducted tour of the society faces it contained.

'Look at the photographs again and you will understand,' he said. 'You'll see there Prince Philip and the rest of our merry bachelors' company.' Ward pointed out Anthony Beauchamp, husband of Winston Churchill's daughter, Sarah, and Arthur Christiansen, editor of the *Daily Express*. He pointed to 'Prince Philip and his cousin David [the Marquess of Milford Haven]. And this is

Nichole. And this is Maggie, I think. Nice girls they were,' he mused as he wandered off to his kitchen to make coffee.

Ivanov dared not steal the photos but he had his Minox camera with him and he fired off snaps of five or six of them, which he later handed over to his KGB boss. When Ward returned to the room with the coffee, he began reminiscing about how he, Prince Philip and the Marquess of Milford Haven had enjoyed themselves in Soho pubs, select clubs and at parties at friends' homes. Then, according to Ivanov, came Stephen Ward's blockbuster. 'That was peanuts compared to what happened recently,' confided the osteopath. 'Prince Philip was considered to be too friendly with Princess Margaret. The habits of one's green years are difficult to break...'

If Stephen Ward's story was only half true, it would throw a new light on the unhappy romance of Princess Margaret, who soon afterwards wed Anthony Armstrong Jones. Ivanov claimed to have met the couple on several occasions, at their wedding, at Ascot and at Henley Regatta. A mutual love of rowing helped the spy befriend the Princess's husband and he claimed to have been regularly invited on to their boat on the Thames.

The idea of a top Soviet intelligence agent being able to observe the Royal Family so closely, whether through Ward's eyes or through his own, is remarkable. That Ward should be made the scapegoat for the entire Profumo scandal was remarkably suspicious. That he supposedly committed suicide before he could give evidence in court was remarkably convenient. Perhaps it is not so remarkable, therefore, that 30 years later Ivanov the spy should state with certainty: 'I collected enough compromising information for a possible blackmail of the Royal Family.'

At a more personal level, Stephen Ward's story might have been his own explanation for a curious sequence of events many years before. It has always puzzled royal chroniclers that Prince Philip put up such a fierce resistance to the affair between Princess Margaret and the one man she ever truly loved, Group Captain Peter Townsend. The events of those early years will never be publicly known but it is clear that in her desperate plea to be allowed to wed Townsend, Margaret expected the same support she had given Philip during his long and unpopular suit for her sister's hand. Was it jealousy of Peter Townsend, rather than antipathy towards him, that caused Prince Philip so vehemently to oppose Princess Margaret's marriage to the handsome war hero?

It is now well accepted that the cruel hurt Margaret suffered at this impressionable time of her young life irreversibly damaged her future. The bitter Princess entered into an unhappy marriage with Anthony Armstrong Jones, sought solace in the arms of playboy Roddy Llewellyn and surrounded herself with the sort of hedonists and sybarites that her sister the Queen would barely suffer to have in her presence. By those early events at Buckingham Palace, the smoking, drinking Margaret was sentenced to a life on the royal sidelines.

If the life of the Queen's sister has been soured by the maladroit workings of the royal machine, what of the Queen's own children? Sadly, scandal has dogged their lives in even greater measure. Indeed, it is difficult to argue that any single one of them has, on balance, enhanced the position of the Royal Family of which they are the principal members.

Hopes ran high for the Queen's oldest child, Charles, as he took his place on the world stage. He was intelligent, well educated, dedicated to the role of the Royal Family and sufficiently aware to raise its eyes to the obligations of the twentieth century. This, then, was the young Charles, invested Prince of Wales, King of England in the making. Friends who feared the influence of homosexually inclined Uncle Dickie were glad to witness a constant string of girlfriends before he settled on the ideal English rose, Lady Diana Spencer. Those same friends were horrified, however, when he began to shun his beautiful wife, preferring to spend his time with a succession of elderly advisers and philosophers. An eccentric seeker of solitude and a communer with plants, he became the royal who always said, 'I want to be alone.' Alone, that is, unless in the company of his married ex-girlfriends, with whom he seemed to feel most at home.

Over the years Charles failed dismally to dispel the depressing rumours that constantly surrounded his marriage. He presented an utterly miserable image of himself and his married life to the rest of the world. For weeks on end, he would avoid seeing his beautiful wife. On the increasingly rare occasions when he deigned to be in the same house as his family, he would remain wrapped up in his own interests, totally self-absorbed, cruelly distant. At private engagements it was more likely to be an ex-flame who played hostess than Princess Diana. The woman who holds Charles's affections most constantly is the great love of his bachelor days, Camilla Parker-Bowles, wife of Household Calvary officer Andrew Parker-Bowles. Charles shares with him a passion for polo as well as an old passion for his wife.

Although they dote on their father, Charles far too rarely sees his sons William and Harry. And in recent years, he has gone to great trouble not to see their mother more than is necessary. It is an expedience that is amply reciprocated by his wife. Yet while seeming distant from his close family, he is nevertheless praised for his compassion for the less fortunate and his concern for inanimate objects — such as office buildings. He is the prince without a cause. Since his distrustful mother announced she will not abdicate, he is also the heir without a throne. It seems unlikely that he will accede to it.

So what went wrong? Is the Queen really such a rotten mother? Is the Duke of Edinburgh really such a bad example as a father? Were all their children brought up wrongly? The answer is important because it is the Queen's children who will shape the course of the Royal Family for the coming decades and so far the signals are not looking too good.

A few anecdotes from the past may provide clues to the answer. Once when the Queen walked past his nursery Prince Charles pleaded with her to come in and play. 'If only I could,' she said and gently closed the door. In a television newsreel Charles was pictured as a young boy welcoming his mother home from a foreign tour with a formal handshake. Prince Andrew, explaining his mother's frequent absences while a young schoolboy, would say miserably: 'Mummy has an important job to do.' Public displays of affection in the Royal Family were indeed rare, which may explain the inability of the Queen's children to form lasting relationships of their own.

Leading psychiatrist Sir Sidney Crown, consultant at the Royal London Hospital, believes the restraints of royal life have left the monarch's children deprived of spontaneous shows of love and affection. He says: 'There is a formality about their upbringing that makes it more difficult for them. They are brought up by nannies and governesses. And of course the Queen herself was very restricted in how she could behave. If you are not used to seeing your parents kiss and cuddle and be affectionate in front of you then it is difficult to do the same when you grow up.' The Queen's children, he said, were also more likely to choose wrong partners because they were under pressure to get married. 'The time comes when they are expected to settle down and they are stuck with whoever they are with at that time.'

However, consultant child and family psychiatrist Dr Sebastian Kraemer believes: 'A third of all marriages now end in divorce. Marriage is an incredibly stressful thing. We should be glad the Royal Family are not gods and are not obliged to keep up pretences like their parents and grandparents were.'

In 1992 the newspapers were full of rumour about the failure of the Prince and Princess of Wales's marriage. In March there was the announcement of a separation between Sarah and the Queen's second son. It was soon followed by the more dignified divorce, after more than two years' separation, of her only daughter, Princess Anne, and Captain Mark Phillips.

Writing in the *London Evening Standard*, A. N. Wilson, author and friend of the Queen Mother, attempted to put the royals' marital problems into historical perspective. He said: 'You do not even have to cite the lurid examples of Henry VIII's wives or the divorce of George IV from Queen Caroline or the newly discovered petition of Prince Albert to the Privy Council asking for permission to divorce Queen Victoria to realise that they are an almost imposs-ible family to marry.' Then he took a stab at the cause of such disharmony: 'Royal couples do not really have any-thing to do. All their activity – whether in the armed services or in the field of charity work – is bogus. Their time has to be filled artificially with "engagements" which eat into their moments of privacy together. It is not really a matter of choice for them ... So if you have come to hate each other, or if one or other is sleeping around, why not get a divorce?'

Why not indeed? Wilson had succinctly pinpointed two of the more unsettling ingredients in the Royal Family's status of late – most of them have absolutely nothing useful to do and they have a propensity for 'sleeping around'.

Conveniently forgetting that the Queen is the head of the Church, the Royal Family must have thought that at least some of their problems had been solved when they at last rid themselves of the damaging 'Fergie Factor', but as columnist John Junor, who always likes to have the last word on royal topics, wrote prophetically in the crisis month of March 1992: 'I just fear that we have far from heard the last of Fergie and that the time may come when historians of the future point to the day she married Andrew as the day the British monarchy went down the tube.'

So what is the state of the British monarchy? Can it withstand the latest attacks upon it or is its accelerating decline unstoppable and terminal? To answer these question we must delve into the monarchy's turbulent history and thereby seek clues to its uncertain future.

CHAPTER ONE

A short history of
the British Monarchy

Baron Acton's maxim, that power tends to corrupt and absolute power corrups absolutely, is nowhere better evidenced than in Britain's long line of absolute monarchs. Murderers, torturers, adulterers, madmen, thieves, devil-worshippers and drunks – all have borne the regalia of this sceptred isle and held sway over an often downtrodden and benighted people. At some time in the past our kings acquired a 'divine right' for all their actions. Indeed, today, there are still those who feel the monarchy is special, if not exactly divine. Yet a short trip through history reveals that many of our sovereigns, far from having divine rights, did not even have any legal right to the kingdom.

Some, of course, have been found to be less black than they were painted at the time. A few have been positively saintly. However, nearly all had feet of crumbling clay.

Opinion in the late twentieth century is that the House of Windsor is not setting a good example of family life. Yet why should we expect it to? The lesson of history is that royal families continually plotted and even fought against each other. Not only did they set examples of extreme violence, usury, avarice, immorality and duplicity, monarchs from William the Conqueror to Queen Victoria have often been the direct cause of armed insurrection.

A SHORT HISTORY OF THE BRITISH MONARCHY

The Normans

Back in 1066, the most evocative date in English history, the fledgling House of Normandy had at least some claim to the English throne, which had been promised to Duke William by Edward the Confessor. Unfortunately, it was also promised to Harold – and at least Harold spoke Anglo-Saxon!

William, a big, headstrong, cunning and violent man, was known as William the Bastard. His birth was the result of an alliance between his father, Robert, and Arlette, the peasant daughter of a Falaise tanner. Nevertheless, as Duke Robert had no legitimate heir, he made his nobles recognise William.

Edward the Confessor was brought up in Normandy and would have favoured the French. It is certainly possible, as claimed in the Bayeux Tapestry, that Harold himself recognised William's claim and even promised his help. Without question, he helped William in a French campaign, fighting bravely and performing various acts of heroism. None the less, the English council gave the throne to Harold and England's most famous battle, at Hastings, became inevitable. Harold was laid low by a stray arrow and the Bastard had become the Conqueror.

William's reign was marked throughout by its extreme harshness. He was absolutely brutal in quelling revolts against him. He dispossessed the Anglo-Saxon gentry, rewarding his Norman followers with their land. Where Anglo-Saxon nobles banded together and fought, he was utterly ferocious, laying waste to large areas. It was small wonder that his most remarkable achievement, the *Domesday Book*, recorded that most of Yorkshire was wasteland. William had laid waste to it himself.

He had no qualms either about making 2,000 people homeless when he destroyed 20 villages to create his royal hunting preserve in the New Forest. His laws with regard to his love of blood sports were draconian. The penalty for shooting at a deer was death. For only disturbing a deer, a peasant could be blinded. When he died in 1087, William confessed: 'I am stained with the rivers of blood that I have shed.'

If he was a cruel and pitiless man, his second son, William Rufus, was a monster. Red of hair and face, the Conqueror's son had inherited his father's vile temper. His accession to the crown caused an almighty family row, as his elder brother, Robert, was passed over. Robert, William and the youngest brother, Henry, loathed each other. Their intrigue and quarrelling began when their father was alive and became all-out war after his death. However, William II did more than any other to stain the House of Normandy with lechery and cruelty. He was a tyrant for 13 miserable years. The *Anglo-Saxon Chronicle* noted that he was 'harsh and fierce in his rule'. He was finally killed while hunting when an arrow, shot by a companion, Sir Walter Tyrrell, ended his reign. History records it as an accident, although Rufus's younger brother, Henry, was also in the party that day and he lost no time in galloping ahead to get back to London and grab the royal treasure. Three days later he had himself crowned king.

In some respects Henry was an effective king. He encouraged scholars, set up a system of justice that laid the foundation of today's crown courts and strove to keep

England at peace. However, he was also an intensely lecherous man who was said to have fathered more illegitimate children than any other English king. Soon after his coronation in 1100, he married Matilda, pious daughter of King Malcolm of Scotland, who had really wanted to be a nun. At the time he was also carrying on a passionate affair with a Welsh princesss called Nesta, who did not take kindly to being supplanted.

Henry also inherited the Norman trait of cruelty, according to the *Anglo-Saxon Chronicle*. In 1125, for example, he had 'all the moneyors in England' summoned to Winchester, where both innocent and guilty were mutilated, many having their hands chopped off, as a punishment for circulating false coin. He was known personally to have thrown someone who opposed him from the battlements of his castle and to have given orders for two of his grandchildren to be blinded when they were held as hostages. He kept his brother Robert imprisoned for 28 years, depriving him of his dukedom.

Henry's only legitimate son, William, was drowned in 1120. So, when the King died after overeating lampreys (eels) in 1135, he handed the succession to his favourite nephew, Stephen, the one and only monarch of the House of Blois.

Stephen was charming, good-natured and gallant, but terribly weak. He could control neither his friends nor his enemies. He was certainly unable to control the powerful barons. He had no stomach for war and inevitably made wrong decisions at critical moments.

He was no match either for the formidable Matilda,

who, being the daughter of Henry II, was the rightful monarch. She married Count Geoffrey of Anjou and built up an army. This proud, disagreeable woman invaded England in 1139, captured and imprisoned Stephen and claimed the throne. She had not, however, bargained for the fighting spirit of Stephen's queen, another Matilda, who rallied forces to his cause and drove her back to France. For a great part of Stephen's reign there was anarchy in England. Towns and villages were burned and destroyed, churches were used as forts, and the barons had their own way. 'Never did a country endure greater misery,' wrote one historian.

Thus the tyrannical rule of this Norman house found an ignominious end in anarchy and mayhem. A new dynasty was to arise – the equally miserable House of Anjou.

A SHORT HISTORY OF THE BRITISH MONARCHY

The House of Anjou

Stephen had made peace with Matilda before his death in 1154 and had agreed that her son, Henry, should succeed him. Henry came from legendary stock. According to an old story, a Count of Anjou had married Satan's daughter, Melusine. Her identity was discovered only when she was made to attend Mass. At the sight of the bread and wine she flew through the roof of the church and was never seen again. The Count's descendants, the Angevins and Plantagenets, were therefore known as 'the devil's brood'.

Henry II had inherited the famous Angevin temper. He was once reported to have flung off his clothes in a fit of anger and writhed on the floor, stuffing his mouth with straw.

A short, powerful man, bursting with fury, he married Eleanor of Aquitaine, a formidable woman who was both politically active and dangerous. She had been the wife of Louis VII of France but their marriage was annulled by the time she was 30. Henry was only 19 when they met but her beauty seduced him. He also had an eye on her great fortune.

They came to England to be crowned but their interest in the country was minimal; they just happened to have acquired a kingdom across the Channel. During his reign of 34 years, Henry spent just over a third of his time in England and Eleanor even less.

Henry was much given to 'fleshly lust' but Eleanor put up with his mistresses. Only when he fell passionately in love with a beautiful younger woman, Rosamund Clifford, did Eleanor unsheathe her claws. When Rosamund expired suddenly it was widely believed that the Queen had arranged for her death.

Eleanor bore Henry four sons. Their family life was appalling. Henry and Eleanor had vitriolic rows. The four princes plotted with their mother against him, and their disloyalty broke his heart. In 1174, Henry turned on his wife and had her imprisoned for inciting her sons to rebellion. Nevertheless, she hung on and outlived him.

Henry achieved much in spite of the bitter feuding but the great cloud on his reign was the murder of Thomas à Becket, Archbishop of Canterbury. Becket had once been his great friend but things changed when Becket made it plain that he would not allow the Crown to dominate the Church. In one of his rages, Henry cried out: 'Who will rid me of this turbulent priest?' Four knights took him at his word. Appalled by the martyrdom of his friend, Henry showed his repentance by walking barefoot through the streets of Canterbury and submitting to a public flogging.

Prematurely aged and full of bitterness, Henry died at the great castle of Chinon in Touraine in July 1189. It was said he called out: 'Shame, shame on a conquered king.'

The son who succeeded him became one of the great folk heroes of English history. Richard I, known as the Lionheart, looked every inch a warrior prince. Tall, with red-gold hair and a fair complexion, he loved nothing better than war and fighting. However, he was a homosexual and his marriage to Berengaria of Navarre was never consummated. The great love of his life was King Philip of France, with whom he went crusading.

In his youth, when not plotting against his father, Richard plotted against his brother, John — known as Lackland because he had no possessions of his own. Brought up in his mother's court in France, Richard never bothered to learn English. He crossed the Channel for his coronation in 1189 but thereafter spent only six months in England in a ten-year reign. His coronation was marred by a massacre of Jewish leaders in London.

Richard used England mainly as a bank to finance his crusades. He was one of the most valiant warriors in Christendom but he bled England dry. Further, he was not the gallant cavalier of legend. In 1191 he ordered the massacre of the 2,700-strong garrison of Acre. One contemporary declared that, although a great soldier, his soul was steeped in cruelty. When he died, it was not on some great crusade but on a petty raid in a minor squabble over money. A crossbow wound in his shoulder turned gangrenous.

Standing by to inherit Richard's throne was his duplicitous brother, John. His early life was spent plotting and fighting against his own family. As king, he upset the Pope to such an extent that the whole country was, in effect, excommunicated. His temper was as atrocious as his father's. He divorced his wife because she bore him no children and finally upset his barons, who rebelled against him and forced him to sign Magna Carta.

John married a second time, to Isabella of Angoulême, who gave him two sons and three daughters. He was said to have been in love with Isabella, but that did not stop him from having a string of mistresses. However, when he suspected Isabella of taking a lover, he had the man murdered and strung his corpse up over his wife's bed.

John's reputation is shocking, yet modern historians say

he was not as bad as rumour pretends. At least he remained in England to govern it! Towards the end, he took to travelling frequently, as if he trusted no one. Wherever he moved, his treasury and crown jewels went too, until, crossing a river that ran into the Wash, the wagon carrying them was lost in quicksand. John collapsed and is subsequently said to have died of a surfeit of peaches and cider.

John's son, Henry, was crowned at the age of nine in a service of dubious legality. He seems to have had little say until he reached majority. Henry was a weak-willed man, kind-hearted critics say, of an artistic temperament – a half-wit, say the rest. Certainly, we have him to thank for many fine cathedrals. However, Henry despised the English, and gave important jobs only to Frenchmen. He signed away England's rights to Normandy and Anjou, and finally brought about a civil war with his barons. Out of this anarchy emerged Simon de Montfort, who set up a council that was to become Parliament.

One other thing of note that Henry III did was to name his son and heir Edward – the first king with an English name since the Confessor (Harold is of Scandinavian origin).

A SHORT HISTORY OF THE BRITISH MONARCHY

The Plantagenets

Edward Plantagenet (named after the Angevin tradition of wearing a sprig of broom, *planta genista*) was a stern, warlike man. He returned from foreign wars to take the crown. In his lifetime he became known as the Hammer of the Scots, because of his harsh treatment of them. He also crushed the Welsh. He broke promises when it was politic to do so and had both the Scottish and the Welsh leaders hanged, drawn and quartered as an example to anyone who might oppose him. He expelled the Jews from England and massacred 7,000 people at Berwick after a battle there.

Nevertheless, at his death in 1307 he left England a better governed country than he found it, and he gave to the English the custom of naming the heir to the throne the Prince of Wales.

Unfortunately, the first Prince of Wales was not a patch on his father. A disaster from the start, this effeminate youth was an open bisexual, whose favours were bestowed on a worthless ne'er-do-well called Piers Gaveston, despite having a strong, intelligent and attractive wife, Isabella, daughter of the King of France, who bore him four children. Finally Isabella, nicknamed the she-wolf of France, plotted the death of Gaveston. Edward was devastated, but then took on new lovers in the Earl of Winchester and his son. Isabella promptly moved in with Roger Mortimer, the rebel Earl of March, and set about removing her husband. Their private army killed the King's lovers and forced Edward to abdicate. Tradition has it that he was murdered in 1327 at Berkeley Castle, by having a red-hot poker thrust into his anus, rupturing his bowel.

His son, also Edward, was a stripling of 14. He was unfortunate in his parentage but was made of the same stern stuff as his grandfather. He bided his time until he was strong enough to revenge his father. In a commando-style manoeuvre, he captured Mortimer and had him publicly hanged, drawn and quartered. Then he locked his mother up for the rest of her natural life.

Edward grew into a strong, good-looking man. He was the first king since the conquest to speak English. He was tough but fair but he was also a lecher and a devil-worshipper. Witchcraft had long been officially ousted as the religion of England but the population still clung fiercely to the old ways. No wonder Edward III was loved as no other Plantagenet by his subjects.

Edward had many mistresses and a horde of illegitimate offspring. His most famous courtesan was the Countess of Salisbury. Legend has it that he was dancing with her when a ribbon or garter fell from her leg, causing consternation in the court. He is supposed to have covered her blushes by putting the garter on his own leg, while uttering the words: 'Honi soit qui mal y pense' – 'Shame on him who thinks evil of it', hence the foundation of the Order of the Garter. However, author Eric Ericson, in *The World, the Flesh and the Devil*, puts it in a different light. He argues that any consternation caused at the ball was not due to outraged modesty, as there was none in the court of the day. Ericson points out that a ribbon worn below the knee signified that the lady was queen of a coven of witches. By tying the ribbon to his own leg, Edward was declaring his faith in the worship of the horned god and the earth goddess.

Edward reigned for 50 years. He outlived his son, the dashing Black Prince, and in 1377 was succeeded by his grandson, the vicious Richard II. A homosexual, although he married twice, Richard's gross tastes and extravagant ways made his court the most exotic in Europe. However, to the common people he gave not a thought. Not, that is, until Jack Straw and Wat Tyler led the peasants in a poll-tax revolt, so successfully that the government was preparing to quit London. Richard is chiefly remembered today for facing the peasants at London's Smithfield — where he ended the revolt with promises he never kept — and for being turned off his throne by his cousin, Bolingbroke. He died at the age of 33, almost certainly murdered.

Bolingbroke's claim to the throne was dubious. He was Richard's cousin and the son of John of Gaunt. Better qualified was Edmund Mortimer, through the daughter of Gaunt's elder brother. None the less, Bolingbroke was crowned Henry IV, and a 14-year reign of turbulence and war with the Welsh was launched. He too had the Angevin/Plantagenet traits of a vile temper and a cruel streak. He contracted a virulent eczema, which he thought was leprosy, and, putting this down to divine retribution, he asked to be buried next to Thomas à Becket, hoping for a way into heaven.

Henry V appears to have been one of the few Plantagenets who was not, one way or the other, sexually motivated. This victor of Agincourt was a warrior who devoted his life to winning the French crown. He died of dysentery at 34, a disappointed man.

Ironically, by his death and that of Charles VI in France, Henry's infant son became monarch of both kingdoms. As he grew into manhood, the young Henry VI became known as the 'saintly simpleton'. He managed to hold on to his throne from 1422 to 1461, although Joan of Arc was to drive the English almost out of France. The Abbot of St Albans complained that Henry was too half-witted to manage affairs of state. Another commentator said a sheep would be more appropriate than a ship on the coins of the realm.

Henry had inherited the mental instability suffered by his grandfather, Charles VI of France. He married a strong, domineering woman, Margaret of Anjou, who was determined to keep him on the throne when he would probably have been happier in a monastery. He loved scholars and ordered the building of two great colleges, Eton at Windsor and Kings at Cambridge. However, he was too weak a king to stop the quarrelling between the rival houses of Lancaster and York, which culminated in the Wars of the Roses.

Queen Margaret's meddling only made things worse. When told she had given birth to a son, the King collapsed (he knew he was impotent) and court gossip said the Duke of Somerset was the true father.

Finally, in 1461, Henry was usurped by the Duke of York's 19-year-old son, Edward, with the help of the Earl of Warwick, the 'kingmaker'. Henry, by then quite insane, was imprisoned, briefly reinstated for political reasons and finally stabbed to death on Edward IV's instructions in 1471.

While Edward, a charming self-indulgent man, allowed his appetite for sex and drink to ruin his health, our next real 'villain' was his infamous brother, Richard, Duke of Gloucester. Shakespeare immortalised the man who became Richard III as an evil, hunchbacked monster, although modern historians think he rather overdid this. However, while Richard could not have committed all the crimes laid at his door, the main reason for his evil reputation still holds.

When Edward IV died in 1483 at the age of 41, he named Richard as Lord Protector of England and guardian of his two young sons, one of them heir to the throne. The two young princes were kidnapped on their way to London, taken to the Tower and never seen again. What could be their bones were found 200 years later by workmen repairing a staircase. Only Richard had a motive for such a murder. After the disappearance of the princes, he accepted the crown but trouble followed him throughout his brief two-year reign. The nobles feared his lust for power and knew that he would sacrifice even those who had served him faithfully. He even poisoned his wife, Queen Anne, when she proved 'unfruitful'.

Nemesis came in the form of Henry Tudor, the young, exiled Earl of Richmond, who landed at Milford Haven in August 1485 to rally his Welsh kinsmen and claim the throne. He fought and killed Richard at the battle of Bosworth Field in Leicestershire, so ending the Plantagenet line of kings. It was said that every man in England slept more soundly in his bed that night.

A SHORT HISTORY OF THE BRITISH MONARCHY

The Tudors

If the monarchs of the House of Tudor had anything in common, it was probably lust for gold. Henry VII certainly made the kingdom the well-organised, highly taxed land it is today. Various ambassadors commented in letters home that he was happier reading his royal expense sheet than state papers.

His son, Henry VIII, was actually the first king to have a number attached to his name. An athlete and a talented musician, he later gave himself over to lechery and love of the table. Crowned king because his elder brother, Arthur, had met an untimely end, he married his brother's widow. When he found she could not give him a male heir, he asked to divorce her. Turned down by the Pope, he created the Church of England and broke with Rome, in order to marry his mistress, Anne Boleyn. He sacked the monasteries but squandered their wealth. When he died – grotesquely obese and riddled with syphilis – England was bankrupt.

Henry had been a terrifying king. Friendship and good service meant nothing. Cardinal Wolsey cheated the executioner only by dying of natural causes, while Thomas More and another chancellor, Thomas Cromwell, both kept dates with the headsman, as did two of Henry's six wives.

There followed a period of chaos. Henry's son, Edward, was a brilliant scholar and would, without doubt, have been the greatest of the Tudors had he not died in his teens.

The next teenage monarch was poor Lady Jane Grey, who personally recognised Mary Tudor's right to the throne but was thrust on to it herself by ambitious relatives. Her reign lasted a week. She was executed on the orders of Mary who, in blood, thus began a reign of sheer terror.

Although extremely well educated, Mary was a bitter, sexually frustrated woman when she was crowned at the age of 37. She was also a Catholic. Her devotion to the Catholic cause led to England's equivalent of the Spanish Inquisition. Hundreds of Protestants were burned at the stake on her order, including Archbishop Cranmer. She came close to losing her throne when she decided to marry Philip of Spain. The populace feared he would drag England into his wars and there were riots all over the country. In the event, Philip cared little for Mary and hardly ever saw her.

Neglected by her husband and hated by her people, she died of dropsy, pathetically believing she was pregnant at last. During the latter days of her five-year reign, France won back Calais, England's last remaining French possession. Mary is said to have declared that when she died, Calais would be engraved on her heart. 'Callous' would have been more apt.

Even Elizabeth, the Virgin Queen, was not without fault. She was especially careful with cash, except when spending it on herself or her favourites. Nevertheless, her achievements were immense, and she left England greater than she found it. If not as cruel as her forebears, she was ruthless enough to execute various court favourites (some say lovers) and also her cousin, Mary Queen of Scots.

A SHORT HISTORY OF THE BRITISH MONARCHY

The Stuarts

It was Mary's son who succeeded Elizabeth to found the vainglorious Stuart dynasty. Another bisexual, James was a spindly little man, who looked bigger than he really was, thanks to his habit of wearing extra-quilted clothes to foil would-be assassins. It is likely that he suffered from the same disease that was to make George III appear mad: porphyria. In any event, he was said to act like a clown, despite his fine education. He it was who invented the doctrine of 'the divine right of kings'.

An ardent Puritan, he commissioned what has become known as the Authorised Version of the Bible in 1611 and he managed to unite England and Scotland without bloodshed. He was fortunate, however, to survive the Catholic-inspired Gunpowder Plot, when barrels of explosives were discovered under the Parliament building. As he grew older, James became obsessed with a fear of witchcraft and demonology and when he died, in March 1625, at the age of 59, he was a prematurely senile figure, worn out by fear and worry.

His son, Charles I, who succeeded him in 1625, also saw himself as God-chosen and was intransigent when his beliefs were called into question. Though upright and honourable in personal affairs, in politics and matters of state he could be devious and stubborn. He was very much under the influence of his strong-willed wife, Henrietta Maria, who did much to fuel the antagonism building up against him. Henrietta Maria, daughter of Henry IV of France, had arrived in England convinced that her role was to support the British Catholics. Her entourage included 28 priests and she would have nothing but French spoken in her presence.

Charles finally drove a conservative Parliament into a civil war. For four years England was in turmoil. When the Royalists were defeated by Oliver Cromwell's armies, Charles was tried as a 'tyrant, traitor and murderer' but a verdict of guilty was reached by a majority of only one vote. At his public execution many people wept.

There could not have been a greater contrast between the tragic figure of Charles I and that of his son, Charles II, the 'Merry Monarch', called back from exile in 1660 to restore the monarchy after Cromwell's death.

Charles was a lazy, good-humoured, witty man who loved women. His court was the most dissolute in Europe, for the King had no morals and did not care what sort of people surrounded him as long as they were amusing. Diarist John Evelyn said it was in the King's nature to 'gainsay nothing that related to his pleasure'.

Charles broke the heart of his queen, Catherine of Braganza, who adored him. Among all his mistresses, the most powerful and dangerous was the beautiful Lady Castlemaine. For a time she ruled Charles largely through her sexual hold over him (he was probably the most highly sexed monarch in our history). Her greed had no bounds. On one occasion the Dutch fleet sailed up the Medway and destroyed English ships lying at anchor there. They were laid up and out of action due to lack of funds, the money having been spent on Lady Castlemaine's houses and jewels! Charles eventually got rid of her but he was never without a mistress for long.

Charles was succeeded by his brother, James II who, in his youth, was an attractive figure and constantly involved in scandals over women. His most famous mistress was Arabella Churchill, sister of the future Duke of Marlborough. James married the Italian princess Mary of Modena and together they planned to turn England back to Catholicism. His whole performance as king was said to be one of 'crass maladroitness'. There were various insurrections, the most famous being the Monmouth Rebellion in the West Country. However, it was when James declared that he had a son (though few believed it) that Parliament and the nobles instigated the so-called Bloodless Revolution. James's nearest Protestant male relative, William of Orange, was asked to be king, and in 1688 William and his wife, Mary II, ousted James.

The House of Orange

William was not an attractive man. It was said when the 15-year-old Mary learned that she was to marry her cousin, she cried for a day and a half. They eventually became good friends but did not manage to produce an heir. Solemn, taciturn and above all dull, William still managed to be unfaithful to Mary with numerous women, most famously the Villiers sisters. As a ruler, he was a success by default – he signed away many of the monarch's rights in return for money for foreign wars. He died when his horse stumbled on a molehill and a fracture led to pleuro-pneumonia. Jacobites, the supporters of James Stuart, drank a toast to 'the little gentleman in black velvet' (the mole).

The last link in the chain was William's cousin, Anne. The daughter of James II, she spent 12 years on the throne, most of them suffering from gout and various other ailments. She produced 17 children, only one of whom lived, and he only to the age of 11. Anne's vices were food – she could eat a whole goose at a sitting – and drink. Poor Anne was a drunk. Known as 'Brandy Nan', she used to keep it in a teapot and call it 'cold tea'. She was the target of Alexander Pope's pithy jibe in *The Rape of the Lock:*

> Here thou, great Anna, whom three realms obey,
> Doth sometimes council take. And sometimes tea.

Above all, Anne is best remembered for being dead. Her health ruined by alcohol and gluttony and continual pregnancy, she was so often unwell that 'Queen Anne's dead' became a morbid joke that is still in the language today.

On her death, England turned to the royal House of Hanover in Germany for its next king.

A SHORT HISTORY OF THE BRITISH MONARCHY

The House of Hanover

If the Hanoverians had one unifying fault, it was their extreme dullness. George I had never wanted to be King of England and he refused to learn the language. He knew little of and cared nothing for English law and customs and was happy to let Robert Walpole do all the business of government for him. A bulging-eyed, pig-headed man, he was also cruel. When his wife took a lover, he had her imprisoned and stopped her from seeing her children ever again. When the lover disappeared mysteriously without trace, it was assumed that George had ordered his murder. George hated his son, later to become George II, and they avoided each other whenever possible. George spent most of his reign in Hanover, where he died unmourned by his British subjects.

George II carried on one tradition: he hated his son even more than his father had hated him. A stupid, dull man like his father, George will be remembered as being the last monarch to lead an army into battle, at Dettingen in 1743. He had an open marriage with Queen Caroline. He was supposed to be devoted to her, but that did not stop him having the usual string of mistresses. Caroline herself chose some of them, for she had a streak of coarseness and apparently enjoyed hearing the lascivious details. At least George outlived his hated son, Frederick, and when he died, in 1760, it was Frederick's son, George, who succeeded, at a time when Britain's fortunes were on the rise.

Tragedy and madness darkened the reign of George III. Grandson of George II, he came to the throne when he was 22 – but it was noted that, mentally and emotionally, he was little more than a child. Unkind critics of the day declared him mad in 1787 when he was seen to address an oak tree which he imagined to be Frederick of Prussia. (Princes who talk to plants today are merely 'eccentric'.) From that time on he was subject to ever-increasing bouts of insanity during which he foamed at the mouth, talked incessantly for 24 hours at a stretch and sometimes screamed sexual obscenities. Doctors of the day were helpless, and tortured him with their remedies. He was gagged, strapped to a chair for hours on end and treated with burning hot poultices. He eventually recovered and thereafter only suffered minor attacks. Only in recent times has his illness been identified as the rare metabolic disease called porphyria, which attacks the brain and nervous system.

George III's reign is usually remembered for just one catastrophic event: the loss of Britain's American colonies in the American War of Independence. However, he was very popular with his people, who considered him a good man. He lived simply and quietly with his queen, Charlotte, preferring a peaceful domestic life to anything else. Because of his very real interest in farming and the new techniques that were being employed on the land, he was called 'Farmer George'. He often walked, plainly dressed and unattended, through the streets and chatted to passersby. Sadly, the King spent the last years of his life as a recluse at Windsor Castle, where he shuffled about in an old dressing gown, neglected by his family and hardly aware of what was going on.

By 1811, George III was considered to be incapable

of ruling and his eldest son became Prince Regent. 'Prinny', as he became known, aroused the greatest resentment. He lived a life of the most ostentatious luxury at a time when the poor suffered squalor and starvation. He opposed every kind of reform. When he was a child his tutor had said: 'He will either grow up to be the most polished gentleman or the most accomplished blackguard in Europe, perhaps both.' His words were prophetic.

Prinny did not become king until 1820, on the death of his father. By then he was 58 years old and had forfeited all respect. The cartoonist Gillray drew cruel sketches of him as a paunchy libertine and he was lampooned all over London.

It was common knowledge that in his twenties he had contracted a secret marriage with a sophisticated and elegant widow called Mrs Fitzherbert. However, the liaison was brushed aside when his debts became so great that he had to make a marriage of convenience with a foreign princess and promise to settle down to a quieter life. The bride chosen for him was Caroline of Brunswick. The marriage of George IV and Caroline was farcical and disastrous. George was a dandy and a roué of exquisite tastes; she was a vulgar hoyden who seldom washed. At their wedding George drank so much claret that he had to be held up at the altar by the Duke of Bedford. On his wedding night he fell into the grate, where Caroline left him.

If today divorce is costing the House of Windsor public respect, the parting of George and his wife was a disaster for the House of Hanover. Her lovers were chosen for the mischief they would cause, and George finally put her on trial for adultery. The gossips had a field day as the terrible couple washed their dirty linen in public.

Although nicknamed 'Silly Billy' by his family, William Duke of Clarence, who succeeded his brother at the age of 65, turned out to be a good king. He had a long liaison with an actress, Mrs Jordan, by whom he had ten illegitimate children, but he had no direct heir. So the last Hanoverian — and our longest-reigning monarch — was his niece, the strait-laced, unamused Victoria.

A SHORT HISTORY OF THE BRITISH MONARCHY

Victoria Regina

Crowned in 1837, when still a slip of a teenager, Victoria was barely sensible enough to choose her own bonnet – or so the politicians thought. She proved a good enough queen when she allowed her ministers to run the country. Inevitably, however, she grew into a hard-headed, self-opiniated matriarch who was dedicated to court ritual and opposed much of the change and reform that were gathering momentum throughout her 64 years on the throne.

During her time, Britain became an empire. Where British armies did not hold sway, British industrial expertise did. Even so, Victoria was the target for much abuse, and worse. At least five attempts were made on her life in the street – one man actually blacked her eye with a stick. The republican ideal, which had been around since the Civil War and had strengthened its hold with the events of the French Revolution, was becoming a force to be reckoned with.

The Chartists put the fear of God into the government when they started to organise the London poor in 1848, the so-called 'Year of Revolutions'. Troops and cannons were out on the streets of the capital and the Royal Family was packed off to the Isle of Wight for safety. The tide of unrest was not to be halted (indeed it was fuelled by the sexual excesses of the bored Prince of Wales, to whom Victoria would give no state role). In 1871 the radical MP Sir Charles Dilke openly called for the Queen to be deposed and a republic to be set up. He was not alone in this view in Parliament nor in the country. The city of Birmingham, whose leading citizen was the radical Joe Chamberlain, moved into the republican camp; and the Irish had long been threatening to revolt.

Victoria's husband, Albert, was her cousin. She chose him despite the fear of in-breeding that was becoming a problem among royal families. Victoria was obsessed by the young Prince of Saxe-Coburg-Gotha and, despite the historians' revelations that Albert once sought a divorce, the marriage was a happy one, producing nine children. However, in 1861, when still only 42, Albert died from typhoid, possibly a result of the bad drains at Windsor. Victoria was shattered and went into everlasting mourning. During the next 40 years she seldom visited London, preferring a secluded life at Balmoral or Osborne. Although she continued to carry out affairs of state, the Queen was hardly ever seen in public. When she did appear, people witnessed a grim-faced, dumpy little lady submerged in widow's weeds. As the years went by she grew stouter, more stubborn and more removed from ordinary people. Eventually the public began to feel cheated. 'To let' notices were pinned to the railings, of Buckingham Palace. People began to ask what was the good of paying vast sums of money for a sovereign they never saw. By the early 1870s more than 50 republican clubs had been founded in various parts of Britain. At a huge rally in Hyde Park, speakers were quite openly anti-royalist.

At Balmoral, Victoria had turned to a commoner for support: her ghillie, John Brown. When she began to appear on the social scene again, it was noted that John Brown was often at her side, that he treated her with familiarity and sometimes addressed her as 'wumman'. Scurrilous verses began to circulate about their relationship and the Queen was referred to as 'Mrs Brown'. Victoria's eldest son, Edward Prince of Wales, urged his mother to break out of her mourning and show herself to the people but she refused to believe there was any kind of discontent.

Victoria's treatment of her son and heir was another factor over which she was criticised. She blamed him, quite unjustly, for his father's death and forced him to live in a kind of limbo for much of his adult life. She would give him no responsibility and would not even let him read her official letters. Edward took the only way out he could think of and lived a high life dedicated to pleasure and women.

Yet such was the deeply ingrained, historical need for the monarchy that when Victoria celebrated her Diamond Jubilee the whole nation turned out to give her the party of the century. By then she had become a grand old lady and when she died, at the age of 81, there was genuine public mourning.

Prince Edward
and the
Jersey Lillie

The British Royal Family has long thought itself a key player in affairs of state, but in reality it has been more interested in affairs of the bedchamber than the workings of international intrigue and diplomacy. Its history is rife with debauchery, lust and immoral excess, and more than one reign has been rocked by the scandal of an illicit sexual entanglement. Yet few were more vulgar or voracious than King Edward VII, the raunchy royal forever derided as Edward the Caresser.

Bertie, as he was known to his friends and subjects during the latter half of the nineteenth century, was a hedonist besotted with the extravagances a man of his wealth and position could buy, and he never failed to exercise his birthright to overindulge his pleasures. He was possessed of an enormous sexual appetite, which he frequently sought to gratify in the high-priced brothels of Europe – or the bedrooms of his friends' wives – and he often regaled his intimates with stories boasting of his carnal prowess.

The Prince of Wales was also a notorious glutton – he could devour 12-course meals – and an excessive gambler who prided himself on being seen at the best racetracks and gambling tables of Europe. A plump, bearded man, he moved from one scandal to the next, never caring that his notorious conduct not only shocked his mother, the very staid Queen Victoria, but also the loyal masses who mistakenly looked up to the monarchy for leadership.

His relationship with his mother and his stern, pious father, Prince Albert, was wavering at best, and appears to be rooted in his miserable, Spartan childhood. He was born on 9 November 1841, and from the time he was old enough to understand, he was schooled in the arts of royalty and groomed for his eventual ascension to the throne. However, Edward was not particularly bright, and his most formative years were divided between dour scoldings from his tutors and frequent beatings from his father. Even his mother was not averse to putting him across her knee and spanking him with her slipper in full view of the court.

One of the few diversions the unhappy youngster enjoyed was his penchant for practical jokes which, needless to say, the Prince Consort frowned upon gravely. Bertie's friends were often the victims of mustard pies, water squirted from bicycle pumps, and pockets surreptitiously filled with sticky confectionery. Once, he and a friend somehow managed to hoist a donkey into the bedroom of an acquaintance. They dressed the donkey in a nightdress, then somehow got the startled creature into the bed!

By the time he was 19, Edward had been packed off to Curragh Camp, outside Dublin, as part of his military schooling. It was there that he lost his virginity when fellow officers smuggled in actress Nellie Clifton, who presumably had no idea of the appetite she would whet that night. Edward's initiation to manhood was soon the talk of society, however, and it wasn't long before it reached the ears of a very angry Prince Albert. By then, Edward was studying at Cambridge and his father, who was not in the best of health, stormed off to challenge his son about the incident. Edward apologised profusely and vowed he had ended the romance, which to all accounts he had. Albert was satisfied with his wayward son's contrition, but, tragically, he had caught a chill during his stay in Cambridge. A few weeks later he developed typhoid fever and died on 14 December 1861.

If Victoria's relationship with Edward had already been strained prior to this, the death of her husband only worsened it. In fact, she even blamed him for Albert's death and wrote: 'Oh, that boy. Much as I pity, I never can, or shall, look at him without a shudder.' Despite Edward's genuine despair at the loss of his father, he couldn't change his womanising ways, not even when he got married, in March 1863, to the beautiful Princess Alexandra of the royal house of Denmark.

Following their brief honeymoon, the happy couple moved into Marlborough House, their London home where, for a brief time, they enjoyed the bliss of newly-weds. Unfortunately, Edward's eye for the ladies could not remain closed for long, despite the best efforts of his lovely wife and the stern admonitions of Victoria. It wasn't long before Edward returned to the ways of the idle rich, cavorting across Europe whenever and wherever the mood took him. Springs were spent basking in Biarritz, the fashionable French seaside resort; summers in the comforting and invigorating surrounds of the best European spas; autumns were for hunting and shooting in Norwich; and winters were spent attending the brightest galas and shows of London's theatre district.

Much to the chagrin of Princess Alexandra, Edward would often bring his wealthy cronies back to Marlborough House, which was quickly turned into a party house where all-night baccarat games were commonplace. Yet, throughout all this, she loved Edward deeply, as he did her and their children. However, her patience was strained to the limit when Bertie was twice hauled into court as a witness in scandals. One involved a gambling debt; the second time he was forced to appear as a witness in the Mordaunt divorce case.

Lady Harriet Mordaunt insisted that he had been one of her many lovers, which, of course, the Prince vehemently denied, and a dozen letters from him to her were produced as evidence. However, they contained nothing untoward, and much of the case rested on the testimony of the lady herself. However, by the time of the trial, Lady Mordaunt had been legally certified insane, and the case was dismissed. Throughout all of this, Bertie's wife and mother rallied to his side, and he escaped the embarrassing ordeal relatively unscathed – and certainly unrepentant – although he was soundly hissed at at the Epsom racecourse.

Although many of his affairs were short-lived – many young women were fêted with royal companionship for one night only – Edward did have a few long-term romances which lasted several years. One of these, with the erstwhile actress Lillie Langtry, became the most talked-about, fascinating and scandalous affair of the era. By the time it was over, the Royal Family, and indeed Britain, would never be the same again.

Lillie, a 'professional beauty' who would become the most shocking 'scarlet woman' of her time, was born on 13 October 1853 in Jersey as Emilie Charlotte Le Breton, the sole sister to six brothers, which taught her how to make it in a man's world from an early age! Her father, the Dean of Jersey, was known as the 'Dirty Dean' because of his many affairs and may have passed on his passionate nature to his daughter. He was such a philanderer that he had to break up Lillie's first love, when she was 17, because the young man in question was one of his own numerous illegitimate children! As Lillie herself later recalled: 'He was a damned nuisance. He couldn't be trusted with any woman anywhere.' However, Lillie, who once ran naked down a country lane for a dare, had many other suitors before long; indeed, the young men of the island lined up to seek her favour.

She was a stunning beauty, with a full figure, long, cascading hair, a flawless complexion and deep blue eyes. The relatively staid, subdued world of Jersey could not hold her long. She was determined to break out of her mundane existence and, during a brief trip to London, where she was overawed by the glamour and glitter of society, she came to realise that her beauty could be her ticket to freedom. 'I learned the magic of words, the beauty and excitement of poetic imagery,' she would remember. 'I learned there was something in life other than horses, the sea and the long Jersey tides. I was possessed by a conviction that my destiny lay in London.'

She cashed in that ticket for the first time in March 1874 when she married Edward Langtry, the son of a well-to-do Irish shipowner who had come to Jersey aboard his 80-foot yacht with the sole purpose of frittering away his family's fortune. Lillie saw the 26-year-old Edward as the answer to all her dreams and would later admit that she loved his yacht more than she ever loved him: 'To become the mistress of the yacht, I married the owner.' She acted quickly, and within 12 months of their wedding she had convinced the hapless Edward to move to London, where she would begin her carefully planned mission to become the darling of British society.

Attending glamorous dinner parties and soirées, she captivated and charmed every man she met with her beguiling beauty – sometimes even the women. The Countess of Warwick, who herself was later to have an affair with Bertie, once remarked: 'The friends we had invited to meet the lovely Mrs Langtry were as willingly magnetised by her unique personality as we were. How can words convey the vitality, the glow, the amazing charm, that made this fascinating woman the centre of any group that she entered?'

At one such social gathering, at the Lowndes Square home of Sir John and Lady Sebright, Lillie met the renowned portrait painter George Francis Miles, who asked her to pose for him. Lillie agreed and before long the painting was gracing cards which sold for a penny apiece. 'My sketches of Lillie during her first London season earned far more than I've ever made on the largest commissions for my most expensive paintings,' Miles recalled more than two decades later. 'She happens to be the most beautiful woman on earth.' Her alluring face and brightly painted red lips became known to the lowliest chimney sweep and the leaders of society. Prince Edward was no exception. He took one look at the portrait, fell instantly in love and asked one of his cronies to arrange an introduction.

On 24 May 1877 the Prince was invited to an intimate dinner party thrown by his bachelor friend, Sir Allen Young, who had ensured that Lillie would also be there. As the formal introductions were being made – and Lillie's fawning husband was bowing his head with great regularity – the Prince knew that this was a woman he had to have. Lillie, no stranger herself to the art of the affair, having cavorted with the King of the Belgians and the social élite of London, was only too willing.

Indeed, they wasted no time. During dinner, the Prince leaned over to her and remarked that the artist had not done her justice and that she was even more beautiful in person than she appeared in the portrait. She murmured her polite thanks, but knew then that she had him hooked. Within one week, they were lovers, but this affair was to be different. In many of his prior liaisons, Edward had been relatively circumspect. During those times, many men of the aristocracy kept mistresses, but they were never flaunted in public. They were kept at a discreet distance, far from the prying eyes of the masses. Moreover, by the time he met Lillie, Edward was the father of six children and the product of the Victorian age which looked down on any overt display of infidelity with a disapproving glare and a wagging finger.

However, Bertie had had enough of what he perceived as the hypocrisy and double standards of the age, and openly strutted his latest 'conquest' for all to see. He built her a house in Bournemouth, which used as their weekend love-nest, and took her on numerous trips to Paris. Neither he nor she cared who saw them together during these romantic forays to France, and once, in full view of the élite dinner crowd at Maxim's restaurant, they brazenly kissed full on the lips! Back in England, however, the Prince was a bit more discreet.

At social gatherings like the Ascot races, they kept a discriminating distance. He would be accompanied by the very forgiving Princess Alexandra, and Lillie would be with her husband. Eventually, however, Edward had had all he could take of this intrigue, and began demanding that his 'Jersey Lillie' be recognised by society as his 'official' mistress, with all the accommodation befitting her 'lofty' status. Oscar Wilde even wrote *Lady Windermere's Fan* for her, but she rejected it!

For three years, they continued their torrid affair, thumbing their noses at the hypocrites who whispered behind their backs. When Bertie was invited to a party, he would simply write Lillie's name on the RSVP and bring her along! 'Each successful season brought with it the same orgy of convivial gatherings, balls, dinners, receptions, concerts, operas, etc., which at first seemed to me a dream, a delight, a wild excitement,' she wrote, 'and I concentrated on the pursuit of amusement with the wholeheartedness that is characteristic of me, flying from one diversion to another, from dawn to dawn.'

Bertie took her everywhere and even had the gall to introduce her to Princess Alexandra and Queen Victoria, who was definitely not amused. However, while Alexandra bit her tongue and ignored Bertie's brazen infidelity, the poor cuckolded Edward Langtry could not. He ran off to a life of alcohol abuse – sometimes getting so drunk he could not even walk – and heavy debt, while Lillie was paraded around the favourite haunts of the European aristocracy.

Admiring crowds followed her through the streets, and everything she wore became an instant fashion trend. Even the colour of her dress could start a fad. Once, she wore a pink dress to Ascot and soon every high-class store in London featured that particular shade in the window.

Unfortunately for Lillie, however, Bertie's roving eye was forever scanning the horizon for new conquests. He became infatuated with French actress Sarah Bernhardt and soon passed Lillie on to his nephew, Prince Louis of Battenberg, a handsome naval officer. Or so he thought. To this day, the rumours are that Lillie and Prince Louis, who would become the father of Earl Mountbatten, were lovers long before her relationship with Edward had ended. In fact, it is believed that Lillie and Louis were lovers for 18 months prior to the break-up with Bertie.

Lillie's relationship with Louis ended when she became pregnant and he cruelly packed her off to France to have the illegitimate baby in secret. She gave birth to a daughter, called Jeanne-Marie, whom she passed off in later years as her niece. Over the next few years, public fascination with Lillie began to die down. In 1881, however, thanks to the encouragement of Prince Edward, who remained a life-long friend, she fulfilled a long-held dream, making her professional acting debut at the Haymarket Theatre in the role of Kate Hardcastle in *She Stoops To Conquer*. The Prince of Wales and most of the social élite turned out to see her and raved over her performance, even if the critics did not. One sniffed: 'She has small ability, no more than that of the respectable amateur.' Wrote another: 'As a novice she should first learn the art of acting.'

Despite the barbs, Lillie was back, and was again the toast of the town. Songs were written about her and her theatrical appearances were sell-outs. Most of her ardent fans were Americans, who had been enchanted by this smouldering woman's affairs with the high and mighty. For the next few years, she travelled Britain with her own acting company, and was eventually hailed as the most prestigious actress of her era. Like a conquering heroine, she also visited America and flitted about the land in her own luxuriously appointed railway coach. It was during that spectacularly successful trip, in 1892, that she travelled to the dusty Texas town of Vinegaroon. The infamous Western character 'Judge' Roy Bean, who had had many a horse thief strung up by the neck, was so smitten with her that he immediately changed the name of the town to Langtry in her honour.

By now, Lillie was a world celebrity, and there followed even more affairs, including the rumour of one with the British Prime Minister, William Gladstone. Then, in 1895, she at last found the great love she had been searching for for so long, wealthy Baronet Hugo de Bathe. When her first, long-suffering husband, Edward Langtry, died in an asylum in 1897 – he had been picked up by disbelieving authorities, wandering around a railway station dazed and mumbling that he was married to the great Lillie Langtry – she was free to marry the Baronet, who was 19 years her junior. Together, they moved to Monte Carlo and Lillie made few visits again to Britain.

Her life was now filled with quiet, happy days, but the cruelty of fate had not finished with this remarkable woman. Her relationship with her daughter ended in a bitter fight when Jeanne-Marie, then 21, confronted her after discovering her father was Prince Louis of Battenberg. When she died in 1929, aged 76, Lillie left an estate worth only a few thousand pounds and was buried in St Saviour's Churchyard on Jersey, not far from where she was born.

She had seen the 'golden age' give way to war, when the best of Europe's young men were slaughtered in the trenches of France and Belgium. She was shattered by the wholesale destruction of life, and many believe she died of a broken heart — not for the loss of one man, but for the loss of an entire generation.

Today, Lillie Langtry is best remembered for her royal liaisons. Yet in an age when women were treated as second-class citizens, Lillie not only stood up to the male-dominated society but used her sensuous beauty to conquer it.

Edward was not so lucky. After his amicable parting with Lillie, he took up with Frances, Lady Brooke, later Countess of Warwick. Nicknamed 'Daisy' by the doting Bertie, Lady Brooke had herself led an active love life, thanks to a husband who was away most of the time following his passion for sport. Unfortunately for Edward, one of her former lovers was Lord Charles Beresford, one of his closest friends. Beresford had dropped Daisy with little thought for her feelings and, when she learned in 1891 that she was pregnant, she flew into a rage. She fired off a vicious letter to her former lover, who did not have the good sense to make sure his wife didn't see it. Lady Beresford not only berated her husband for being a philanderer, she also threatened to publish the letter! Only

Edward's intervention saved them all from what would have been a devastating scandal.

However, not even Edward could save himself from the 1890 scandal surrounding the Tranby Croft case. While playing baccarat with some friends, it was believed by some present that Sir William Gordon Cumming, Regimental Lieutenant-Colonel of the Scots Guards, was cheating. When it was brought to Bertie's attention, he insisted, on pain of exposure, that Sir William sign a pledge never to play cards for money again. Soon afterwards, however, the matter came to public attention, Sir William sued for slander and Edward was cited as a witness. The Prince was forced to admit that he gambled at cards, which he had long denied. One critic wrote:

> Another year has brought sadness and sorrow to the bosom of our gracious Queen and a diminished spirit to meet the responsibilities of her high position; while over the throne the black shadow of a ghastly spectre has fallen. Among us has risen a second George IV in the heir to the throne of this vast Empire. He has been convicted of being concerned in an infamous abomination, and the awful spectacle is presented of an heir to the throne publicly acknowledging complicity in gambling transactions.

When Queen Victoria died in January 1901, Bertie at last found himself with more to fill his time than just women and gambling. Throughout her lengthy reign, Victoria, who correctly thought her son an irresponsible playboy, had kept Edward at a distance, never allowing him to become involved with matters of state. Indeed he was fully 51 years old before his mother would even let him see (but not keep!) copies of the Prime Minister's reports on cabinet meetings. Suddenly, here he was, King Edward VII. He threw himself into his new role as leader of the British Empire and developed an interest in foreign affairs, although he exhibited none of his mother's acumen and was loath to involve himself in the actual intricacies of international politics.

Despite his new-found responsibilities, old habits died hard. Throughout his reign, he had yet another mistress, Alice Keppel, and he continued to accommodate his passion for food and drink, which he pursued abroad for up to three months every year, often without a single minister in attendance. Bertie would then complain to friends that his ministers told him nothing! Yet he really had little interest in public affairs, was easily bored and lazy and made several diplomatic gaffes, including one at a dinner thrown by the King and Queen of Italy, in which he praised the Anglo-Italian alliance. It was a nice sentiment, but unfortunately for Bertie such a pact had never existed. On another occasion, when he was to visit the German Emperor at Hamburg, the Foreign Secretary, Lord Lansdowne, gave him some confidential papers which might help him in dealing with his German counterpart. Bertie let the Emperor's nephew, the Kaiser, read them!

Within five years, Bertie's health began to falter, thanks to a lifetime of overindulgence. On 6 May 1910, following a series of heart attacks, Edward the Caresser died. Lillie Langtry went to the funeral.

A SHORT HISTORY OF THE BRITISH MONARCHY

George V

So ended the reign of the libertine Edward VII. It ended, however, with rumours of a dark skeleton in the closet. The British Royal Family has been accused of many dastardly deeds over the centuries but the tales that emanated about one of the senior members of the House of Saxe-Coburg-Gotha were among the most dreadful ever. Most people at the time found them beyond belief. With the advance of forensic science, however, they have since begun to gain real credence.

The theory is that Edward's eldest son and heir, popularly known as 'Prince Eddy', was under suspicion of being the most notorious murderer in the annals of crime. Had he lived, had he succeeded to the throne, Britain might have been ruled by Jack the Ripper!

Controversy still rages as to the true identity of the knife-wielding stalker of 1888, and the truth will probably never be known, but rumour at the time when the Ripper's reign held London's East End in terror centred, as it does now, on a royal connection. The finger pointed at Prince Eddy or, to give him his full title, Albert Victor Christian Edward, Duke of Clarence and Avondale, heir to the throne and great-uncle of the present Queen. It is perhaps fortunate (certainly it was for the Royal Family) that Prince Eddy died in 1892 of pneumonia – Buckingham Palace-speak for brain damage, brought on by syphilis.

A hundred years later, world-renowned forensic psychiatrist Dr Harold Abrahamsen declared in his book *Murder and Madness: The Secret Life of Jack the Ripper* that the killer was indeed Prince Eddy, but aided and guided by his mentor, tutor (and homosexual lover) James Kenneth

Stephen. Abrahamsen suggested that coroners and Scotland Yard alike were slow to pursue any clue that pointed towards the throne. He took this as evidence of a royal cover-up.

Whatever the truth of that dark autumn of 1888, Prince Eddy was still a royal liability. A victim partly of the education system instituted by his grandmother, he was a homosexual already suffering from syphilis when he formed an intense relationship with his woman-hating tutor, James Stephen.

None of this could remain secret today, of course. No prince or princeling, no consort or hanger-on could long evade the close scrutiny and snapping lenses of the world's press, but it was not like that at the time of Prince Eddy and his younger brother, the man who eventually did make it to the throne, as George V. The newspapers' self-censorship spared George a lot of unwelcome publicity. Yet it was George, more than any king, who opened up the royals to the public and founded the constitutional monarchy we know today.

George V, who came to the throne in 1910, was even more of a German mouthful than his ancestor Prince George of Brunswick-Luneberg. He was a Saxe-Coburg-Gotha. Happily, the King cut his family's last connections with its German origins by adopting the title of the House of Windsor in 1917. It was not an act of altruism, however. The name-change was forced upon the monarchy by deep anti-royal sentiment. The real reason for this amazing 'disguise' of royal roots was that on 7 July 1917 London rioted after a daylight raid by 24 German twin-engined

Gotha bombers, which killed 44 people and injured 125. German-owned property was attacked by enraged mobs. Ten days later the King judiciously changed the name of his dynasty to Windsor!

George ushered in a relatively peaceful period for the Royal Family despite, or perhaps because of the Great War. Even if George's penchant for visiting seaside prostitutes had made news, there were more important matters to think of. For the man in the street, who all too soon was to become the Tommy in the trenches, there was the small matter of survival.

Survival, at all costs, was the name of the game for the more exalted, too. When the Tsar of Russia, faced with the Communist revolution, sought asylum for himself and his family in Britain, the government readily agreed, but the idea did not suit His Majesty. George took the view that the public would resent the presence of the Romanovs. Quite likely, he saw the potential threat to the throne of sheltering a monarch deposed by the masses.

In any event, he began an active campaign to get the government to change its collective mind. His view ultimately prevailed, and his own cousins and their young family were doomed to the violent slaughter that, seven decades later, was uncovered in Ekaterinburg in the Urals.

His Queen, Mark of Teck (previously the fiancée of Prince Eddy) also played her part in stitching up the Romanovs. She certainly profited from the 'fire sale' of Russian jewels that were saved from the Bolsheviks to extend her own beloved collection of valuables. Her greatest coup, however, was ten years later when George

V persuaded Grand Duchesses Xenia and Olga, who had escaped the slaughter along with their mother, the Dowager Empress, to send their jewels to be appraised and sold in England. Queen Mary is alleged to have held on to the fabulous collection until 1933 (the height of the Depression) when they were offered for sale at rock-bottom prices. The present Queen must have been shocked to discover just how much blood is attached to the stones she now owns.

There was scandal, too, closer to home. George, like his son, Edward VII, did not confine his womanising to pros-titutes. Like his son, he had a penchant for the occasional woman of quality. One of these affairs, with Queen Maria Cristina, widow of the Spanish King Alphonso XII, resulted in the birth of an illegitimate daughter, Helle Cristina Habsburg Windsor. She was quickly whisked away to Malta where she posed no threat to the monarchy, right up to her death in 1990, aged 100.

None of this set the pages of the popular press alight. Had it done so, the royal divorces that are becoming the norm today, would almost certainly have started then. Queens Alexandra and Mary may have felt able to turn a blind eye to their husbands' philandering, but if they had been forced to read about the monarchical misbehaviour along with the unwashed *hoi polloi*, could they have stood the strain?

Paradoxically, George realised that the public wanted their kings to have less to do with affairs of state and to become more of a soft focus for the fawning masses. Even the austere matriarch Queen Mary joined in and allowed the popular magazines to have their way. George, seeing the fate of less flexible monarchies around the world, moved the family out of the political spotlight. It was George who, in his efforts to protect the very notion of royalty, bowed to the public distaste for all things German during the First World War. So, as German Shepherd dogs became Alsatians, the dynasty of Saxe-Coburg-Gotha became, overnight, the simpler, and very English, Windsor. It probably went some way to preserving the monarchy through a difficult period.

George certainly believed in the survival of the most royal! Those who feel there are too many royals around today have him to thank that there are not even more with spectacular titles and privileges. George decreed in 1917 that only children of the sovereign should be styled prince or princess, and that children of daughters should not be so honoured. George rightly saw the success of the monarchy as being its exclusivity. He even foresaw the public resentment of the extended Civil List.

Finally, after a reign spent bending the rules of royalty to fit the nation's democratic aspirations, George V died. Terminally ill, he was put to sleep by his doctors overnight – so that his death would first be reported in the serious morning papers, rather than the more downmarket evenings.

George was in a coma at the time, but such was his preoccupation with the royal heritage that he would undoubtedly have approved as, in fact, years later, did his terminally ill widow, Mary. She agreed to her own mercy killing ten weeks before the coronation of the present

Queen. Mary knew that if she lingered on a week or two longer, the coronation would have been postponed for the period of official mourning that is required after the death of a sovereign or consort.

So, in 1936 the King was dead, but the monarchy he fought so hard to preserve was soon to face its greatest challenge of modern times — the abdication crisis brought about by his son. This time, it would be in the full glare of world publicity.

CHAPTER TWO

The Duke of Windsor

While George V was a stable, stately monarch, his son and heir, Edward VIII, was a blot on the royal horizon. Just as George V was rigidly upright even throughout a loveless marriage, so Edward bowed in the wind towards every pretty woman.

George V had an unshakeable sense of duty towards his country; Edward was a threat to state security, who had neither the foresight nor the intelligence to see how his actions exposed Britain to its enemies. He failed to inherit that sense of nobility that would have protected the institution of the Crown and he almost brought about the fall of the Windsors like a collapsed house of cards. The abdication crisis in 1936 was to threaten the monarchy in the same way the Gunpowder Plot almost wiped out Parliament.

Edward Albert Patrick David became King on the death of his father in January 1936. Within 12 months he was in exile, looking a fool. Today he is regarded as a great romantic, prepared to sacrifice all for the sake of the woman he adored. The enduring view is that his staid and stodgy family and machinating politicians insisted that he did 'the right thing', while he allowed his love for American divorcee Wallis Simpson to eclipse the call of duty. On close inspection the flaws in Edward's character shine out like beacons. He was born to be king but never merited the title and quickly proved his inherent weaknesses for all the world to see.

When his sexual tastes came to the attention of his family and the government, a scandal brewed, but between the Windsors and the ministers of the day, the crisis was safely covered up.

As Britain edged towards war with the European fascists, the British people were filled with genuine distaste for the activities of the dictators. Yet Edward chose to consort with British fascist leader Oswald Mosley and even went as far as meeting Nazi Führer, Adolf Hitler.

The government soon pinpointed Edward as a threat to state security. His father called him a cad and wrote in a diary that Edward would almost certainly ruin himself. Even his mother, Queen Mary, seemed to have little love for him. His sister-in-law, Elizabeth, now the Queen Mother and everyone's favourite granny, was stone-hearted towards him.

How did such a dashing and popular Prince of Wales become such a sad and derided ex-king? What made a man with everything – wealth, rank, privilege and respect – throw it all away? Can it all be laid at the feet of the twice-wed but many times bedded Wallis Simpson, the American socialite and vamp whose power over men was legendary? Certainly, she dominated her weak, spoiled and foolish man but, in doing that, she met the only condition he demanded of her. The man born to be king needed to be ruled.

Who can say what influences were to hold sway with a small boy growing up in a royal nursery, distanced, spurned even, by the one person he needed most, his mother? On Queen Mary's death, years later, he was to write to Wallis: 'The fluids in her veins have always been as icy-cold as they are now in death.' Yet, throughout his notorious love life, the women he sought out to become his mistresses had one thing in common: he always seemed to be seeking the mother figure he claimed to have been deprived of. Indeed, his final words were: 'Mama, mama.'

At 13, Edward embarked on the Naval career his father had picked out for him and became a cadet at Osborne Naval College. After passing the entrance exam with flying colours, he left his sheltered royal life for the brutish, homosexual-oriented life of the college, where he witnessed friends enduring appalling and humiliating degradation at the hands of other cadets. He, himself, was also an object of fun. Having his hair dyed red with ink was just one of the harsh pranks played upon him. However, he emerged from these adolescent trials a handsome man who was most attractive to the opposite sex. His superficial charm and clean-cut good looks set him on the road to destruction.

Edward saw action during the First World War, well away from the front lines. He lost his virginity in a French brothel in 1916 to a girl called Paulette. Although he expressed some disgust at the time, he returned time and again. In fact, by 1917 his advisers were concerned at the level of the Prince's whoring, and with good reason — eventually there was to be a blackmail threat, based on certain letters he had written.

At home he turned to Viscountess Coke, daughter-in-law to the Earl of Leicester and 15 years his senior. From their first meeting, in March 1915, he found a willing confidante in Marion Coke. When she gave birth to a son at the end of that year, the Prince of Wales agreed to be a sponsor at the christening and the child was named David after him.

Edward's next amour was Lady Rosemary Leveson-

Gower, who was a Red Cross nurse in an army hospital in France when they met at the end of the war. However, protocol put paid to any hopes of a lasting romance. Although Lady Rosemary herself was above reproach, she was a woman whose family history precluded a royal liaison. Her mother, Millicent, Duchess of Sutherland, had married within a year of being widowed. With even more unseemly haste, she then divorced her new husband, at the age of 52, and married Lieutenant Colonel George Hawes, whose name had already been linked to a homosexual scandal of the day. Rosemary's uncle was the freespending Harry Rosslyn, the earl who inspired the song 'The Man who Broke the Bank at Monte Carlo'. He became a professional gambler with his £17,000 income (£340,000 in today's terms). He was to be married three times and bankrupted three times and was estimated to have gambled away a quarter of a million pounds.

The King summoned Prince Edward to tell him in no uncertain terms that the marriage he proposed was out of the question. Who can tell whether it was this stern lecture regarding affairs of the heart that finally set Edward on a collision course with his father and the state?

Edward subsequently found solace in the arms of Freda Dudley Ward, wife of Liberal MP William Dudley Ward, vice-chamberlain of the royal household. Her own marriage was a façade and she daydreamed about a lasting love with the Prince. However, in her heart she knew that a divorced woman would never be accepted by the royals. Edward might talk about resigning from his high office – he discussed the idea even then – but fear of his father's fury stopped him making the fateful decision.

Much later Freda admitted: 'Yes, I could have dominated him. He made himself a slave to whomever he loved.' She showed admirable restraint during the 12 years they were close friends and the relationship survived plenty of knocks from the establishment, mainly from the King himself, who branded her 'the lace-maker's daughter' because her father had made his fortune in the Nottingham lace-making industry.

Already the King's passion for correctness and formality had been severely affronted by his son. As the Roaring Twenties got underway, Edward threw himself body and soul into the frivolity of the times. During one interview with his errant son the King was heard shouting: 'You act like a cad. You dress like a cad. You are a cad. Get out of my sight.'

Freda remained a close friend and heard plenty of laments from her miserable young Prince. Socialite Lady Cynthia Asquith noted: 'Saw the Prince of Wales dancing around with Mrs Dudley Ward, a pretty little fluff with whom he is said to be rather in love.' However, there was more to this relationship than heady romance and the Prince's cousin, Dickie Mountbatten, was far closer to the truth when he wrote in a letter: 'He has only had one "mother", though he'd be the last person to admit it, and that is his great friend Freda who is so nice and about whom you've probably heard, oh, such wicked lies. She's absolutely been a mother to him, comforted and advised him and all along he has been blind in his love to what the world is saying.'

Following a highly successful public tour of Canada and the United States in 1919, Edward developed a taste for everything and everybody American, long before Wallis Simpson appeared on the scene. When he attended Leicester Fair he met vivacious 25-year-old American, Thelma Furness, recently married to the much older Viscount Furness. Soon, their relationship progressed to intimate dinners at the Prince's own residence. Six months on, she joined him on an African safari. 'This was our Eden,' she wrote 'and we were alone in it. Each night I felt more completely possessed by our love, carried ever more swiftly into uncharted seas. I felt content to let the Prince chart the course, heedless of where the voyage would end.'

This time, however, Edward refused to let his fascination with a trans-Atlantic siren rule his life. He continued his courtship of Thelma in tandem with that of Freda Dudley Ward although, of course, neither was ultimately to win his favour. Yet, strangely, Thelma was to play a key role in his romance with Wallis. She was hosting a house party in Burrough-on-the-Hill, near Melton Mowbray, in 1931 to which her lover, the Prince, and Wallis Simpson were both invited. The ambitious Wallis set her sights on Edward immediately. As she sat down next to him at lunch, she set the tenor of their relationship with a domineering riposte. When the Prince asked her if, as an American, she was shivering in Britain's lack of central heating she replied: 'You disappoint me, Sir. Every American woman gets the same question. I had hoped for something more original from the Prince of Wales.' Whether she knew it or not, Wallis had set her bait with perfection. Edward could not resist the lure of a dominant woman. Their relationship went from strength to strength. Onlookers were bemused at their behaviour together. She called him 'my little man' and gave him public reprimands. He was besotted both by her and the treatment she doled out.

As the romance deepened, the King, along with the rest of the country, was asking: 'Who is that woman?' When his question was answered, it was probably worse than his bleakest imaginings. Wallis was the daughter of Alice Montague, who went from rags to riches through her marriage to wealthy Teackle Wallis-Warland, and back to rags again following his untimely death. 'Bessiewallis', as she was known, was a baby when her father died and knew more of the seedy world her mother inhabited as landlady of a Baltimore guesthouse than she ever did of the flashy upper-crust home where she was born.

At nineteen Wallis met and married a US naval pilot, Lieutenant Earl Winfield Spencer. Before the honeymoon was over, however, she realised she had married a lush whose relentless drinking would transform him from a dashing uniformed hero to a violent ogre. They first parted when Winfield decided to move in with a new girlfriend. Yet, months later, he was begging for a reconciliation in Washington where he was based. Wallis's mother was in the capital, too, working as a hostess at the Chevy Chase Club. Wallis relented and rejoined her husband. The marriage foundered once more but by this time Wallis had found herself a new niche in society. The rich and beautiful welcomed her with open arms and she launched herself on a string of affairs.

Finally, she met her first real love, Argentinian attaché Don Felipe Espit, 35, rich and a shameless Romeo. Although she did not name him, Wallis wrote in her autobiography: 'He was the most fascinating man I ever met. He was both my teacher and my model in life.' She learned many of her skills in pursuit and manipulation in order to capture him, but her scheming wasn't enough to hold him and she was furious when she discovered there were still other women in his life. Heartbroken, she agreed to a third reunion with her husband, newly appointed commander of the *Pampamga*, a third-rate gunboat in the South China seas. Wallis joined Winfield in the Orient, in September 1923, the very week that China's civil war escalated. Earl Winfield Spencer sailed into the heart of the conflict, but no one really knows what became of Wallis at that time.

What is known, however, is that she was in Paris by January 1924. Even then Naval Intelligence were keeping her actions taped. She and her widowed pal, Corinne Mustin, decided to cheer themselves up with a riotous time in France. They led a lavish existence despite the fact Wallis had only a small income from her husband. How did she afford her champagne lifestyle? The society gossips had a field day. By the summer, she was back in the States, again reviewing her unhappy marriage. However, she and Winfield joined forces once more and Wallis began a new and illustrious adventure in China, that was to dog her romance with the Prince ever more. She and her husband visited the 'singing houses' of Hong Kong, not, as they sound, cabaret shows but high-class brothels favoured by senior Naval staff. Here, young teenage girls, trained in the art of sensual and erotic lovemaking, satisfied a huge range of sexual desires. Entranced by the goings-on, Wallis joined in with the sexual practices. Later, she claimed she was part of a threesome excluding her husband. Intelligence sources insist she was eager to learn the Oriental way of lovemaking called *fang yung*, involving massage of every part of the body. It invokes deep relaxation and prolongs sexual arousal in men. Wallis soon had the art of fatal attraction at her fingertips.

British Intelligence revealed this and much more to King George V when he wanted the woman's background probed. The China Report, as it is known, showed just why Wallis could never be royal. As the abdication crisis loomed, Prime Minister Stanley Baldwin saw two other, equally lurid, reports which sealed the fate of the nation.

The Spencers' rocky marriage finally cracked when a Naval ensign confessed to Win his love for Wallis. Win was livid and kicked her out, which left Wallis heading for the American court in Shanghai, determined once and for all to end the marriage with a divorce.

Shanghai was a place of mystery, mayhem, prostitution, drugs and destitution – and Wallis loved it. She met a fellow American called Robbie who introduced her to the varied expatriate community in the city. She describes the meeting innocently enough. 'He came towards me, young and handsome, beautifully dressed. We had a drink together, very pleasant. Then he suggested dinner, and it proved to be even more pleasant. This was the simple beginning of a delightful friendship.' Wallis became a paid hostess at the house of her boyfriend's partner, close to some of Shanghai's most exclusive brothels where no Chinese were allowed. In the dens, the hookers carried out an erotic 'tao of loving' in which sex is held to be important both physically and mentally to men and women. Wallis Simpson was intrigued.

Although she was at the very centre of the party set, she eventually fled Shanghai. Again, no one knows why. In her autobiography she claimed it was to go on a shopping trip to Peking. But Peking was an uncomfortable thousand miles away across a war zone.

In one of China's finest hotels, Wallis ran into Gerry Green, a serviceman she knew from her months in Paris, now working for the US legation Guard. Moments later, she met old pal Katherine Moore Bigelow, now married to wealthy American Herman Rogers. These revived friendships led her into a fabulous social whirl where, she wrote, 'every woman could be a Cinderella and midnight never struck'. For every single woman there were ten men and few, she admitted, had honourable intentions.

Still under the watchful gaze of US Intelligence sources, Wallis consorted with Count Galeazzo Ciano, who was to be Italy's consul general and was son-in-law to the dictator Mussolini. Wallis also discovered the joys of gambling and became a poker addict, playing with chips provided by her wealthy escorts. They also showered her with gifts of jade and cash with which she bought clothes or more jewellery. It was said that she would do anything for money — indeed, she had to as she had none of her own, and that is how she managed to remain in Peking, living the society life, for almost a year when she had originally planned to leave after a fortnight.

In the end she departed again quickly and without proper explanation. Not a shopping trip this time, but an illness is her stated reason for going. However, it was thought that she was pregnant, probably by the fascist Count Ciano. An ensuing abortion led to a raging infection which left her cripplingly ill on the trip back to the States. As soon as her boat docked she went to a hospital in Seattle for a further operation. She never became pregnant again.

Years afterwards, when the contents of the China Report were put to her, Wallis made vehement denials. While she admitted having been in a Hong Kong singing house, she insisted it was not by choice. How she explained her society lifestyle against her meagre income isn't known. She was clearly unaware that her first marriage had aroused the interest of the security services which thereafter tracked almost all her movements.

However, it wasn't only Edward and Wallis's questionable sexual tastes that came to the attention of the secret services. Edward's younger brother, Prince George, Duke of Kent, was a notorious bisexual whose affairs fascinated court circles for years. Noël Coward and black singer Florence Mills were among his conquests, as was a young man in Paris who later had to be paid substantial amounts to return his love letters. Edward's cousin, Louis Mountbatten, and his wife, Edwina, were also at the centre of scandal. Edwina kept company with her lesbian sister-in-law and was fascinated by black men and Indian politicians. Her husband was a womaniser who is also thought to have had homosexual affairs. Even Edward was accused by some of homosexual leanings.

By early 1935, although still married to her second husband, Ernest Simpson, Wallis was ruling Edward's life. She ran his private home, Fort Belvedere, near Ascot, and even had her own wardrobe installed there. One guest recalls a dinner party there:

It was a very lively evening with a great deal of conversation and jollity. The party went on until around 2 a.m., I suppose. As a house guest I retired to my bedroom. I do know that night Edward went to Wallis's room. Those of us who knew him well enough could see that he, and all of us, were heading for trouble. The man whom I admired so much was going to destroy his great heritage, and those of us who attempted to offer words of caution were, I am afraid, brushed aside. He was blinded and astounded by Wallis and nothing could move him from the path he was taking. He believed, in his distorted thoughts, that he could make everything work out in a way that would suit everyone, that he could take Mrs Simpson as his wife and she would sit beside him when he became king. That was how the infatuation with her had taken over his thoughts. I think sometimes he did allow himself to consider the worst, that he would be prevented from marrying her. And I think that in those moments he had decided, long before the abdication, that he would quit his royal life for her. Sad, but true.

*   *   *

With Wallis Simpson's known Nazi sympathies and Edward's right-wing beliefs, it is hardly surprising the Fascists wanted to capitalise on the duo. Diplomats from Germany and Italy were expressly told to court them. Wallis was often a guest at dinners given by the homosexual German Ambassador, Leopold von Hoesch. She was thought once to have been the lover of his successor, Joachim von Ribbentrop. MI5 were even concerned that she was being paid by the Nazis for information. In the beginning, however, it's more likely that her passion for status led her to show off by passing on titbits or simply that she let slip certain items during conversation. She was consequently tailed by security men who carefully noted her relations with the Germans.

Edward, the man who sided with the upper classes during the General Strike, happily backed both Hitler and Mussolini. He said: 'It was no business of ours to interfere in Germany's internal affairs, either re Jews or re anything else.' He added: 'Dictators are very popular these days and we might want one in England before long.' In 1935, he informed the Italian Ambassador in London that Britain's opposition to Mussolini's invasion of Abyssinia and the League of Nations' sanctions were 'grotesque and criminal'. He followed with interest Hitler's grasp of power in Germany and apparently admired his iron-fist brand of politics. An enthusiast of Fascism, he kept in regular contact with Sir Oswald Mosley throughout the thirties. German documents which fell into British hands revealed the dangerous degree of support the Prince was showing to Hitler at the start of 1935. His stand alone could have prompted a crisis as his opinions were directly opposed to those of the government. Moreover, he had no place involving himself in politics. Certainly, Edward found the art of politics irresistible but he had not the mental agility nor the aptitude to be a success. At one point, he even encouraged the formation of a King's party around him, so deluded and arrogant was he in the belief that he had a role to play.

As world tensions tightened in 1935, Edward and Mrs Simpson decided on a holiday in Europe. They went to a lunch at the British Embassy in Paris, attended by French Premier Pierre Laval. At his trial after the war, Laval revealed that Edward spoke up totally in support of the French pact with Mussolini, which gave the dictator the green light to invade Abyssinia.

While Edward took the throne, Hitler was giving orders that the new King should be brought into the Nazi fold by forging a powerful friendship with him. The Duke of Coburg, a disgraced nobleman, became the Führer's personal emissary to the palace. Hitler was regaled with details of their meetings.

When Hitler marched into the demilitarised Rhineland in March 1936, effectively ripping up the restraining Locarno Treaty, he awaited repercussions. In Britain his ambassador, von Hoesch, appealed to the King to intervene and ensure that Britain took no action. Hitler took comfort, believing the King to be on his side.

Most worrying of all was the way a number of top-secret documents went straight to the Nazis after Edward became King. Historian A.J.P. Taylor reported in *Origins of the Second World War* that confidential Foreign Office documents were inside the German Foreign Ministry even before they reached the British Embassy in Berlin. The guilty agent was named Herr Doktor by spycatchers. Officially the identity of this spy has never been revealed. However, as they tried to plug the leaks, Intelligence came to realise that Herr Doktor was none other than Wallis Simpson. To prove it, false information was included in state papers that went only to Edward. Within days agents reported that these red herrings were on the desk of Ribbentrop. After that the King himself was screened by security and he was no longer trusted with state secrets.

Edward signed his abdication papers on 10 December 1936. The next day he told his country: '... it is impossible to carry the heavy burden of responsibility and to discharge my duties as King as I would wish to do without the help and support of the woman I love.' Edward went into exile on 12 December 1936.

Edward's father had died on 20 January 1936. Mountbatten always believed that if George V had lived longer, Edward would have found the nerve to tell him he had chosen love before his country. Said Mountbatten: 'He would have mustered the courage if the King had lasted one more year.'

To compound further the huge catalogue of errors made by Edward, he chose, following his abdication, to retreat to a French chateau owned by a known German agent, Charles Bedeaux.

Charles Bedeaux had cowtowed to the Nazis in the

hope of retrieving a business venture they had confiscated. In 1943 he was captured by the Americans while working for the Germans in North Africa and he eventually committed suicide in a Miami jail.

At his home in Chateau Le Cande, Charles Bedeaux watched the exiled Edward and recently divorced Wallis marry on 3 June 1937.

In Berlin the Windsors stayed at a 26-room mansion belonging to Dr Robert Ley, the Labour leader. It had once been the home of a Jewish banker. SS troops stood guard outside as Edward and Wallis fraternised with the likes of Ribbentrop and Goebbels. There was a tour of factories and housing projects before Britain's recent king met Hitler himself.

As the sun poured down on the Führer's home in Berchtesgaden, the pair met and chatted. Finally, Hitler shook the new Duchess of Windsor by the hand and then gave the Duke his Nazi salute, to which Edward replied 'Heil Hitler'.

However, the Windsors did not appear to greet the Germans with such ardour when they invaded France only four years later. Now they were forced to join other refugees on the road to Spain. At the border, the Duke had to haggle with officials because he had no visa. In Barcelona he sent a telegram to the Foreign Office in London saying: 'Having received no instructions have arrived in Spain to avoid capture. Proceeding to Madrid.'

Both Britain and Germany wanted the Duke and Duchess on their side. Hitler, ready for Britain's capitulation, was planning to instal Edward on the throne with Wallis as his queen and a puppet Fascist government. Precisely because of this danger Britain was not ready to relinquish links with the Windsors. Seizing his opportunity, the Duke refused to return to Britain unless he was given a proper job and his wife was recognised as a royal. The government responded with a job offer of Governor in the Bahamas, the least vital of all British assets. There was a flurry of diplomatic activity as go-betweens tried to find a compromise. In the end Churchill threatened the Duke with a court martial unless he complied with instructions. He telegraphed: 'Your Royal Highness has taken military rank and refusal to obey direct orders of competent military authority would create a serious situation. I must strongly urge immediate compliance with the wishes of your government.' Edward was furious but he obeyed.

Meanwhile, in Berlin the Germans were plotting to kidnap the Duke and Duchess in order to keep them in Spain. The benefits of this would be tremendous and Hitler backed the plan with hard cash. He was prepared to offer 50 million Swiss francs (£45 million in today's money) for Edward to speak out against the actions of the British royals and government and to remain as 'king-in-waiting' in Spain. Hitler always remained convinced of the Duke's importance. In October 1941 he said: 'He is no enemy of Germany... when the proper moment comes he will be the only person capable of directing the destiny of England.'

Churchill may have thought he scored a victory when the Duke and Duchess finally embarked on the Canadian ship *Lady Somers*, leaving Portugal bound for the Bahamas, but blundering Edward could not be kept out of trouble even in that far-flung outpost. His shadowy dealings in the colony were later to force a split with Britain for ever.

Wallis describes their arrival on 17 August 1940. 'David had been on the bridge of the ship as we entered the harbour and the captain picked out Government House, our future home. At a distance it looked like a rambling Southern plantation house with spacious verandah, jalousied windows and surrounded by palm trees.'

Even here the Nazi tentacles reached out to them. One of their first acquaintances on the paradise islands was Axel Wenner Gren, a Swedish millionaire and a Mr Fixit who had strong links with the Third Reich. It was Gren, the founder of Electrolux, the international electrical company, who had visited Goering in 1939 in order to secure peace. Goering asked him to meet Chamberlain and Gren actually entered Downing Street armed with a letter of introduction from the Swedish Crown Prince, Gustaf Adolf, in which he related Goering's outpourings against war and restated German terms. Chamberlain refused an audience with Gren, however, and the self-appointed ambassador returned to the German corridors of power until he sailed for the Bahamas on the outbreak of war.

Both British and American Intelligence observed Gren as he returned to his Pacific mansion. He quickly resumed a friendship with the Duke and Duchess which had begun in pre-war France when they were first introduced by Charles Bedeaux. When the Duchess fell ill with toothache and stomach pains, he happily offered the services of his yacht so that they could sail to America.

Once again, the Windsors made a foolish error. Without informing Churchill, they headed for America on the yacht of a known Nazi sympathiser. Although they insisted the visit was strictly private, the newspapers on both sides of the Atlantic had a field day. Churchill sent another acid telegram.

There would be no objection if your Royal Highness cared to make a cruise in the West Indian Islands. It would be impossible, however, for HM Government to approve the use of Mr Wenner Gren's yacht for such a purpose. This gentlemen is regarded as pro-German, with strong leanings towards appeasement and suspected of being in communication with the enemy. Your Royal Highness may not realise the intensity of feeling in the United States against people of this kind.

American files already had the Duke down as a Nazi sympathiser and his wife as being on Hitler's payroll, so Roosevelt knew the score. Later, in an American magazine called *Liberty*, shortly before the bombing of Pearl Harbor, Edward revealed his uncertain loyalties by saying: 'America will help Britain more by not engaging in actual fighting but remaining a keystone for the new world which must be created when the war is over. There will be a new order in Europe, whether imposed by Germany or Britain.'

Despite their now somewhat humbler position in society, Edward and, in particular, Wallis continued to wallow in luxury to the point of losing a grip on reality.

While war was waged and thousands of people, not least the British, went hungry, Wallis used rum and whole eggs to shampoo her hair. She insisted her dirty laundry was sent to New York for cleaning. This was so excessive a demand that the security forces became convinced it was a cover for Nazi activities. J. Edgar Hoover himself scrutinised their activities and claimed the couple should be locked up until after the war.

Wallis complained about the official residence, and the island parliament finally set aside £1,500 for refurbishment. Wallis spent five times that amount by bringing in interior designers from New York and insisting on only the best. However, their generally absurd behaviour is put firmly in the shade by a far more sinister episode involving a notorious American gangster and a ruthless killing. The hood was Meyer Lansky, a murderer and high-ranking Mafia godfather. One of the original cast of Murder Incorporated, which claimed 800 lives, he had always managed to give the police the slip. Lansky teamed up with Nassau lawyer Stafford Sands and property dealer Harold Christie in a bid to bring gambling to the Bahamas. Their first stroke of luck came within months when Stafford Sands was appointed legal adviser to the government and quickly started moves towards legalisation.

Christie introduced the Duke of Windsor to Meyer Lansky in Palm Beach and the former British king lent his weight to the Mafia man's cause instantly, excited at the prospect of a Riviera-style casino. However, there was a hitch when island bigwig Sir Harry Oakes tried to stall the plans. He couldn't bear the thought of more wealthy tourists shattering the tranquillity of the islands and was determined the idea should be ditched. In May 1943, Lansky offered Sands a $1 million backhander if gambling was legalised on the islands. Sands knew Sir Harry was against it, yet he also knew how desperate Lansky was to get started.

At 7 am on 8 July 1943, Harry Oakes was murdered and his body set alight in his bed. Curiously, the fire did not spread, save to char the bedclothes and mosquito netting. Apart from the victim, Harold Christie was the only other person in the house. It was at this point that the Duke of Windsor, as Governor, intervened in an unseemly, almost suspicious, manner and for no obvious reason. Using wartime emergency laws, he banned press reports of the death. Then he decided to take personal charge of the murder probe. He could have asked local police to help. Beyond them was the FBI in the States, while detachments of Scotland Yard men were on hand in New York and Washington, but instead the Duke telephoned Miami police headquarters and asked for one Captain James Barker, whom it is possible, although unlikely, he had met before.

Could the Duke have known that this was a Lansky man, bought and paid for by the Mafia and who had once tried to entice a whole police department into a deal with the Mafia? Later, Barker was to become a hopeless heroin junkie, shot dead by his own son who was eventually acquitted of murder on the grounds of justifiable homicide.

The Duke visited the scene of the crime later in the day and was told that Sir Harry's son-in-law was the prime suspect. Sir Harry had hated his daughter's husband, Count Freddie de Marigny, believing him to be a gold-digger. That same day de Marigny was charged and thrown into jail. The penalty he faced was death by hanging and it was a fate he almost met through an appalling miscarriage of justice. Witnesses rolled up to tell the court how much de Marigny hated his father-in-law. The world was agog to hear detectives claim that their suspect was in the area on the night of the murder and that there had been a bust-up between Oakes and de Marigny. Details about his failing finances certainly pointed to a motive but the clinching details were fingerprint evidence, lifted from a Chinese screen by Oakes's bed, and a singed hair on de Marigny's forearm.

The defence produced their own witnesses who had seen de Marigny burn himself trying to light a candle. Then a fingerprint expert from New Orleans proved that the police print could not have been taken from a rough surface like the etched screen but must have come from a flat surface. The prosecution case was not only left in tatters, it seemed to have been forged from start to finish.

As the trial got underway, the Duke and Duchess began a seven-week holiday in Miami. There was apparently no question of the Duke staying to give his version of events. Defence laywer Godfrey Higgs asked Captain Barker: 'May I suggest that your desire for personal gain has caused you to sweep aside the truth and fabricate the evidence?'

Barker: 'No, Sir.'
Higgs: 'Did not His Royal Highness the Governor visit

you at Westbourne and come to Sir Harry's room at the time you were processing fingerprints?'
Barker: 'He did.'
Higgs: 'I don't think it would be proper for me to inquire as to why he came or what was said.'

Chief Justice Sir Oscar Daly, who presided at the trial, fiercely attacked Barker for the dubious quality of the prosecution case and de Marigny was acquitted, but with no thanks to the Duke of Windsor who might have left an innocent man to hang while he sunned himself in Miami. It was never explained what had gone on between the Duke and Barker while the policeman fabricated the evidence; not even the judge pressed for the truth.

We can only speculate as to whether the Duke was lured into mob deals with the promise of a payout at the end. Would he once again have allowed himself to be shamelessly used by the ruthless and scheming? A disturbing pointer comes to light in a report by US Intelligence in May 1943. It reads: 'The Duke of Windsor has been finding many excuses to attend to private business in the United States which he is doing at present.' It is certainly true that the pair loathed the Bahamas and escaped to the States as much as possible. The Duke finally resigned his position on 15 March 1945.

However, the Bahamian scandal would not die down. Lansky and Sands continued in their efforts to bring gambling to the Bahamas. While the Mafia gangs concentrated on their interests in Cuba, Sands again produced an application for a casino licence. This time he claimed a syndicate of businessmen was behind the venture and that British Earls Dudley, Derby and Sefton and Viscount Camrose were all members. All were friends of the Duke of Windsor. According to Lord Derby, however, they knew nothing about the syndicate or its application. At this stage the Duke refused to be involved himself, despite approaches from Harold Christie. The application was refused.

Repercussions of the murder still had Bahamian society trembling. Sixteen years on the leader of the black Progressive Liberal Party and editor of the *Bahamian Times*, Cyril Stevenson, pushed for an inquiry. 'This whole business has been one big whitewash from start to finish,' he declared. 'People in high places know who the killer is. It is time the true facts were brought out into the open so that this nightmare of violence this colony has suffered be ended.' He was referring, of course, to Lansky, helped by Harold Christie. Yet, despite a vote by the Bahamas House of Assembly to call in Scotland Yard, the facts remained cloaked in mystery. For, as detectives boarded an aeroplane to fly to Nassau, there was more double dealing. When they landed, the British police were immediately sent home. The Governor of the day, Sir Oswald Raynor Arthur, declared: 'There will be no new inquiry. The case is closed.' The Mafia finally had its way and made the Bahamian casinos its own.

*   *   *

On the day that Hitler shot himself, the Duke and Duchess sailed from Nassau. They knew Britain did not want them and maintained that unless the Duchess was given full recognition, they would not return. Their destination was France. Although they had homes in Paris and Antibes, abandoned following the German invasion, their future was full of uncertainty. The Duke returned alone to London in October with a plan for his future. His suggestion was that he should become a roving ambassador, concentrating on America. He proposed to emulate the successes he had had while touring years before as the Prince of Wales. Patently, it did not dawn on him that he had proved beyond doubt that he was a totally unsuitable emissary, even in the tamest capacity. He twice met his brother, the King, and spoke with the new Prime Minister, Clement Attlee. He pledged not to make speeches or statements without British government approval nor to take on public engagements without permission but his promises were not enough to instil faith at Buckingham Palace or at Downing Street. No job offer came his way.

Six years on, Churchill tried to heal the rift. 'We are like stateless persons. We have nowhere to go, nowhere to live, no purpose in our lives,' the Duke said when Churchill visited them in Paris. Churchill epitomised the respected voice of reason but he soon realised that the King and his family wanted nothing to do with the disgraced black sheep and was forced to abandon his attempt.

The message was loud and clear. The Windsors would forever be on the outside. They tried to make the best of it, choosing a lifestyle they thought befitted their status. They hosted lavish dinners in fine style, entertaining the rich, fashionable and powerful, but their extravagance could not mask an inner misery. Wallis had to face the simple fact that she would never have the title and status she coveted. Meanwhile, Edward was fearful that his marriage was under threat as Wallis embarked on a sexual adventure reminiscent of her youth. The object of her desire was Woolworth heir Jimmy Donnahue, about whom Noël Coward was cutting: 'I like Jimmy. He's an insane camp but he's fun. I like the Duchess; she's a fag hag to end all but that's what makes her likeable. The Duke... well, although he pretends not to hate me he does because I'm queer and he's queer. However, unlike him I don't pretend not to be. Here she's got a royal queen to sleep with and a rich one to hump.'

* * *

One final mystery about the Duke remains under wraps: the identity of his illegitimate sons. One is said to be the result of a fling he had while apart from Wallis in September 1934, when he ran into the younger, married sister of an old flame. A child was born nine months later and rumour has it that this Old Etonian is identical to his father.

Another love child is said to be Anthony Chisholm, the Duke's godson. Chisholm, who died in 1987, was born nine months after the then Prince of Wales visited Sydney, Australia, with the Navy and met his mother, Mollee Little. Again, the young man bore the hallmark good looks of the Duke and he visited his 'godfather' in later life.

* * *

The ice between the monarchy and the rogue Prince was finally broken years later when he met his niece, the present Queen, several times and saw her only days before his death. Despite this, a coolness remained and it wasn't until he died of throat cancer on 28 May 1972 that the Duke of Windsor was once again accepted back into the ranks of royalty. His family were determined to bring him home for a traditional family burial at Frogmore. He had been absent from Britain for years and had done nothing for his country during his exile, yet still-loyal subjects queued to see his body as it lay in state in St George's Chapel, Windsor. In the event, his funeral service was a quiet one attended by family and specific friends picked by the Duke himself before his death in the arms of the woman he loved so much.

The Duchess agreed to be driven by Prince Charles to see her husband lying in state but she returned to Heathrow as soon as the funeral service was over. Without even pausing for a backward glance, she boarded her flight to Paris where she bitterly maintained: 'Not one member of David's family showed any real sympathy.'

The acrimony between the Duchess and her British in-laws was not to end there. Lord Mountbatten was keen that some of his dead cousin's papers and belongings, including some family jewellery, should be returned to Britain where they would be preserved for the sake of history. The Duchess was not only bitter about her treatment by the royals, her memory and general health were failing her too. Following their first painful meeting she was certain that Mountbatten was after her money. He tried twice more, even offering to be executor of her will. Perhaps the Duchess would consider setting up a foundation with Prince Charles at the helm? The Duchess would hear nothing of it. She wrote to Mountbatten: 'I confirm to you once more that everything has been taken care of according to David's and my wishes... It is always a pleasure to see you but I must tell you that when you leave me I am always terribly depressed by your reminding me of David's death and my own and I should be grateful if you would not mention this any more.'

Buckingham Palace did finally reclaim the Duke's papers for the royal archives, together with some ceremonial uniforms, apparently with full permission from the Duchess, although her lawyer and aide, Maître Blum, denied that this permission was ever given and claimed the items were simply taken, probably by Mountbatten.

In 1976 the Queen Mother decided that 40 years of hostilities should end. While visiting Paris she attempted to visit the Duchess, now bedridden and in failing health. When the embassy called to arrange details the Duchess only had to think for a moment before saying: 'No. It is too late, too late. I don't see any point in meeting her now.' She still remained aloof the next day when the Queen Mother's page, Reginald Wilcox, arrived bearing a basket of 72 pink roses and a handwritten card which simply said: 'All Good Wishes from Elizabeth R.' Refusing the gift, Wallis said: 'Why now? We have never even exchanged Christmas cards or birthday greetings. We have never spoken on the telephone. Why now?'

Wallis survived her husband by 14 years, spent mostly living in the past. His room was never altered. By 1980 she was paralysed by arteriosclerosis and she died on 2 April 1986. She was buried beside her prince at Frogmore with a simple inscription on her coffin: Wallis, Duchess of Windsor, 1896–1986. Even in death she was denied the three letters that she craved: HRH.

CHAPTER THREE

The Queen Mother

It is 7.30 a.m. and the world's favourite great-grandmother is roused from slumber by a lone Scottish piper playing in the grounds below her powder-blue bedchamber. Forty miles away, her younger cousin is gently woken by a nurse. Other patients are being stirred by staff as a new day dawns within the public ward's walls of flaking, cream paint.

At Clarence House, just off the Mall, the Queen Mother is served a fine cup of her favourite, unsweetened Lapsang Souchong tea. It is accompanied by an ironed copy of *Sporting Life*, the 'bible' of the horse racing fraternity, from which, with an expert eye, she will select the day's winners and losers.

In the mental hospital, Katherine Bowes-Lyon is washed and dressed before being fed a bowl of cornflakes, her favourite food, followed by a cooked meal, perhaps of baked beans on toast. She can vaguely recognise her name but has not the faintest inkling that she is in any way connected to the Royal Family.

Katherine Bowes-Lyon, 25 years her serene cousin's junior, is the living skeleton in that family's closet – the tragic figure with a mental age of six who unwittingly brought unthinkable shame and condemnation upon the Queen Mother in April 1987 when it was revealed that, since 1941, she had been consigned to the ironically named Royal Earlswood mental hospital in Redhill, Surrey, along with her sister Nerissa and other female cousins. One of the cousins died in hospital soon after admittance.

Patients at the Victorian hospital are known by the nurses as 'the forgotten people', but Katherine and Nerissa were not simply forgotten. They were, somewhat prematurely, officially listed as *dead* in *Burke's Peerage*, the who's who of the royal and noble. Katherine was 'killed off' by Burke's in 1961. Nerissa 'died' in 1940. In truth, they lived together in the Royal Earlswood's Margaret Ward for many years until Nerissa did die, of pneumonia, in 1986, a year before the scandal of their sad existence broke. She was buried in an unmarked pauper's grave at a cemetery a few miles from the hospital. Katherine and the two other cousins – twins Indonea and Flavia Fane – continued to live out their twilight years in that same ward, without comprehension of Katherine's high-born ancestry or the global furore of which she was the focus. She may have watched the news bulletins on a communal TV as the revelations unfolded, but she could not have known that her story brought an unwelcome scent of disgrace to the most untouchable, most loved and revered royal of all, her cousin the Queen Mother.

Hardened cynics among the legion of media royal-watchers will tell you how even they are drawn into the family's carefully oiled image-preservation machine by the sheer magnetism of the nation's favourite granny. The Bowes-Lyons scandal, however, brought the hitherto untouchable into sharp, critical focus and there were even more skeletons to be found in the cupboard.

Mystery surrounds exactly *where* the Queen Mother was born. It is known that Elizabeth Angela Marguerita Bowes-Lyon, ninth of the ten children of Lord Glamis (later the fourth Earl of Strathmore) came into the world on 4 August 1900 but nobody knows where the birth took place. Some say it was at the family's London home in

St James's Square. Others believe it to have been at their English seat, St Paul's Walden Bury, Hertfordshire. Yet another school of thought suggests Elizabeth's birthplace was fairytale Glamis Castle in Scotland – or even some point between there and London.

The Queen Mother herself remains strangely vague on the subject, always responding with a cry: 'I was too young to remember.' Although she was the first commoner to marry into the Royal Family this century, it defies logic that there should be no official trace of where her high-born entry into the Glamis dynasty actually took place.

What the records do reveal, though, is that her father had to pay a fine of seven shillings and sixpence (now 37½p) for registering her birth seven weeks late.

The original Bowes-Lyons were descended from medieval Scottish robber barons; clannish and brutal in their founding of the dynastic traits that remained through the ages. In 1537 Lady Glamis was seized by King James V of Scotland's soldiers and accused of plotting to kill him by practising sorcery. She was burned at the stake as a witch on Castle Hill, Edinburgh, and the castle and its estate were confiscated by the Crown.

Two hundred years ago, when he stayed at Glamis, the novelist Sir Walter Scott became the first literary witness of the castle's ethereal inhabitants. He wrote of a night of terror after a servant had escorted him to his room: 'I must own that when I heard door after door shut after my conductor had retired, I began to consider myself far from the living and somewhat too near the dead.'

The family history is not only as mind-bogglingly

eccentric as it is aristocratic, it also contains precedents of mental illness and disturbing deception, for romantic Glamis Castle, which has played host to murderers, witches, ghosts and even a 'monster', houses a forbidding, locked, secret room.

It was in this secret, shuttered room that the Bowes-Lyons are said to have incarcerated the Queen Mother's hapless great-great-uncle, Thomas, for more than half a century. He was born in 1841, mentally deficient and hideously deformed – looking like a hybrid of Quasimodo and the Phantom of the Opera – and, even in his early years, was cruelly dubbed the 'Monster of Glamis'.

The eleventh Earl was said to be so horror-struck by his heir's stooping, misshapen body, covered in thick black hair but with only tiny arms and legs, that he banished the poor child to a locked, icy chamber measuring only 15 by 10 feet. Almost two generations passed before a workman repairing the roof spotted Thomas, whereupon he was banished to Australia to live out his remaining years. The Bowes-Lyons pretended he had died at birth, and the earldom passed to the second-born son.

It is almost certain that the Queen Mother knew of the existence of the room where Thomas spent most of his pathetic life. During the First World War, when Glamis Castle was turned into a sanitorium, she spent many months there, rolling bandages and reading books to wounded servicemen.

Did she know about the Monster? Royal biographer James Wentworth-Day pointedly asked that question of the Queen Mother's sister, Rose, Countess Granville, shortly before her death in 1967. She replied: 'We were never allowed to talk about it. My father and grandfather refused absolutely to discuss it.'

*   *   *

Even as a child Elizabeth's great beauty had been apparent. A full ten years before her marriage, Lady Buxton remarked: 'How many hearts Elizabeth will break!' She was the belle of every ball and without a doubt the best dancer on the floor, turning every eligible head with her looks and *joie de vivre*.

At parties, she would break the ice by urging guests to have their fortunes told. Once, when she had her own palm read, she was told: 'You will have a great and glamorous future.' The young debutante simply laughed and ordered more champagne. At a ball in London she met Albert, then Prince of Wales, whom she had known as a child. Awkward, stuttering Bertie, then 24, was instantly charmed by the blossoming beauty who could make him laugh so easily and forget his own painful shyness. Three times he begged for her hand until she agreed with the words: 'Oh Bertie ... yes, yes, yes!' Five years after her Great War efforts at Glamis, the Queen Mother was wed. A nation rejoiced as the future King George VI walked his dazzling 23-year-old bride down the aisle at Westminster Abbey, on 26 April 1923. The fortune-teller's words had come true and she became the Duchess of York.

The Yorks had two children, Elizabeth, born on 21 April 1926, and Margaret, born on 21 August 1930. Life was idyllic. With the spotlight on Bertie's elder brother, David, who was heir to the throne, the couple could enjoy tremendous freedom. Today's multi-media pursuit of young royal jetsetters simply didn't exist then.

However, it was not to last. In 1936 that freedom vanished for ever as the abdication crisis became the royal feud of the century and threw Elizabeth to centre stage of a scandal that shocked the nation. Both she and Bertie were devastated when his elder brother, then King Edward VIII, relinquished his throne rather than give up the woman he loved. From the moment Elizabeth first set eyes on the tall, willowy Wallis daggers were drawn.

In public, she displayed a dignified façade, but privately she fumed: 'In her ruthless disregard for her marriage vows and in her relentless determination to wed David that woman has ruined several lives. That is bad enough – but her conduct has brought disrespect to the Crown, which is unforgivable.'

She could not even bring herself to refer by name to Wallis, whose sexual exploits were well known in London and New York society circles. Instead, she called her simply 'that woman'. In the ensuing cat-fight, to the delight of scandal-mongering royal courtiers, Wallis, in turn, referred to Elizabeth as 'that fat Scottish cook', or plain 'Cookie'.

When one close confidante suggested that Wallis's influence had curbed the ex-king's drinking habits so that he no longer had bags under his eyes, Elizabeth responded by pointing to a photograph of Bertie and saying angrily: 'Yes – but who has the lines under his eyes now?'

When Bertie died of lung cancer in 1952, aged 56,

Elizabeth unforgivingly laid the blame on Edward and Mrs Simpson, convinced her husband would have lived longer had the abdication crisis not thrown him into a monarchy he was self-confessedly completely unprepared for.

By her ninetieth birthday, on 4 August 1990, the Queen Mother was still the darling of the nation; in opinion polls she was only just pipped by Princess Diana for the accolade of 'favourite royal'. Inside the family itself, she is very much the matriarchal figure, dispensing tea, sympathy and priceless advice to its younger members. They may have brought glamour and glitz to the palace, but her word is still regarded as law.

In the unique role she occupies, she has become no stranger to scandal. Both the Princess of Wales and the Duchess of York have sought her wisdom as they have struggled to come to terms with royal life and with the often intolerable strain it can place on marriage. The Queen Mother also has to display her innate diplomacy, when handling members of her household staff, among whom homosexuality has been rife. One below-stairs unfortunate, arrested in a public lavatory, spent the night in a police cell wondering what her reaction would be. The next morning, she sent her official car for him with a bunch of flowers and a note saying: 'Naughty boy!'

All Clarence House staff are aware that, when at home, it is the Queen Mother's custom to be served a large gin and tonic at 7 p.m. sharp. Once it failed to arrive on time and no amount of pressing the servants' bell brought any response. She stormed downstairs and approached the pantry just in time to hear two footmen squabbling. 'Perhaps,' she said, 'when you two old queens have finished quarrelling, you'll serve this old queen a cocktail.'

Not even her elder daughter, the Queen, is spared her dry tongue. Once, at lunch, unusually for her, the Queen ordered a second glass of wine. Despite her own love of fairly generous measures of gin, the Queen Mother turned to her and said: 'I shouldn't if I were you, my dear. After all you do have to reign all afternoon.'

Aside from the immediate family, the Queen Mother's more distant relatives – in true keeping with Glamis dynastic traditions – are eccentric, to say the least. On the Outer Hebridean island of North Uist lives Earl Granville, her 73-year-old nephew. He has become a hermit on his 60,000-acre estate of lochs and peat bogs, rarely bothering to answer letters or pick up the telephone. Aboard the royal yacht *Britannia*, while sailing to her Balmoral holiday, the Queen is said to have called in and found the Earl washing his socks on the rocks.

Another royal cousin who spurned convention was John Bowes-Lyon, whose father, Major General Sir James, was a gentleman usher to the Queen and whose mother, Mary, was the daughter of a millionaire racehorse owner, Sir Humphrey de Trafford. A bachelor art expert, John became known as the 'black sheep' of the Royal Family when he joined New York's jetset nightclub and party scene. Bowesie, as he was nicknamed, used to hang out with the camp followers of pop artist Andy Warhol. In London, he became a regular at the Embassy Club, a raffish haunt of male models and pop singers in the eighties.

Most publicly outrageous of all her relatives, however,

remains Teresa d'Abreu, daughter of the former Margaret Bowes-Lyon. After attending convent school, she formed a bizarre pop group called the Sadista Sisters. Dressed in a black corset and fishnet stockings and brandishing a bullwhip, she performed with her oddball group in working men's clubs.

While such relatives may have caused the Queen Mother private disquiet, her own intimate dinner-party secrets were revealed by a regular guest, writer and gossip columnist A. N. Wilson. He caused a furore in July 1990 with a telltale article in the right-wing, weekly *Spectator* magazine. Wilson was blasted as 'ungentlemanly' for breaking the strict but unwritten rules of protocol in penning the piece, which rocked the Queen Mother's ninetieth-birthday celebrations.

Ignoring tradition that guests who mix with the royals never betray confidences or repeat gossip, Wilson told how the Queen Mother was once in love with King Edward VIII, her husband's brother, years before the abdication crisis. Wilson claimed that the Queen Mother confided that she had fallen for him in the 1920s, while he was still the Prince of Wales. There had, indeed, been newspaper speculation at the time that they might wed, although, eventually, of course, she settled for his younger brother.

Wilson also revealed the Queen Mother's dinner conversation about other royals, including Prince and Princess Michael. She said of them: 'I can't understand a word Prince Michael says. He will mumble into his beard. As for Princess Michael ... [she laughed]. But golly, I could do with the £100,000, couldn't you?' This was a reference to Princess Michael's royalties for a book, publication of which brought accusation that she had plagiarised other authors' work.

This reference to money – a subject never normally discussed openly by the royals – was one of several details revealed by Wilson. In another he claims the Queen Mother expressed fears about getting into financial difficulties and even joked that her bank manager had scolded her over the size of her overdraft.

Other Wilson revelations were tame by comparison – such as the Queen Mother's love of detective novels and her dislike for the newly formed Social Democratic Party. However, the damage was done and the Queen Mother was plunged into a scandal in which she was lampooned with newspaper headlines like: 'You should have kept mum, Ma'am!'

It was the references to money that were the most hurtful, making public her notoriously eccentric attitude to the subject. When Norman Hartnell died, it was said that all the leading designers dreaded the prospect of being taken on by the Queen Mother. 'Was it,' asked one of Hartnell's more malicious customers, 'because of her distinctive, not to say appalling taste in clothes?'

'No,' replied another courtier. 'It was because she had never been known to pay a bill.'

As so often when tracked by scandal, the Queen Mother found herself loyally supported by a sympathetic public, with outrage directed, by and large, towards the indiscreet Wilson. One opinion column epitomised, perhaps better than any other, the reason why the public simply won't tolerate their favourite great-grandmother being tainted by scandal. It said: 'The Queen Mother is a largely mythological being. This is not to say that she is a bogus character... a hard haughty aristocrat pretending to be a homely old body. It is more that her vision of her public role and her distinctive personal appearance exactly match the job requirements, if not actually some profound need for a mother-figure on the part of the collective subconscious.'

That caring wise-owl mother-figure image was tested as never before with the revelations about her relatives consigned to a mental hospital. As media attention focused on their existence, events began to take a darker twist.

It was the Queen Mother's brother, John Bowes-Lyon, who, among his five children, fathered Nerissa, 'officially' dead, and Katherine, who remained in the Royal Earlswood Hospital. As children, the girls would have spent summer holidays with their mother, Lord Clinton's daughter, Fenella, at Glamis Castle, the home of their grandparents.

When the Queen Mother married the Duke of York in 1923, her niece, Nerissa, would have been four years old. Katherine was born three years later. Their father died in 1930, aged 44, and their mother, Fenella, in 1966.

When the Duke of York unexpectedly became King George VI in 1937, his two nieces by marriage would normally have enjoyed front pews at the coronation but there is no record of them having attended. Nor were they guests at the present Queen's wedding to Prince Philip even though their other sister, Diana, was one of Elizabeth II's bridesmaids.

A burning question remains over Katherine and Nerissa:

was the announcement of their 'deaths' by their mother in 1963, just three years before she herself died, simply the slip of an ailing old lady or something far more sinister? A newspaper investigation revealed that, at the time, Fenella was engaged in a bitter and protracted battle to gain the title of Baron Clinton for her great-nephew, Gerard Fane-Trefusis. The baronetcy dates from 1299 and is the twelfth oldest in England. When the twenty-first baron died in 1957, Fenella and her sister, Harriet, had been left co-holders of the title. Harriet had died almost immediately and Fenella, then in her seventies, wanted the title to go to her great-nephew. However, because it is so ancient, the title does not devolve by pure heredity. It is covered by ancient land laws which date from the Norman Conquest. In simple terms, that means the title can be divided by the family, who can co-hold it until an heir is designated by them to become the next baron.

When that co-ownership was split between Fenella and Harriet as senior co-heirs, it meant that their respective families — the Bowes-Lyons and the Fane-Trefusis — had to decide among themselves who should hold the baronetcy next. Even under normal circumstances, such monumental decisions affecting the British nobility can take years. One theory is that Fenella feared that if she died before the wrangle was resolved, rights to the title would devolve to her children, the two mentally handicapped daughters, Katherine and Nerissa, who would be incapable of making a sane decision. To that end, did she 'kill them off' by registering their deaths in *Burke's Peerage?*

In an interview with London's *Today* newspaper, royal

genealogist Hugh Peskett said it was 'entirely possible' that she did so, trusting instead her favourite nephew. He added: 'My hunch has always been that the author of this cover-up was Fenella. She may have believed she was saving the family from embarrassment and unnecessary wrangling.'

In the end Fenella's wish, however she achieved it, came true and Gerard Fane-Trefusis did inherit the title of Lord Clinton in 1965, eight years after it fell vacant. At his 65,000-acre farm in Devon, he spoke of Fenella, saying: 'My great aunt was a somewhat vague person.' He believed her actions did not have 'any bearing' on him taking the title, but insisted: 'Really I feel it is a family matter and it is not something I want to talk about.'

Katherine Bowes-Lyon and her two surviving cousins were not the only well-to-do inmates at the Royal Earlswood Hospital, which spends £5½ million a year in caring for 412 patients. (By rough calculation this means it costs £39,000 a year of British taxpayers' money to look after the Queen Mother's three relatives.) Most patients live in small wards, like Margaret Ward, which Katherine shared with others her own age.

A member of staff said: 'These people are her friends. But although they have been together for many years, they aren't really close. They behave like small children. They get upset and they squabble like toddlers. One might spit at a nurse or throw a chair because someone's been teasing them or has stolen a bar of chocolate.'

The only places Katherine and the two Fane sisters could really call their own were the special lockers they had been given. A hospital visitor said: 'What they keep in there is totally up to them. It may be a little toy or a piece of cloth they especially like. None of the nurses is allowed to look inside any of the private lockers.'

Much has changed at the hospital – originally called an asylum for idiots when opened in 1855 – since the royal relatives first arrived. Then the girls would have slept in crowded wards, holding as many as 70 patients, and would have remained locked up for most of the day. There are no locked doors now, and rubber-walled cells and straitjackets have vanished too. A spokesman said: 'Staff are trained to defuse situations with modern drug therapy.'

Once, it was revealed, Katherine, nicknamed Tinky by hospital staff, wandered off and was discovered walking along the road outside the main gate late at night. On occasion, said the spokesman, troublesome patients are still locked up in 'rare emergencies'.

The scandal of the beloved Queen Mum's relatives languishing in their mental hospital came as a shock to the nation, but it was a scandal softened again by her sense of duty and diplomacy when the *Daily Star* revealed how she regularly sent massive donations to the National Health Service hospital, cloaked in anonymity, via its League of Friends. The scandal dissolved completely when, on 11 April 1987, a call for the Queen Mother to resign as patron of Mencap, the society for the mentally handicapped, was unanimously thrown out.

It is not known if she ever visited her cousin Katherine.

CHAPTER FOUR

Elizabeth II

To the millions of loyal British citizens who revere their cherished monarchy, Buckingham Palace is not simply the ancestral home of the Royal Family, it is, in every way, a magnificent monument to the grand and glorious traditions of empire and crown, a proud, noble structure that, for many people, encapsulates the very best of British achievement. Likewise, even to the hundreds of thousands of foreign tourists who come each year to marvel at its hallowed portals and stately façade, Buckingham Palace is a much-envied symbol of tradition, of continuity, of a nation at peace with its past and confident in its future. Versailles may dwarf it in grandeur but no other royal enclave can compare with its ongoing importance.

Despite its undoubted serene majesty, the 600-room Buckingham Palace is first and foremost a home. For many years, the Royal Family has found both privacy and protection behind its imposing wrought-iron railings and perimeter walls, safe in the knowledge that they are far removed from the faithful and the curious who gather outside each day for a glimpse of regal activity.

All that was to change in the early summer of 1982 when an itinerant, unemployed decorator named Michael Fagan not only broke into the 'impenetrable' palace but even got as far as a bedside chat with the Queen herself! His brazen foray into a world usually restricted to aristocrats, presidents, ministers of state and visiting dignitaries shocked the world and numbed a nation.

However, that daring midnight raid did a lot more than simply expose the bumbling security forces whose sworn duty it is to protect the monarch at all costs. It also shone a spotlight on some dark and embarrassing corners in the palace that its regal inhabitants and guardians had carefully kept hidden from the loyal masses.

*   *   *

The story of Michael Fagan began humbly enough on 8 August 1950 when he was born, the son of a poor building contractor, at Paddington General Hospital. A bright and eager student, Fagan seemed destined for better things than his circumstances would indicate, and he excelled in his early years at primary school. Somehow, however, along the way, that early promise and application dissipated. At 15 he had already dropped out of school, and quickly drifted into a transient world of part-time decorating and painting jobs. People who knew him from his teenage years remember him as a loner who was quick to spend whatever money he earned. In 1972, at the age of 22, he appeared to settle down somewhat when he met and married a Welsh-born woman, Christine, two years his senior and already the mother of two children. Within the next few years, Fagan and Christine added four children of their own and there were numerous visits from social workers, worried about the children's upbringing. Fagan and the family moved 12 times in just ten years, and they lived literally from week to week, largely dependent on unemployment benefit and child allowances from the state. On those rare occasions when he did land a part-time decorating or repair job, Michael soon wasted the money hoping to fulfil his fantasies of leading a nomadic existence. His mother

Ivy recalled: 'If he got any money he would take Christine and the kids off to Wales where they would travel about until it had all been spent. He told me he would like to live on the top of a Welsh mountain.'

By 1982 his life had hit rock bottom. In June Christine walked out on him yet again and when he finally traced her to a foul squat in Islington, North London, there was a heated row. Local police were summoned to the scene and Michael was hauled away and charged with assaulting his stepson, who had moved with his mother. While he was being held on remand at Brixton Prison, Christine came to visit him and gradually they set about trying to patch up their differences. Social workers, who helped them to find another flat, quietly hoped that they had finally heard the last of Michael Fagan and his problems. They couldn't have been more wrong!

What they and the rest of Britain did not know was that Michael had already done the unthinkable by making an uninvited call at Buckingham Palace – a full four weeks before his infamous bedside encounter with Queen Elizabeth. That first break-in came on the night of 7 June. At approximately 11.15 p.m., the slightly-built decorator climbed over the railing and jumped quietly into the stately grounds. Somehow avoiding every 'fail-safe' security device – including pressure pads embedded in the ground, high-tech infra-red beams, trained guard dogs, hand-picked police patrols and veteran military men – Fagan calmly wandered across the massive courtyard. He then climbed a 50-foot drain pipe and nonchalantly gained entry into the palace through an open bedroom window. When a housemaid spotted him and screamed, Fagan simply slipped into one of scores of corridors and coolly began looking at some of the famous artworks that line the palace walls. He then made his way through the vast, complicated interior of the palace until he found a store room where he helped himself to a bottle of wine.

After a while, he would later explain, he became bored and left the palace just as quietly and as easily as he had entered. 'I went downstairs, slipped out and made my way home,' he recalled many years later. 'I reckoned I would see the Queen some other time.' He was right.

Although the 7 June break-in was hushed up at the highest levels, it caused a sensation in official circles, and not just because it was the Queen's residence. American President Ronald Reagan and his wife, Nancy, were in London at the time, and the Queen was to receive them on the lawns of Buckingham Palace. Thus, security was supposed to be even tighter than ever, yet it had been penetrated, apparently with ridiculous ease. The incident was so embarrassing to those concerned that not only was it kept from the British public, but the authorities also decided not to inform the American Secret Service, which protects US presidents!

All this, of course, was of no concern to Michael Fagan. He had merely wanted to see the Queen, tell her his troubles and then, as if by waving a magic wand, he presumed she would solve everything and send him happily on his way. He had failed the first time but on his second attempt, he promised himself, nothing would deter him from having his private audience. 'This time I'd made up my mind that I had to see the Queen,' he would say later. 'I had to tell her my problems. Maybe, I thought, she could help me get back my kids.'

His second climb occurred in the early hours of 9 July 1982 as the Royal Family slept peacefully in their apartments inside the palace. 'I climbed over the railings, as there was no one about,' he said. Once on the ground, he stealthily made his way towards a temporary canvas awning that had been put up to shield some ongoing construction work. He quickly found his entry point. 'I got in through an open window on the gound floor,' he said. Fagan found himself inside the room which houses the vast royal stamp collection, a £14 million treasure trove of some of the world's rarest stamps. However, robbery was not his motive and he went quickly to the door. It was locked from the inside. 'When I couldn't get out through the inside door, I climbed back out of the window and up a drainpipe on to a flat roof. It was easy. Nothing to it at all.'

Unbeknown to Fagan, however, his daring climb had triggered one of many infra-red alarms. Incredibly, a bumbling policeman manning a substation in the palace actually turned it off, thinking it was 'a bloody malfunction'. When Fagan at last reached the roof, he took off his shoes and socks and walked carefully across a narrow ledge to another open window, which was guarded by taut wire netting to keep the ever-present pigeons at bay. He pulled back just enough of the wire to gain entry and squeezed inside. He was now in the office of the Master of the Household, Vice-Admiral Sir Peter Ashmore, who, in an ironic twist of fate, was the man in charge of the Queen's security while she was inside Buckingham Palace. Thoughtfully, Fagan stopped to wipe his hands on the velvet curtains (because they were covered in pigeon repellant from the wire) before leaving the room.

For the next 15 minutes or so, he recalled, he continued wandering through the maze of hallways and rooms of the palace. Although he was actually seen by a maid, his early-morning 'tour' went totally unchallenged. The embarrassed maid would later tell security officials that the man she had spied had not acted suspiciously and therefore she hadn't reported his presence to anyone. Fagan eventually made his way into the glittering throne room, where he remembers 'sitting down on each one, trying them for size'. Moving on, he soon found the private apartments and, by a stroke of luck, found a secret door leading to the Queen's chambers. He remembered being amazed at the complete lack of security he had encountered on his trek.

At approximately 7.15 a.m., Fagan, holding a piece of glass from an ashtray he had broken in an outside ante-room, quietly turned the knob on the bedroom door. The Queen, who slept alone (Prince Philip preferred the privacy of his own bedroom) stirred but did not wake. 'I opened the door and there's a little bundle in the bed,' he recalled with some amazement. 'I thought this isn't the Queen, this is too small. I went to the curtains and lifted them. A shaft of light must have disturbed her.'

The official version of what happened next was neatly packaged so that the Queen came out in the best possible light. Page after page of newspaper accounts told a breathless world how Her Majesty had calmly listened to the disturbed young intruder, then spoken to him of her own family. The official story also claimed that the Queen had tried to trick Fagan by ordering a cigarette – she abhors smoking – and how her calm, royal bearing even dissuaded the poor man from committing suicide by slashing his wrists with the shard of broken glass.

However, Fagan paints a vastly different picture of the Queen's reaction and has sworn repeatedly that he was not contemplating suicide. As he tells it:

> She sat up and looked at me. Her face was a mask of shock and incomprehension. 'What are you doing here? Get out! Get out!' she said.
>
> Her cut-glass accent really startled me. I just looked at her and replied: 'I think you are a really nice woman.' She just repeated: 'Get out! Get out!' and picked up a white telephone, said a few words, then hopped out of bed, ran across the room and out of the door. I was surprised at how nimble she was. She ran like a girl. It was all over in about 30 seconds. I really felt sad and disillusioned. It was a complete shock because the Queen wasn't what I had expected. I felt so badly let down. The conversation never took place. I just sat down on the bed crying my eyes out.

For the next six minutes, as Fagan sat inconsolable on the Queen's bed, the bumbling palace aides failed to heed Her Majesty's terrified calls for help. Then a chambermaid finally arrived and the intruder was ushered into a pantry where the Queen's footman, Paul Whybrow, had just arrived after taking the corgis for their morning walk. Whybrow poured Fagan a whisky, on the Queen's advice, and offered him a cigarette. While he calmed himself, the Queen went on the rampage. 'All the time I could hear the Queen bawling down the phone, demanding to know why the police hadn't arrived,' Fagan said, later.

Eventually, the plodding police did arrive, and the intruder was quickly bundled off, fingerprinted and jailed on breaking and entry charges. Fagan revelled in the bizarre courtroom procedures that followed, which focused on his first break-in. During the madcap hearings, he ranted to the court that he was the son of Rudolf Hess, Adolf Hitler's war-time deputy and faithful lap dog, and chastised his lawyer when Queen Elizabeth's name was mentioned. After his committal for trial, his lawyer issued a brief statement to the media, explaining how upset Fagan was at the fuss he had created: 'What has distressed my client most in seeking help for himself from Her Majesty is that he has caused an invasion of her privacy, because of the publicity, far greater than he could ever have imagined. Having started this chain of events, my client sincerely hopes that he can help to put an end to the continuing intrusions into Her Majesty's privacy by asking me to state on his behalf that he trusts speculative reports concerning Her Majesty's life will cease.'

Of course, they did not. The remarkable break-in would see to that, especially the gossip surrounding her relationship with her husband and his choice of sleeping arrangements. Eventually, Fagan was found not guilty of stealing the wine, which belonged to Prince Charles. Later, however, when he confessed to stealing a car, he was, surprisingly, packed off to a maximum security psychiatric hospital, home to some of Britain's most notorious killers and psychopaths, until his release in January 1983.

'That had to be the worst time of my life,' he said. 'All right, I flipped and did something I'll regret for the rest of my life. Crazy? Of course it was. I mean, who in their right mind would shin up a drainpipe, break into Buckingham Palace and talk to the Queen? But I paid the price, I was sent away from my kids, and that hurt more than anyone will ever know. They were way out of line sending me there. After all, I never meant to harm the Queen. In fact, I did her and the country a bloody big favour by pointing out how easy it was to break in, not once, but twice!'

Britain did indeed come to learn what a shambles the so-called 'steel security' cordon around the Queen really was. The Keystone Kops had not only ignored the very alarms installed to protect her but had also ignored the Queen herself! Home Secretary William Whitelaw summed it up when he said the scandalous incident revealed 'an appalling lack of security' and 'slackness and weakness in supervision'. Assistant Police Commissioner John Dellow put the blame squarely on his own men, saying the break-in was 'a failure by police to respond efficiently and urgently. If police officers had been alert and competent, Fagan would have been apprehended well before he got close to the private apartments.'

For his part, Fagan managed to overcome his sudden

and unsought celebrity status. He and Christine eventually divorced and he settled in a London flat with three of his young children. By all accounts, he is today a model father and insists that his children 'respect the Queen and the Royal Family'. However, his brazen break-in had affected far more people than he ever realised. Despite all the efforts by security men and public-relations handlers, the earnest gaze of the world was firmly fixed on the palace. The aura surrounding both it and the Royal Family has never been quite the same.

It was as if, from that moment, the doors of Buckingham Palace had been thrown wide open for the first time. As if the Queen's principal home had at last become public property (which indeed it is – Balmoral and Sandringham are her private homes, Buckingham Palace is not). Michael Fagan had pulled aside more of a shield than the wire netting on a window. He had drawn aside a veil which, until then, had kept prying eyes averted from the palace portals. Suddenly, the intimate workings of 'the Firm's' London HQ were examined by the press and pored over by the public. Her Majesty's own lifestyle, a tantalising glimpse of which had been given by Michael Fagan, became a matter for intrusive conjecture.

The public had vicariously walked the corridors of power with Fagan and found it a fascinating experience. Now they wanted to know even more of the Queen's secrets, even her bedroom secrets. The mystique that the Royal Family had nurtured over the years, intended to distance themselves from their subjects and to prevent awkward questions being asked about their private lives, had been removed in the most extraordinary way. Suddenly it was OK to ask: 'Just *who is* the Queen?'

* * *

Elizabeth Windsor was born at 2.40 a.m. on 21 April 1926 at 17 Bruton Street, just under a mile from Buckingham Palace. Present at the birth was the Secretary of State for Home Affairs, Sir William Joynson-Hicks, as was the custom at the time. A medical bulletin referred to 'a certain line of treatment', meaning a Caesarean section. It had been a tough birth for her mother, the Duchess of York. It was a toughness her first child inherited.

Even from her earliest years she seemed to possess the qualities that would one day mark her long reign as Queen. Unlike her younger sister, Margaret, Elizabeth was a serious, self-possessed child, quick of temper and not afraid of using what former nanny Marion Crawford described as a powerful left hook whenever her ire was raised.

Third in line to the crown when she was born, no one could have predicted that by her twenty-fifth birthday she would become monarch of the British Empire. By 1936, when she was just ten years old, her life changed for ever. George V died and his eldest son became King Edward VIII. His reign lasted less than a year when he dramatically abdicated to marry Wallis Simpson, and suddenly Elizabeth became heir to the throne when her father was crowned George VI. It was a tumultuous time for the Royal Family and particularly so for young Elizabeth, who was abruptly thrust into the spotlight as the future queen. She was a naturally shy youngster, a trait she inherited from her father, and never even attended school. Instead, like so many royals before her, her education came at home, under the careful attention of hand-picked tutors. Indeed, her early life was guided by a series of nannies and tutors almost from the very beginning. Soon after her birth, she was left with nannies for six months while her parents toured Australia and New Zealand.

In 1939, as the clouds of war approached, the 13-year-old Princess Elizabeth met the man she would later marry – her third cousin, the dashing Prince Philip of Greece. Although she was just a child at the time of that first meeting at the Royal Naval College at Dartmouth, she was immediately taken by the handsome, fair-haired, 18-year-old Philip. Nanny Crawford remembered that meeting very well, and recalled afterwards how she 'noticed that Lilibet began to take more trouble with her appearance. Then suddenly she started to play her gramophone more than usual. Her favourite tune was 'People Will Say We're in Love', from the musical *Oklahoma!* Because discretion was necessary, they could not dance together at parties too often, athough they would glance longingly at one another.'

Their love for each other remained a secret to many of those around them, but eventually the courtship became more open as Elizabeth matured to womanhood. As the relationship grew more serious, there were doubts that Philip would be an acceptable husband. After all, he was a 'damn foreigner', and many people openly questioned whether he was suitable to become the husband of Britain's future queen. Even Elizabeth's parents were unsure of the budding courtship, and her father took her off on a three-month tour of South Africa, which he thought would be long enough to make her forget Philip. However, the young Princess was determined to follow her heart. Eventually, the King gave his blessing and, on 20 November 1947, Elizabeth and her Prince Charming were wed in a lavish ceremony before 2,500 guests at Westminster Abbey. It was a marvellous occasion, and helped buoy up a depressed Britain, still hurting from the ravages of the Second World War.

Just six days shy of their first wedding anniversary, Princess Elizabeth gave birth to their first child, Prince Charles. Some two years later, in August 1950, the 24-year-old Elizabeth had their only daughter, Princess Anne. For the next three years, the Princess and her husband lived a comparatively carefree existence. Even though they knew her father had cancer, no one in the royal household thought he was in danger, so, just seven days before the King's death, in February 1952, Elizabeth and Philip set off on a goodwill tour of East Africa, New Zealand and Australia. They were in Kenya when word finally reached them about the King's death. Together, they had spent the night of 5 February watching the exotic African wildlife from a platform perched some 25 feet up in the trees. Although she did not know it then, by the time she climbed down from her overnight vigil, Elizabeth was a queen.

When the news reached her, it came from her husband, who asked her to accompany him on a walk by the river. Together, they walked and talked for almost an hour before the saddened young Princess was ready to accept condolences from her hosts and entourage. Although privately devastated, Elizabeth summoned enough of her royal bearing to appear composed when she arrived back in Britain. Clad in black as she stepped from the plane, she was greeted by her uncle, the Duke of Gloucester, and all the leading political figures of the day, including Prime Minister Winston Churchill. It was a sad day to mark the beginning of her long reign. The day also marked the inevitable change in her relationship with Philip – literally and figuratively, he would now have to walk one step behind her as she carried out the duties of her office in lonely isolation.

Her coronation, on 2 June 1953, was a day of international celebration as the young Queen led a glittering procession of dignitaries down the central aisle of Westminster Abbey. Looking resplendent in a white dress with a lined velvet cloak, Elizabeth wore St Edward's crown and carried the orb and sceptre of her lofty office. More than 300 million people around the world watched the historic ceremony on television – the young Queen had insisted her coronation be televised throughout the Commonwealth – while hundreds of thousands of faithful Britons lined the streets of London in pouring rain to catch a glimpse of the monarch as she and Philip arrived at the abbey from Buckingham Palace in a golden coach pulled by eight horses. It was a day to remember as bells peeled and cannons roared across the British Commonwealth. Finally, at midnight, the Queen appeared on the palace balcony just as the news of Sir Edmund Hilary's conquest of Mount Everest spread.

Soon after that glorious day, Elizabeth and the Duke of Edinburgh embarked on a lengthy trip to meet her new subjects. The world-wide tour began in November 1953 and didn't end until a gruelling six months later. Due to the demands placed on them in the early days of her reign, the Queen and Philip even had to put off having more children, until Andrew's birth in 1960 and Edward's four years later. Together, the Queen and the Duke have undertaken 60 or more state visits and numerous less formal trips to all corners of the globe. She has been carried aloft in the South Pacific, graciously accepted a taste of cooked rat at a banquet in her honour in Belize, and been pelted with eggs by protesters in New Zealand.

Yet through it all, the Queen remembered her bearing — always correct, always regal, always in control. According to various palace insiders, that is also exactly how Elizabeth is in private. Even among members of her own immediate family, she staunchly insists that they observe all the correct formalities. In her country homes, far removed from the more formal air of Buckingham Palace, family members must bow and curtsy to her upon arising and before retiring. Likewise, they must dress properly for dinner and make certain that they do not arrive after Her Majesty has entered the room. Similarly, anyone wanting to leave the table before the Queen has finished is sure to get one of those famous withering looks. Even the Duke of Edinburgh is not excepted from such imperious rules of the royal household. When not all together for family gatherings or holidays, her children more often communicate with her by letter, rather than by telephone.

Given such stiff, formal, some may say starchy, rules of conduct, it is astonishing just how many breaches of those rules were revealed in the aftermath of Michael Fagan's break-in of 1982. For Fagan not only made the security men look fools, he made a laughing stock of the entire Buckingham Palace machinery. No longer could the Queen expect the public and the press to avert their eyes modestly from her household. Suddenly it was hot news, and every aspect of 'the Firm' has been put under the microscope ever since. In the years since the Fagan security fiasco caused quizzical eyes to focus on palace affairs, many more scandals have been exposed, including other serious breaches of security, drug busts, homosexual activity and bed-hopping orgies.

One of the most startling of many palace scandals emerged early in 1990 when a royal butler blew the covers off the sordid lifestyle of some of the Queen's staff. Christopher Irwin, who worked at the palace and Clarence House, the Queen Mother's official London residence, for 11 years, shocked and dismayed Britain with his claims that: 'Life among some younger members of [the Queen's] household employees is a bed-hopping free-for-all. The turnover rate in partners is staggering. And the royal quarters are the easiest places in Britain to take drugs. No one ever checks the rooms.'

Irwin, father of five children, also disclosed an amazing lapse in security screening procedures for would-be palace employees. By his own admission, he had 29 criminal convictions to his discredit, including assault, drug possession and theft. Yet he said he 'sailed through' all the security checks to land a job at Britain's most important and closely-watched home.

'It terrified me how lax security was,' he said. 'I was given full security clearance. It would have been the easiest thing in the world to have planted a bomb in the palace. It really worries me how vulnerable they are.' Irwin, a drug addict for all his adult life, also claimed he was given cocaine numerous times by a royal footman and once even served Prince Charles and Princess Diana at dinner while zonked out on mind-altering amphetamines.

However, it was his tales of palace orgies that really stunned loyal Britons. He claimed that after guests had left the many lavish banquets hosted by the Queen, the staff and servants would often hold booze and sex parties well into the dawn hours. 'Once everyone had gone some of us would have a free-for-all with the food and wine,' he recalled. 'There was often a race to sit in the Queen's seat and give mock orders. One palace waitress, after a particularly long session, whipped off her top in an impromptu striptease. Some of the girls there are really wild.'

Indeed, the acute drinking problems facing some of the Queen's staffers became front-page news when servant Paul Brown fell from the roof of the palace after a boozy 1991 Christmas party. Police said the footman, who had been at a party with friends at a nearby restaurant, was climbing on some scaffolding above the staff quarters at the palace just for a lark when he slipped and plunged 20 feet to the ground. Fortunately, he survived the crash but security officials were enraged that he had managed to scale the scaffolding undetected. If a drunken servant could do it, what was to stop a madman, or even a trained IRA terrorist?

Homosexual lust has also been a highly embarrassing problem among the servants inside the palace walls. In 1989, one of Her Majesty's top chefs was brought before the bench on a gay sex charge. One cook at the palace, who often prepared meals for the Queen, was charged with importuning another man in a toilet in central London. That same year, yet another trusted palace worked was nabbed on similar sex chages. The royal aide, who had been a clerk for the Queen since 1979, was accused of propositioning a man at a lorry park. In 1991 a personal footman of the Queen was caught in a gay sex act with another man in a public lavatory near Buckingham Palace. The 25-year-old man, who was considered one of the Queen's most trusted footmen (his main duty was to care for Her Majesty's cherished corgis), worked at the palace for five years until he was caught red-handed by a police officer.

The following year, three royal footmen were in disgrace after they were discovered having a gay orgy in one of Buckingham Palace's large Victorian enamel baths. Another servant opened an unlocked door in the top-floor staff quarters and recoiled in shock as the miscreants rubbed each other with bath oil and scrubbed each other with loofahs.

A proportion of the palace footmen are homosexual but are valued for their loyalty and attention to detail. Certainly, there must be some attraction to keep them at the palace. Their duties are dull – they include pressing clothes, running errands and walking the Queen's corgis –

and their wages are only £6,000 to £8,000 a year with accommodation thrown in.

These examples of impropriety and breaches of security came years after the Fagan affair, and yet officials continued to claim that the Queen couldn't be safer. Indeed, there were several more break-ins after Fagan's. In 1990, Stephen Goulding got three months behind bars for twice breaking into the grounds. He claimed he was Prince Andrew and when shown a photograph of the Queen, he exclaimed: 'That's my mum!' Irishman Eugene Smith was caught in the palace grounds that same year, claiming that he just wanted the Queen to help him find his lost lover. Smith, 32, climbed into the garden at a spot near Grosvenor Place and Constitution Hill. Fortunately, he triggered alarms as he scaled the palace walls and this time security guards didn't ignore them. Police said the Royal Family was in no danger but the incidents renewed all the old fears over Her Majesty's safety and forced embarrassed security chiefs to re-examine their precautions, just as they were forced to do in the wake of the notorious Trooping the Colour parade in June 1981.

As the Queen, dressed in the uniform of the Welsh Guards, was riding out to review the troops on Horse Guards Parade, a disturbed youth fired six blank shots at her. The terrified Queen struggled to control her horse, Burmese, as the shots rang out. Prince Philip and Prince Charles, who were just behind her, rode up to protect her as police and soldiers grabbed the 17-year-old culprit, unemployed Marcus Sergeant. Although she was uninjured, Her Majesty later confided to her family that she had spotted the gun in the milling crowd not long before Sergeant fired it. From that day on, the Queen has not ridden on a horse to the Trooping the Colour ceremony, and now rides in a carriage.

Of course, the Queen's safety is of paramount import- ance to those who are charged with the special task of protecting the palace. Yet there is also unimaginable wealth stored behind those huge walls, and that, too, must be taken into consideration by the teams of security experts. Inside is a vast horde of priceless paintings, jewels, stamps, antiques and furniture, which make up part of the Queen's immense fortune. Their value, and indeed, the worth of the Queen's entire personal fortune, are almost as closely safeguarded as the monarch herself. According to the best estimates, the Queen is by far the richest woman in the world, with assets reaching a staggering £7 billion, and she pays not one penny in taxes.

An exact figure is, of course, impossible to ascertain. Her wealth is shrouded in mystery and protected by law. For instance, royal wills are never published, and only a few trusted officials are ever given access to them. Her shareholdings cannot even be identified, although her portfolio, which has interests in several major companies around the globe, is estimated by some to be in the region of some £2.5 billion. The portfolio, which is managed by royal stockbrokers Cazenove & Co. and Rowe & Pitman, is believed to contain vast shares in companies like British Telecom, electronics giant GEC and mining conglomerate RTZ. She also owns the 100-acre West Ilsley stud in Berkshire, as well as her two private holiday homes, Balmoral and Sandringham Castles, each worth tens of millions of pounds. Queen Victoria bought the massive 50,000-acre Scottish Balmoral Castle in 1848, and today it boasts excellent grouse shooting and salmon fishing plus a nine-hole golf course and a two-lane bowling alley. The Jacobean-style Sandringham in Norfolk has 274 rooms and sits on 20,104 acres. The estate contains some of the best farmland in England.

Aside from that, the Queen owns the world's largest private art collection – some 5,000 paintings and 30,000 drawings, including works by Renaissance masters Leonardo da Vinci, Michelangelo and Raphael. The amazing collection boasts well over 750 drawings by da Vinci, 26 paintings by Van Dyck, oils by Frans Hals, Rubens, Correggio, and Titian, numerous portraits by Gainsborough and four works by Rembrandt. One rare Vermeer painting alone is valued at a mind-boggling £28 million.

Likewise, the royal stamp collection is considered the best in all the world. It takes more than 320 volumes to hold it, and it includes such rare treasures as samples from the initial printing of Britain's first stamp, the legendary penny black, issued on 6 May 1840, the first colonial stamp, issued in 1847 for use by the master of the steam-ship *Lady McLeod*, and nearly priceless 1847 Mauritius stamps engraved by a local jeweller named J. Barnard. Only 26 are known to be in existence.

The Queen also oversees the most expensive and largest jewellery collection in the world. Even the fabulous Crown Jewels, which are on public display at the Tower of London, are just a portion of the incredible haul. For instance, the

Queen Mother's ermine-fringed coronation crown holds the dazzling 108-carat Koh-i-noor diamond, the huge gem that the British East India Company confiscated from the treasury of the Maharajah of Lahore and presented to Queen Victoria. Its value alone is an ice-cool £7 million. Other impressive gems include a sapphire from the Stuart line and a ruby from Edward the Black Prince, both of which are in Victoria's coronation crown.

Then there is Her Majesty's Fabergé eggs and figurine collection, including three imperial Easter eggs worth about £2.5 million each. The Queen also owns a fortune in porcelain, and the collection includes several masterpieces, like the *Table of the Great Generals*, which Louis XVIII gave to George IV. The work, which was commissioned by Napoleon in 1806, took six years to complete. The royal car collection – including a prized 1954 Rolls-Royce Phantom IV, valued at around £400,000 – is worth several millions.

So is the furniture. In the eighteenth century, the Crown commissioned William Vile to make cabinets, bookcases and bureaux for the palaces. Vile's jewellery cabinet, built for Queen Charlotte, ranks among the finest pieces of furniture of the period.

On top of all that, the Queen also gets paid! From the Civil List, she gets approximately £8 million a year, which goes towards paying costs for many of her homes, catering for the numerous state banquets, wages for some 300 staffers and so on. She also receives another £3 million from land holdings in the north of England, and that is used primarily for her clothes, staff pensions and the maintenance of the mansions she owns privately, Balmoral and Sandringham. Besides these personal possessions, of course, the Queen and her family get the enviable use of their official residences, Buckingham Palace and Windsor Castle. The costs of these are astronomical. Although Her Majesty often looks for ways of saving herself money, she sometimes forgets to be quite as frugal when taxpayers' money is at stake.

A crane once dominated the skyline of the Royal Borough of Windsor for several years. It was needed as part of the massive, multi-million- pound restoration work which took place at Windsor Castle. So extensive was the project that for the first time in many years the Royal Family were unable to spend their Christmas at Windsor.

The good folk of Windsor thought it pointless to complain over the length of time their town was blighted by cranes and scaffolding, clearly visible for miles around. They had protested before in vain when they discovered that, like all other 'tenants' in the area, the Queen qualified for a local council grant towards the cost of double-glazing her 'house' to cut down the aircraft noise from Heathrow Airport. The cost of double-glazing Windsor Castle had been almost incalculable. Yet despite all the residents' expressions of dismay and despite all the Queen's wealth, the thrifty monarch still claimed the grant.

During the restoration work of the late 1980s and early 1990s it was decided the castle's historic Round Tower needed repainting. Almost a year's work went into its renovation and the result, as far as the contractors were concerned, was perfect. However, it was not perfect as far as the Queen was concerned. She announced that the freshly painted, rust-coloured tower was not to her liking and work began all over again – this time to paint the edifice a more royal blue!

Apart from castles of stone and mansions of bricks and mortar, the Royal Family also owns multi-millions of acres of land. Their principal boon is the cash-rich Duchy of Lancaster, their ownership of which stems from the thirteenth century. Henry III seized the original parcels of land – which today total 52,000 acres – from a pair of earls following the Barons' War of the 1260s. He gave the land to his son, Edmund, who hoped to become King of Sicily and needed an inheritance.

Whenever and wherever the Queen travels, it's first class all the way: on the road, in one of her five Rolls-Royce Phantoms; on special occasions, in one of the seven magnificent horse-drawn coaches. The Queen's Flight, which has a staff of some 200 people, has three BAe146s – which could seat 128 passengers if they were used as commercial planes – at a cost of about £45 million, and two helicopters. Then there's the stately royal yacht *Britannia*, all 412 feet of it, which needs a crew of 286. In one year alone, some £10 million was needed just for its upkeep. The Royal Family also have exclusive use of a private 12-car train, which costs another £1.5 million to operate every year.

Despite her almost unbelievable wealth, the Queen is notoriously frugal. Aides have remarked that she is so tight with her money that she even saves pieces of string. Once, she sent out a team of bodyguards to scour her estates with metal detectors when she misplaced a dog lead. During one of her many chauffeur-driven rides around London, she banned apples from the palace after she spotted the price per pound and considered it way too much, even for the royal table. There have also been numerous stories about how she throws a royal fit if lights inside Buckingham Palace are left on (she is said to wander the palace at night, switching off those lights she deems unnecessary) and how she insists that curtains be mended, rather than replaced.

There is no waste in the royal household. Once, when one of her beloved corgis killed a hare, she carefully picked it up and presented it to the palace kitchen staff. 'We can eat this,' she announced. Her Christmas gifts to family members include gardening gloves, hot water bottles, sometimes even compasses! Her taste in everyday things also belies her wealth. She prefers bland food, with no spices or rich sauces, enjoys nothing better than a good cup of tea, and loves traipsing through the countryside with her dogs or horses.

Although there is little doubt that the majority of British people have a deep respect for the Queen, there is a growing call throughout the kingdom that she should, at the very least, start paying her fair share of taxes, especially in these tough economic times. Her Majesty has never paid taxes on her immense personal fortune or investments, unlike other members of the Royal Family, though she does pay indirect taxes. No British monarch has paid income tax since Queen Victoria and she did so voluntarily. Now, public demand for a change is growing.

Surveys in both 1991 and 1992 found that an increasing proportion of Britons (as many as four in five) felt that the Queen should pay taxes.

It is unlikely that the Queen will ever do so within her lifetime. However, from a reliable source close to the senior royals, the authors can reveal that Prince Charles holds a different view. The Prince and Princess of Wales, who reportedly have a net worth of some £230 million, live handsomely on their £2.3 million annual income from the Duchy of Cornwall. As all of this income is his own, Prince Charles is not on the Civil List. When he eventually accedes to the throne, it is very likely that he will make a deal with the government of the day. He will undoubtedly accept his full dues as monarch from the Civil List, but in return he is likely to bear voluntarily the full burden of taxation on his vast income. That, it is believed, will be the concerned Prince's firm commitment to enhance the standing of the Royal Family in the twenty-first century. It would be a sacrifice that would win him instant national support.

Many of the other royals, concerned about their image, now also try to appear to be working for their money. Aside from Prince Andrew, who was in the Royal Navy, and Prince Edward, who was bent on theatrical life, during the 1980s, family members doubled the number of yearly public appearances to nearly 3,000, led by Princess Anne who managed more than 700 appearances in 1991. As she was getting 'only' some £230,000 a year in government allowance, many saw her as by far the hardest-working royal. Andrew was getting slightly more, at £250,000, while Edward pulled in £100,000. By comparison, the Queen Mother was raking in £640,000, Prince Philip £360,000, Margaret £220,000 and Princess Alice £90,000.

The untold and ever-increasing wealth of the Royal Family came under its closest scrutiny in the summer of 1992. There were demands for an inquiry into what then amounted to £9 million a year of Civil List money to support the monarchy in the style to which it had been accustomed. The furore could not have come at a worse time. Members of the family were receiving handsome amounts for very little coverage of any official engagements. No one could remember when Princess Margaret or Prince Edward had last fulfilled a public duty; the Duchess of York had been 'struck-off' the royal rota of good works and charitable appearances because of her split with Prince Andrew, and the private squabbles between the Prince and Princess of Wales were interfering with the scheduling of their official itinerary.

So in July 1992, when Members of Parliament were barred from launching an inquiry into how the Civil List money was being spent, the whole question of public subsidy for the royals was blown wide open. The Civil List row was over the government's deal, two years earlier, which not only guaranteed the Royal Family an automatic 7.5 per cent annual increase until the year 2000, but also guaranteed the secrecy of negotiations as to how the tax-payers' money was being spent. This ten-year code of silence, effectively gagging any debate about public funding of the royals, only became known when the House of Commons' independent Public Accounts Committee pushed for an inquiry. One member complained: 'If there is nothing to hide, why is the Establishment trying to prevent Members of Parliament asking questions?'

Fabulous wealth, luxurious surroundings, pre-eminent social status – such are the rewards of being born into the House of Windsor. With it, as we have seen, comes inevitable (though often avoidable) criticism. In the Queen's case it has, of late, largely been aimed at her appearance and her sense of fashion. Even her couturier of four decades, Sir Hardy Amies, spoke out about her frumpiness. 'I sometimes wish she had been a bit more of a clothes person,' he said. 'She doesn't care, basically. She listens to our advice, then goes off and wears shabby shoes because they're comfortable.' Her dowdy trademark attire – boxy outfits, clunky handbags and unfashionable glasses – has been lambasted from Blackpool to Brisbane.

Of course, compared to other members of her family, the Queen has largely remained above reproach and is still widely popular with her subjects. Yet there can be no doubt she has suffered much through the public humiliations and scandals of her more wayward relatives. So much so, in fact, that many people have for years wondered if the Queen would one day abdicate her throne in favour of Charles but Her Majesty appears to have no intention of making way for her eldest son, despite his growing impatience. In her 1991 Christmas speech, she left little doubt about her future intentions when she said: 'I feel the same obligation to you that I felt in 1952. With your prayers, and your help, and with the love and support of my family, I shall try to serve you in the years to come.'

Some intimates claim, however, that Elizabeth would dearly like to abdicate but has decided that she simply cannot. She remembers too well her uncle, the Prince of Wales, whose abandonment of the throne for Mrs Simpson forced her shy father to become king. Advisers have also reportedly told her that, given the conduct of some of her children, she must remain in power to ensure the survival of the monarchy. Indeed, Fleet Street editorials have warned many times in the recent past that the younger royals' ongoing public antics threaten to bring down the House of Windsor.

Despite the Queen's own misgivings about the frenzied media coverage devoted to her family, she seems to understand that it is she, and probably she alone, who can ensure that the monarchy lasts well into the next century as Britain moves closer and closer to a homogenised Europe.

There is no doubt that the monarchy is secure as long as Elizabeth reigns. Over the vast majority of her life, she has earned the respect and admiration of her subjects. Even before she was Queen, a war-torn nation admired her courage and determination during the worst days of the German blitz. Today, more than 50 years later, she is still a popular figure and an integral part of British heritage. One day the mantle of ruler must inevitably pass to Charles. Although he has been well schooled in the ways of the monarchy, what effect will the long, debilitating wait have on him? Given the family's strong genes, the Queen could well rule the House of Windsor for another 20 years – or more. By then, Charles will be well into his sixties, most probably a grandfather, and hardly the invigorating presence his youthful mother was when she ascended the throne so many years ago. Will today's generation of young Britons have anything in common with an elderly, old-fashioned king?

That is the challenge facing Queen Elizabeth. In the time she has left as sovereign, she must restore pride and dignity in the monarchy. To some, it would seem an impossible task.

CHAPTER FIVE

The Duke of Edinburgh

When Prince Philip was born on 10 June 1921, a lucky star must have twinkled in the cloudless Greek skies, for none of the royals has enjoyed endless good fortune like the Queen's husband – lucky because he was once penniless despite his own distinguished ancestry. Uprisings around Europe left him not only hard-up but without a country or even a name he could call his own. When he courted Princess Elizabeth he was earning only £11 a week in the Navy. Yet if she knew of his straitened circumstances, she clearly didn't care a bit and he went on to marry the world's richest woman.

More than that, his sisters had all wedded Germans. While Philip was hoping for the hand of the Princess in war-time Britain, his in-laws were bombing the country she was one day to rule. At a time when everything German was reviled by the British people, the man with relatives close to Hitler was yearning to be accepted. He was eventually welcomed into the Royal Family with barely a whisper heard of his Teutonic links. While royal marriages all around have failed, his own seems strong and flourishes despite gossip and rumour-mongering which have the Prince involved in all manner of scandal.

Indeed, he was lucky to be born at all. Philip was the fifth and final child of his parents, Prince Andrew of Greece and his mother, born Princess Alice of Battenburg at Windsor Castle. His mother was 36 and the youngest of his four older sisters, Sophie, was seven at the time. As the family were already struggling to survive, it's certain the new arrival was something of an accident. Prince Philip's family were only occupying the Greek throne because nobody else wanted the job! Sixty years before he was born, Philip's Danish grandfather obliged the concerned European royals by taking the job. His father, Prince Andrew, was kept in pocket by royal patrons, like so many of his cousins in Europe at the time. He was bowled over when he met the stunning Princess Alice at the coronation of King Edward VII in 1901. Never mind that she was quite deaf, having been born with severe hearing difficulties. She could lip read in four different languages so it hardly mattered. Despite opposition from her father, she married the charming Prince and seemed stoical about the life of relative poverty she was to face.

These were turbulent times. Just a few years before his birth, Philip's family were in exile when the Greek King Constantine, his uncle, abdicated, having, it seemed, been a supporter of the Germans after failing to join the Allies during the First World War. However, the royals were later restored by public demand and Prince Andrew brought his family back from exile in Switzerland to Corfu in time for Philip's arrival.

The place of his birth was a holiday villa called Mon Repos on the island of Corfu. This was no luxury pad of the type favoured by other royals of the era. There was neither electricity nor hot water in the rundown rambling home. Princess Alice had to be heaved on to the dining-room table to give birth – it was the only piece of furniture strong enough to hold her during labour. Young Philippos, as he was named, was sixth in line to the Greek throne with not a drop of Greek blood in his veins.

Their English housekeeper Agnes Blower told how they

were 'as poor as church mice. He was the sweetest, prettiest baby; what a joy he was to us all. I can see him now, kicking his legs in the sunshine and for 18 months in Corfu I watched him grow up. It was a lovely outdoor life although he didn't have many toys, hardly any. They were very poor.'

The chubby tot would have seen little of his father, as Prince Andrew was leading a Greek division against the Turks as a bitter struggle between the two nations continued. Through a crisis in command, thousands of Greek soldiers were lost in a desperate and unsuccessful campaign. Philip's father returned to Corfu in the wake of the disaster, only to be hauled off to Athens to face charges of disobedience and desertion. A military tribunal found him guilty. He was sentenced to be shot along with fellow convicts.

Here Prince Andrew was to experience some of the luck that blessed his son much later. His frantic wife contacted her brother, Lord Louis Mountbatten, who used his royal links to alert King George V. With hours to go before the scheduled execution, British agent Commander Gerald Talbot visited Pangalos, the Greek Minister of War, who was unmoved by the British officer's pleadings until he discovered a British warship, HMS *Calypso*, had sailed to Athens and had its guns pointed towards the city.

Instead of execution, Prince Andrew was banished from Greece for life. He and his family sailed on the *Calypso* away from the only homeland they had known. Sailors used a discarded orange box to make a cot for the infant Philip, who was too small to sleep in a bunk.

Following a brief stop in Britain, the family settled in France, but the troubles had taken their toll of his parents' marriage. By the time Philip was eight they had split. Prince Andrew went to the Riviera, took up with another woman, began gambling and remained virtually penniless until the day he died in 1944.

Philip's mother became increasingly eccentric, perhaps showing the first symptoms of nervous depression, from which she suffered for years. She donned nun-like clothes and returned to Greece to work for the deprived with a close woman companion. She lived out her final years at Buckingham Palace with her only son close at hand, until she died in 1969.

Once his parents had separated, neither figured largely in Philip's life. It was now that his British relatives came to the fore. He spent more and more time with his grandmother, Victoria, Dowager Marchioness of Milford Haven, his Uncle George, Marquess of Milford Haven and Uncle Louis, Lord Mountbatten. He was to receive a firm grounding in how to be British.

However, his sisters were anxious that they should have a say in his upbringing too. Princess Sophie was just 16 when she married Prince Christopher of Hesse in November 1930. The second youngest was Cecile, who wed George Donatus, heir to the Grand Duke of Hesse and the Rhine in the same year when she was 19. They were later killed in an aircrash before the Second World War. Philip's eldest sister, Margarita, 25, married Gottfried, Prince of Hohenlohe- Langenburg, her mother's second cousin, in March 1931. Finally Princess Theodora, 24, married a cousin, Berthold, Prince and Margrave of Baden.

All of the girls' husbands were German and two in particular were spellbound by the lure of the swastika. Prince Gottfried joined the army as a corps commander. Prince Christopher took a far more prominent role in the Nazi regime in the Luftwaffe and in a vital, top-secret Intelligence department until he died when his plane was shot down over Italy. However, it was Christopher's brother, Philip of Hesse, who was close enough to Hitler to cause major concern. He acted as a go-between for the dictator and the likes of the Duke of Windsor and Mussolini, earning accolades from the Führer. However, 1943 brought his downfall when his father-in-law, the King of Italy, dramatically switched to the Allied cause. Philip of Hesse was taken to Dachau, while his wife, Mafalda, was sent to Buchenwald where she died in an American bombing raid. Philip of Hesse survived the war, was tried for war crimes and finally returned quietly to life at home in the same year that Philip married Elizabeth. Nobody made the connection.

Hitler was only just beginning to tighten his grip when the young Prince Philip visited his sisters in 1933. They were determined he should attend school in Salem where headmaster Kurt Hahn was producing exciting results, but then Hitler unwittingly intervened. Hahn was a Jew, so naturally he ended up in prison. It wasn't until his supporters lobbied long and hard that he was released and allowed to depart to Scotland where he chose to put his educational ideas into practice at a new school called Gordonstoun.

Meanwhile, Philip's own brother-in-law, Bertold of Baden, was appointed head of the Salem school. It seemed the perfect place for 12-year-old Philip to receive his education but the move was a disaster. For a start, Philip had no time for Nazism and its paraphernalia. He thought goose stepping was ludicrous and he treated the 'heil Hitler' salute as a joke. Fortunately, as a 'foreigner', he wasn't compelled to join the Hitler Youth Movement where he would have been exposed to far more propaganda. His brother-in-law found it a struggle to make the school work. Some teachers followed Nazi ethics to the letter while others abhorred the regime, which led to an atmosphere of suspicion and fear. When Bertold decided to shut the school rather than sell out to the Nazi cause, he was threatened with jail. It was then that both the headmaster and Philip's sisters realised that Germany was no place for him. He was sent back to Britain – and went straight to Gordonstoun, a school he has championed ever since.

At Gordonstoun, there's plenty of emphasis on the importance of physical pursuits and prowess. Philip was a star pupil and the cutting edge of his competitiveness has shone out ever since. The school moulded him, if any shaping were needed, into the most British of men. Although the German links could not be denied, they could, however, be hushed up. None of his sisters appeared at the Prince's wedding and all his visits to them in Germany have been kept strictly private.

In April 1946, when Philip was publicly courting the British princess, an incident overseas threatened to put

Philip's close family on all the front pages. His sister Sophie, widow of Prince Christopher, wished to remarry, this time to another prince, George William of Hanover. As the family castle at Kronberg had been commandeered by the Americans, she and her sisters had to seek official permission to reclaim their jewels from the castle vaults. Their horror, when they discovered the strongbox had been raided and their gems were missing, can be imagined. Prince Philip himself was on hand to comfort his weeping sisters, who had been crying for joy only hours earlier at their reunion after the end of the war.

Three Americans were to blame, investigators discovered. They were Captain Kathleen Nash, her boyfriend Colonel Jack Durant and pal Major David Watson. They had rifled the castle as the war ended and transported much of the haul to America to sell it off. There were necklaces, tiaras, brooches and rings set with the finest-quality stones and precious metals. In total the loot was vauled at £1.5 million although plenty had been sold off by the crooks already. In addition there were other heirlooms, including nine leather-bound volumes of letters from Queen Victoria. However, quite the most shocking item to come to light was a solid-gold swastika. If Philip's allegiance to Britain was beyond question, it was clear that his own sister's perhaps was not.

It could have been a major embarrassment to Philip and smothered any chances he had of marrying into British royalty, but his lucky charm worked once more. The newspapers failed to spot the link between Philip and the troubled Hesse dynasty. One man who must have breathed a huge sigh of relief was Lord Louis Mountbatten, Philip's uncle and self-style mentor.

Mountbatten himself had felt the chill wind of anti-German feeling in Britain and for this reason had translated his German name of Battenburg to Mountbatten. Something had been lost in the change, however, and that was the right to call himself HRH. He was deeply ambitious for the sake of his family lineage and desperately wanted a royal match for his nephew, so he started a campaign that would make Prince Philip of Greece the perfect suitor.

With the help from Mountbatten, 17-year-old Philip entered Dartmouth as a Naval cadet. He was to become a prize pupil. While at Dartmouth, Mountbatten managed to engineer a meeting between the pair, who would be married inside the decade. Elizabeth was only 13 and her sister, Margaret, nine when they arrived at Dartmouth aboard the royal yacht *Britannia* with their parents on 22 July 1939. Uncle Dickie made sure that it was Philip who entertained the girls while their father performed his official duties. At 18, Philip was blond, blue-eyed, handsome and manly. He amused the girls by jumping over the tennis net with considerable panache. They had a prawn tea followed by banana splits aboard the yacht before it was time to return. As the royal yacht set sail, a flotilla of boats crewed by the boys headed off in hot pursuit. The last to turn back was a rowing boat oared through the water by Philip under the watchful gaze of an admiring Princess Elizabeth.

It was in 1939, on his first ship, the *Ramillies*, a posting again secured by Uncle Dickie, that Philip himself revealed that the plotting had begun. The ship's captain was Vice-Admiral Harold Tom Baillie-Grohman. In a 'welcome abroad' chat Philip dropped a bombshell.

'My Uncle Dickie has ideas for me; he thinks I could marry Princess Elizabeth.'

The Captain was shocked. 'Are you really fond of her?'

'Oh yes, very. I write to her every week.'

Baillie-Grohman counselled the young Prince to say nothing of the attachment while aboard. Anyway, there were more pressing matters to consider. War was beckoning. However, at that point Philip was still a Greek, not a British, subject and as such had no quarrel with Hitler. All his efforts to be naturalised had come to nothing. Once more it was Uncle Dickie who helped him out by issuing orders to the Admiralty that ensured that Philip could continue the Naval career for which he was so eminently suited. Dickie wasn't the only member of his family eager to see a royal partnership. Six and a half years before any engagement, Philip's aunt, Princess Nicholas, declared to party-goers in Athens that Philip would be the husband of Princess Elizabeth and that, of course, was why he was serving with the British Royal Navy.

According to her governess, Elizabeth was in love. The young couple began a correspondence that endured through the trauma of the war years during which Philip sailed on dangerous missions for Britain although he still failed to get his British citizenship, despite strenuous efforts on his behalf by his uncle. Mountbatten made overtures to the Home Office, the Foreign Office, the Prime Minister – even to the King himself. Still the essential documents were not forthcoming.

In actual fact, the King had reservations about the love match — and love match it was, for anyone could see that the young Princess had fallen for her dashing hero Prince. None the less, Philip remained without a state and Elizabeth was young. The King also had to consider how his subjects would react to such a union. Even if most people didn't know of the German links, the King was painfully aware of them.

While the King tried to put the brakes on the romance, Philip and Elizabeth continued to see each other as often as possible. In 1946 there was even an unofficial engagement after Philip proposed following a long, romantic walk on heather-coated turf by a pretty lake. Still prevaricating, the King ordered a statement to be issued denying rumours of the engagement. He knew that documents recently uncovered by the Allies had linked his errant brother, the Duke of Windsor, with Philip's brother-in-law, Prince Christopher. It could be the blast that would shatter all hopes of a union.

Little did Philip realise that his incredible luck was still holding fast. Simply by playing the waiting game, the King, Philip and Elizabeth began to realise that the German ghost was not about to rear up and haunt them. At the end of February 1947 Philip's naturalisation papers were made ready.

Of course, becoming a British citizen meant renouncing his claim to the Greek throne and he thus lost his title of prince. It also meant he had to have a proper surname. Until then, he had been plain Prince Philip of Greece, with no other needed. It seemed appropriate that he should choose his mother's Anglicised maiden name, Mountbatten, which naturally delighted his uncle.

The engagement was finally announced in July 1947 and a November wedding day was set. There were public misgivings about a foreigner joining 'the family firm' but the occasion also acted as a joyful celebration to lift everybody's spirits in those dreary post-war days. Ever-cautious, the King refused to grant Philip a royal title. The honeymoon was at Broadlands, the home of Mountbatten, followed by a spell at Balmoral. Philip got a baptism of fire as the press and public clamoured to glimpse the newly-weds. He was irritated by their intrusion and showed it. At Balmoral he caught a cold. Living the life of a royal was perhaps not as wonderful as it appeared.

For the first time Philip had a home of his own. This was at Clarence House and he worked hard to give it his mark. He brought the few possessions he had into the marriage and has maintained a comparatively frugal outlook ever since those hard-up Navy days. He enjoyed the first years when their first two children, Charles and Anne, were born. He continued his career in the Navy and his wife later joined him in Malta, getting a taste of real life for the first time. They combined official duties with his work and having fun. Then, in February 1952, life changed dramatically on the death of King George V. This signalled the end of Philip's Naval career – he was now needed to support his wife at home. It also put paid to any small freedom he had so far enjoyed. Now he was to find out what living in a goldfish bowl was really all about. Mountbatten was thrilled to find a close relative even closer to the throne, but not everybody shared his joy. The Queen Mother was among many who distrusted Mountbatten as a meddler, remembering his allegiance to the Duke of Windsor during the abdication fiasco. Worse, Mountbatten bragged that the House of Windsor was now in fact the House of Mountbatten and peerage experts Debretts felt bound to agree.

However, Mountbatten had reckoned without the interference of Queen Mary, the ageing family matriarch, who insisted that the name of the House of Windsor be preserved. The birth of Charles and Anne passed without the need to publish their surname; their titles were simply Prince and Princess. To clear up any later confusion, however, Churchill and his cabinet colleagues then agreed that Windsor was the proper name for the royal children no matter what marital name had been introduced. On 21 April 1952 it was officially proclaimed by Order in Council that it was the Queen's 'will and pleasure She and her Children shall be styled and known as the House of Windsor'.

Mountbatten must have been most gratified, only seven years afterwards, on the birth of Prince Andrew, when the Queen changed the family name to Mountbatten-Windsor.

The grand Coronation Day was set to be the most prestigious and moving ceremony of Elizabeth and Philip's lives but it was marred by a crisis about to hit the royals in the form of Princess Margaret's affair with Group Captain Peter Townsend. The RAF hero, now comptroller of the Queen Mother's household, had fallen in love with Margaret and she with him, but he was a divorcee, following his wife, Rosemary's, adultery. A liaison was unthinkable.

Although Margaret had given her full support to Elizabeth and Philip during their long wait for official approval, she now discovered this would not be reciprocated as far as Philip was concerned. Perhaps he suspected that Townsend, as equerry to the King, had held up his own plans to wed.

When the Margaret–Townsend affair 'went public' in the summer, Philip felt the royals were being made to look silly. He was adamant that there should be no marriage and therefore no constitutional crisis or split with the Church.

Later Townsend said:

I was not against Philip's marriage to the Queen. I know of the rumours but believe me, I have never told anyone who they should or should not marry. I would not interfere with my own sons let alone other people... To me, Philip seemed a fine up-standing man... The one thing we did do was fight battles against each other on the courts – badminton and squash. Philip would fight me to a standstill. He played to win every time. One time he was so intent on the game he nearly broke my wrist.

After Margaret renounced her love, Philip gained more power when Churchill suddenly realised that if anything happened to the Queen, it would be Margaret who would take over the reins of power. Thanks to the Regency Act of 1953, Philip was made regent, guardian to the sovereign in the event of the Queen's death. This left Margaret even more in the wilderness. Relations between them were forever spoiled and she now referred to him scathingly as the 'con-sort'.

Margaret continued to hope for marriage with Group Captain Townsend but Philip barred the way. In frustration, she blurted out to the Queen the latest gossip surrounding her fun-loving husband. It wasn't the first time scandal had bubbled around Philip, but the Queen was furious that Margaret had listened to such tales.

One abiding story linked his name with that of cabaret star Helene Cordet, mother of two children, Max and Louise, both conceived out of wedlock. Philip had known Helene since boyhood, when her father had paid for holidays for the little prince. Just as her family cared for him when he had nothing, he lent a hand when Helene was penniless in the 1940s.

At first Helene failed to quash stories of an affair with Philip, merely by virtue of her lack of denials. Then she finally admitted that the children were the result of a passionate affair with a fickle French airman called Marcel Boisot, who had left them destitute.

Philip was godfather to both children. Max was sent to Gordonstoun to follow in Philip's own footsteps, even though Helene was a woman of slender means. Later, during the royal tour of China in 1986, Philip dropped out of the entourage to visit Max, a professor of economics at the Euro-Chinese Business Centre in Beijing.

Max insists that Boisot is his father. 'I have heard these rumours all my life,' he said. 'But they are ridiculous. My father, my real father, lives in Paris.' Helene continues to be friendly with Philip and has once met the Queen.

Another enduring rumour involved actress Pat Kirkwood. Her name was linked with the Prince after they danced the night away at a London club. Who could fail to notice the glittering pair as they twirled on the floor, she dressed in a delicate coral gown? However, most observers failed to mention that Kirkwood's boyfriend Baron, a long-time pal of Philip, was also there. There was no affair, just some good, old-fashioned fun.

None the less, the stories dogged Kirkwood and led to a humiliating telling-off for Philip from the King himself. After all, his darling daughter was heavily pregnant at the time. Philip learnt another lesson of royal life the hard way.

In addition, actress Anna Massey, niece of a former Governor General of Canada, and novelist Daphne du Maurier, whose husband General 'Boy' Browning is comptroller of the Prince's household, have also felt bound to deny any suggestion of affairs.

Philip's men friends also gave cause for concern. He was involved with the Thursday Club, a curious men-only group featuring some wacky personalities who specialised in drinking, flirting and playing pranks. Among the regulars were mouth organist Larry Adler, actors Peter Ustinov and James Robertson Justice, photographer Baron and artist Vasco Lazzolo. This harmless-seeming association came near the knuckle during the Profumo scandal when it was revealed that Dr Stephen Ward was an occasional guest alongside Prince Philip at the Thursday Club. The shady Ward, who committed suicide while on trial for living off immoral earnings, claimed that Philip visited his flat for parties at least once, possibly twice.

Ward had done a series of sketches of Philip and other royals. When the scandal broke, these drawings were on display in a London gallery. They were suddenly bought by a smartly-dressed man who arrived one morning and produced cash from a briefcase. They were never seen again and their whereabouts now are a mystery.

There's little doubt that Philip found it hard to adjust to life in the hot seat. Now that his good fortune had landed him at the top of the pile, he found his charmed existence was in jeopardy. No longer could he indulge in horseplay or japes; the staid palace-dwellers frowned upon such behaviour and the press would have a party with any juicy titbits that came to light.

His friend and private secretary, Commander Michael Parker, connived with Philip to provide some freedom, some loosening of the chains. Philip nicknamed the two of them 'Murgatroyd and Winterbottom' when they were off on jaunts away from the palace. Together, they seized the opportunity to take a five-month world tour, culminating in the opening of the Melbourne Olympic Games in 1956. The Queen tolerated this lengthy absence, but Parker's wife, Eileen, became fed up and decided to end the marriage.

This served to cast a shadow over Philip's own marriage. Speculation became rife that the romance was over between him and Elizabeth and that they were leading separate lives. Parker felt bound to resign his post, to Philip's fury and dismay. He flew home before the end of the tour to face the furore. Meanwhile, the Queen had to face the press when she was reunited with her roving husband in Malta. Critics were silenced, however, when she created for him the English title 'Prince' in 1957 in recognition of his services to the country. They went on to have two further children.

Stories of flings and love children continue to haunt the Prince. According to one insider, however: 'If the Queen believes that the sexual side of his nature has been catered for elsewhere, she accepts it as part of life.'

It must be said that often the Prince does little to promote his own cause, having some amazing public gaffes to his credit. He is ferocious about press interference in his affairs even though it is the British taxpayer who pays for his activities. While he won't tolerate stupidity in others, he often fails to see the folly of his own words and actions until it is too late.

At the Kenyan independence ceremony, the Duke was handing over the colony to President Jomo Kenyatta before 50,000 cheering Kenyans, not to mention a host of international politicians. He couldn't resist quipping, in a private aside to Kenyatta: 'Are you sure you want to go through with this?' Alas, he hadn't realised the loudspeaker was still on so the joke was shared with the entire audience, not to mention the world's press.

In China in 1986 he commented to a British student: 'If you stay much longer, you will get slitty eyes.' He seemed oblivious to the offence such a clumsy remark would cause and obviously still had not learned his lesson on his return when he told the joke: 'If it's got four legs and it's not a chair, if it's got two wings and it's not an aeroplane, if it swims and it's not a submarine, what is it? A Cantonese dinner. They eat anything that moves.'

A Chilean representative, who turned up to receive the Queen wearing a lounge suit, felt the sharp edge of Philip's tongue. Philip asked: 'Why are you dressed like that?'

The Chilean responded: 'We are poor, I could not afford a dinner suit so my party told me to wear a lounge suit.'

Philip retorted: 'I suppose if they'd said wear a bathing suit, you would have done that too.'

A Canadian journalist at a press conference in Toronto asked the Queen and Philip what sort of flight they had had. Philip growled: 'Have you ever flown in a plane? Yes. Well, it was just like that.'

To the Sultan of Oman, he growled: 'I'm not one of the corgis.' To the singer Tom Jones: 'What do you gargle with, pebbles?' To the managing director of a Manchester knitting firm to whom he had just been introduced: 'I suppose you are a head nit.'

Prince Philip, who always has to walk a pace behind his wife, was once asked if he was a male chauvinist. He replied: 'I'd find it difficult in my position.' The Queen was once asked by Queen Juliana of Holland how she managed to overcome Philip's obviously strong-willed demands. She said sagely: 'I just tell him he shall have it and then make sure he doesn't get it.'

CHAPTER SIX

Princess Margaret

The teenage princess was used to flirting. She knew she was pretty and she exploited this to full advantage. Her father, King George VI, doted on her to the extent of spoiling her terribly. The laughter and joyful chatter of young Princess Margaret echoed through the Royal Family apartments of Buckingham Palace. Despite the dark blanket war had thrown over her country, Margaret was determined to enjoy life.

'I'm so lucky to be me,' she told friends, hugging herself and giving a broad, beaming smile. Years later, Margaret was to smile bitterly when she remembered those words. For into her life came a dashing new member of the royal staff who was to turn her world upside down and damn any chance she ever had of finding real happiness.

No one could have ever guessed what effect Group Captain Peter Townsend would have on the fun-loving, precocious Margaret. She was just 14 when she was introduced to him – an impressive RAF war hero taken on as the King's extra Air Equerry. Everyone believed that the way Margaret looked at Townsend was simply a schoolgirl crush but that immediate, dangerous spark of attraction was to end in heartache for her. It was to change her life irrevocably, as well as changing the attitudes of the entire Royal Family – and the public's attitude towards *them*. It was also to force a hard-hearted decision on the unbendable Royal Family to avert a constitutional crisis.

Townsend was 29 at that first meeting in 1944. An ex-Spitfire pilot, he had come through the Battle of Britain with a shining reputation and had ended the Second World War with a tally of 11 enemy planes shot down, a DSO and a DFC and bar. He was dashing, handsome, debonair and exactly the sort of chap the King would have wished for as a son; indeed, he was once heard to say so. The young Princess Margaret was even more charmed by the newcomer. She was infatuated from the moment her father introduced him to her. Many years later she said: 'Peter appeared when I was 14. I had a terrific crush on him.'

After the war, Prince Philip of Greece arrived on the scene and began courting Margaret's elder sister. He was accepted easily into the royal circle but Townsend and he had little to do with each other. They were opposites. The dry-witted, quietly-spoken RAF officer found Philip less than subtle company. Equally, the bluff, hearty Philip failed to disguise his lack of respect for Townsend. Also, the equerry was far too close to the King for Prince Philip's liking.

In 1947 the King ordered Townsend to accompany himself, the Queen and the two princesses on a three-month tour of South Africa. In part, it was planned as a test of the strength of feeling between Elizabeth and Philip. The separation was indeed a trial for Elizabeth, but it was a delight to Margaret. She was overjoyed that she had to spend three months in the company of her secret beau.

The closeness that was to develop between the impressionable 17-year-old and the 'crush' twice her age was reinforced by the fact that Townsend was to act virtually as 'minder' to the Princess while abroad. Of course, the RAF officer would be travelling alone. His wife, Rosemary, was to remain at their home in the grounds of Windsor Castle.

However, romance had to bide its time. Elizabeth completed her African duties, returned to Philip and married him in November that year. Margaret returned to pass her time with a bunch of seemingly ephemeral friends known by gossip columnists as the 'Princess Margaret Set'. Foremost among this crowd of rich, amusing young people were the late Billy Wallace and the Hon. Colin Tennant, who was later to make a gift to her of a plot of land on his Caribbean island of Mustique.

Margaret continued to harbour a deep yearning for Peter Townsend but in that less liberal, post-war age she had no real hope of realising it. Then, in 1951, came her chance of happiness. Townsend's marriage hit the rocks.

The failure of his marriage had not really been his fault, much less Margaret's. During a brief war-time romance, Townsend had become engaged to Rosemary Pawle, the daughter of a brigadier. They had wed during a snatched leave and had two sons. His RAF duties obviously meant long separations but his wife had assumed that all this would end in peace-time. Peter's job with the royals, however, ensured that this was not the case. In 1950, he was given the even more demanding post of Deputy Master of the Royal Household and spent far more time with Margaret than he ever did with his wife. After advising the King, Townsend determined to divorce Rosemary quietly on the grounds of her adultery with wealthy merchant banker Johnny de Laszio.

Townsend told Margaret of his divorce plans on 14 August 1951, just four days before her twenty-first birthday, when the two of them were out riding in the romantic setting of the wooded grounds of Balmoral Castle.

Margaret's heart must have leapt with joy. The stage was set for a new romance to blossom.

Soon afterwards, however, the couple's actions had cause to make the mild-mannered King George vent his wrath on them. He came across Townsend carrying Margaret up a flight of stairs. 'I asked him to carry me, Papa,' she said. 'I ordered him to!'

In February 1952, King George VI died. Adoring Margaret was heartbroken. At his funeral the card on her wreath bore the touching message: 'Darling Papa, from his everloving Margaret'. The King had doted on his younger daughter and, while Elizabeth withstood the shock with fortitude, Margaret was distraught with grief. The pivot of her life had vanished and she now expected Townsend, 16 years her senior, to fill the void.

When her sister acceded to the throne Margaret moved to Clarence House, taking on the effective role of constant companion to her newly widowed mother. If anything, it made it easier for the illicit lovebirds to meet, for in May the Queen Mother appointed Peter Townsend comptroller of her household, in which role she came to rely heavily upon him. Townsend recalled in his autobiography, *Time and Chance*: 'We found increasing solace in each other's company, with the change in her own family situation, living alone with her mother (whom she adored) and the break-up of mine.'

Inevitably, the couple had to break the news of their love affair to the senior members of the Royal Family. Their feelings for one another had taken no heed of wealth, rank or convention. The question they were desperate to have answered was whether or not they would be allowed to wed, he being a divorcee and she being third in line to the throne. The moment of truth came when Margaret and Townsend, by now further promoted to Queen's Equerry, were invited by Elizabeth and Philip to join them for dinner at Buckingham Palace. The Queen took the news of their marriage bid sympathetically and calmly. Philip seemed to make light of the difficulties – a line that soon changed to one of diametric opposition. The Queen Mother was also informed. She knew the couple faced dire problems but was too kindly and charitable to say so.

The family had been told. Tact and charity had been the response. As the nation looked forward to the new Elizabethan Age, Margaret looked forward to a life with Peter Townsend. She even asked him to help decorate her quarters at Clarence House, believing that he would one day share them with her. They would slip away to dine quietly together. Sometimes they would stay at a friend's house. Sometimes they would simply go to the cinema together. They were never recognised. Although by now their romance was known to the Royal Family its seriousness had not dawned on them. All that was about to change.

It seems strange now that the loving couple did not know how to conduct their affair to a successful conclusion. After all, they had the best advice money, power and prestige could buy readily to hand. Perhaps the advice was too kindly. Perhaps it was ingenuous. Perhaps the couple wanted to believe their sentiments were so strong that they could overcome centuries of tradition. Perhaps love really *is* blind.

The seriousness of their predicament did not begin to dawn until Townsend announced to the Queen's senior adviser, Alan (always known as 'Tommy') Lascelles, that he was resigning from the Queen Mother's household. He told Lascelles, an awesome figure of authority and a pillar of the establishment, that his decision was a matter of honour now that the woman he loved was living at Clarence House. Townsend regarded Lascelles as a friend and, although he expected no great favours, he did at least expect sympathy for his plight. He received neither. Out came the oft-quoted remark: 'You must be either mad or bad.' Recalling the ructions caused by the last similar attempt by a divorcee to set up house with a member of the Royal Family, Lascelles suggested that Townsend should not only resign his position but should accept an overseas posting immediately and have no further contact with the lovesick, vulnerable Princess. Townsend was shocked by the senior royal adviser's reaction, but Lascelles, haunted by recollections of the abdication crisis of Edward VIII, saw this developing situation as a rerun of the events of 1936. He had decided that it was his duty to protect the new Queen from another damaging scandal that might mar the inauguration of her reign.

If the loyal Lascelles had foreseen what scandals would emanate from the Royal Family over the following decades of the 'New Elizabethan Age' he might well have thrown his hands in the air, considered the plight of Princess Margaret and Group Captain Peter Townsend small beer and said: 'OK, old chap, marry the lady. The Queen has just married a penurious emigré. You at least are an all-

British war hero. And the people of Britain are behind you. Yes, marry her.'

Instead, Lascelles played it by the book. He went straight to the Queen and reminded her that, under the Royal Marriages Act of 1772, Margaret would have to obtain her consent to any union before her twenty-fifth birthday. Thereafter, she would be exempt from this requirement but would still need the consent of the British Parliament and of the parliaments of all her dominions. More problematic, said Lascelles, was the Townsend divorce. It mattered not a jot that he was an innocent party in the matter. The Queen was head of the Church of England and, under canon number 107 of the year 1603, could give her consent to such a marriage only if the Prime Minister and his cabinet agreed.

It was still not a firm knockback for the lovers. The Queen asked whether, despite all the obstacles he had outlined, a marriage was still possible. Lascelles said it was – but sought her agreement to his urgently alerting Prime Minister Winston Churchill. This he did most diplomatically but none the less effectively. Lascelles sent for Sir John Colville, a former courtier who was now Churchill's private secretary, and left him in no doubt about his feelings towards the marriage: it must be stopped! Colville reported as much to Churchill the following weekend at the premier's country house, Chequers. Churchill's first reaction was: 'What a delightful match.' He thought war hero Townsend a perfect partner for the beautiful Princess.

Then he began to have second thoughts. Here were the makings of another royal scandal only 17 years after the abdication crisis of Edward VIII had shaken the monarchy. Churchill had been heavily attacked at the time for taking the side of Edward and Mrs Simpson. Now, as Prime Minister, he worried lest a trauma of 1936 proportions hit the Royal Family. As he dithered, his wife, Clemmie, interrupted. According to Lady Longford's book *The Queen: The Life of Elizabeth II*, Clemmie told him: 'Winston, if you are going to begin the abdication all over again, I'm going to leave. I shall take a flat in Brighton.' Winston sighed resignedly.

Tommy Lascelles had got his way. Churchill made up his mind to do his level best to separate Princess Margaret and the only man she had ever loved. A cruel strategy was put into play that largely disregarded the hurt being done to the young Princess.

First, Winston Churchill went to see the Queen to put his well-structured argument against the marriage. He said that it was an identical issue to that which Prime Minister Baldwin had faced when Edward VIII applied to marry Mrs Simpson. Winston argued that if the Queen and her children died or were killed, Margaret would become sovereign. Because her marriage to a divorced man was not fully recognised by the Church, any children they had would be denied the right of accession to the throne. The solution, Churchill said, was to 'exile' Peter Townsend. He should be given a foreign posting far away from Margaret, who would no doubt forget her beau and get on with her royal life.

To her credit, Elizabeth resisted this final act of cruelty. She could not bring herself to exile a man who had been such a devoted servant to her father. Instead, she ordered that Townsend remain at the side of the Queen Mother, who she knew relied heavily on his abilities. However, Prince Philip's long dislike of Townsend showed itself again at this critical time. The old seadog firmly and steadfastly campaigned to end the romance between the Battle of Britain flier and his pretty sister-in-law.

The Queen was sympathetic yet torn between the choice of her sister's personal happiness and the very serious constitutional and Church issue involved. Princess Margaret later told a confidante that while everyone else was deciding her future, she felt utterly helpless. As a result, she may well have accepted the 'inevitable', a stern instruction from her sister never to see Peter Townsend again.

The problem was that nobody ever said it! No one ever told Margaret: 'No, you cannot marry the man.' Not Lascelles; he had merely offered advice to the Queen and her Prime Minister. Not Churchill; he had merely suggested that Margaret bide her time and apply again later. Not the Queen herself; she had charitably offered future hopes of happiness to her sister. Only Philip had been forthright; he had said: 'Forget it.' And forget it, for the moment, Margaret had to do, for her sister's coronation was being planned and the eyes of the nation and most of the civilised world were upon the new monarch. Nothing must mar her moment of supreme majesty.

It seems ludicrous in this day and age that the fate of two grown-ups should be decided by committee, in secret and entirely against their interests, and, as would later be proved, entirely against the wishes of the British people. Yet, over the crisis weeks, the future of Margaret and Peter was being mapped out by virtual strangers, fearful of further damage to the institution of British royalty. The machinations that ensued revealed just how little control senior members of the Royal Family had over their own destinies. If Margaret, sister of the Queen, wilful and with more influence than almost anyone else in her realm, was not allowed to make a simple, personal choice as to how to run her own life, then who could?

While all this was going on, the British public remained blissfully unaware of the drama unfolding as a backdrop, a sub-plot, to the greatest post-war spectacle to grip the nation: the coronation of their Queen.

All that was to change on Coronation Day, 2 June 1953. All eyes at Westminster Abbey were on the young Queen Elizabeth II – except the eyes of two people. One was Princess Margaret, whose admiring glance was directed at the man standing a couple of paces away from her: slim, tall, handsome Peter Townsend, wearing his wartime decorations on his RAF uniform. The other was an American reporter, who was intently watching Princess Margaret because he had heard rumours of a romance between her and the Group Captain.

Margaret, bejewelled and radiant, tried throughout the ceremony to avert her eyes from Townsend. She failed. Turning slightly and looking up at him, she stretched out her white-gloved hand and picked a piece of fluff from his uniform. As her hand brushed proudly across his tunic, the eagle-eyed reporter spotted this simple touch of love.

Princess Margaret had innocently given the game away.

The following day the *Journal-American* carried the tale. It was immediately picked up by other American newspapers. One said that the Group Captain had held out his hand to her and that Margaret had seemed about to fall into his arms. Suddenly the world's press was full of the story of the love of a princess for her gallant knight.

British newspapers, prevented from announcing the romance by the palace, knew that the secret could not be suppressed for much longer. Tragically, neither the palace nor the government thought to forewarn the couple. Townsend said later that, had Richard Colville warned him or Margaret of the stories building up in the foreign press, 'there would have been time for me to fade out before the storm burst'. That there was no warning was the first of a series of incomprehensible blunders. It took 14 days before a British newspaper, the *Sunday People*, plucked up the courage to mention what the foreign papers had been trumpeting. Even then, the *Sunday People* discounted the love story as 'utterly untrue', reporting: 'It is quite unthinkable that a royal princess, third in line of succession, should even contemplate marriage with a man who has been through the divorce courts.' The *Sunday People* had opened the floodgates. Suddenly the whole of the British press was full of 'the Margaret Affair'.

It was at this moment in history that the couple desperately needed the sound counsel of palace advisers. Peter Townsend needed the support of his superiors. Margaret needed sympathy and comfort. However, Prince Philip, for whatever reason, sided with the anti-marriage lobby. He told senior courtiers that the Crown had been drawn into a damaging public debate and accused Margaret of being the one who had let the side down. His principal concern was getting the whole business quietened and out of the headlines.

Another quiet move at the time was the so-called Regency Act of 1953, which made Philip regent in the event of the Queen's demise. It effectively removed Margaret's most important constitutional role in favour of Philip.

The Royal Family got round the Townsend–Margaret 'problem' with typical brutality. The Princess and her mother were dispatched on a tour of Rhodesia, while Lascelles finally got his way and 'exiled' Townsend to Belgium with the trumped-up posting of air attaché in Brussels. Privately, the devoted couple were told that they could say their farewells once Margaret returned from Rhodesia. Thereafter they must separate for a year. Reluctantly, they agreed to what they assumed was a temporary parting. Margaret told a friend: 'We were given to believe that we could marry eventually.'

As Townsend prepared to leave Britain for his foreign posting, the Princess telephoned twice a day from Africa. They looked forward to a farewell tryst before the day of his final departure for Brussels but Townsend was suddenly given fresh orders by Lascelles. He was told to report for duty in Belgium on 15 July, the day *before* Margaret was due back in Britain. She was furious but was apparently unable to prevent the powerful Lascelles getting his way once again.

While Margaret was still in Africa, the Queen and Prince Philip did show Townsend some compassion. They asked him to accompany them on a visit to Ulster. Upon their return to London, the Queen stepped from the plane and made a public point of stopping for a chat with the Group Captain as he stood in line with other courtiers and RAF officers. With eagle-eyed reporters watching and photographers snapping away, she shook Townsend's hand and smiled warmly. This display of affection was seen by the press as being the green light for the lovers. The following days' papers were full of stories backing the couple. Opinion polls revealed a vast public upswell of support for Margaret. Headlines urged the lovers to ignore the constitutional stuffed-shirts and to announce their engagement. When Margaret drove through the streets of the East End of London a woman shouted at her: 'Go on, marry him.'

Such popular support only reinforced the official line. Townsend was bundled off to Belgium. When Margaret returned to Britain the following day she was told by her sister that the family had decided she must bide her time before any thought of a renewed romance. Yet the Queen still held out to Margaret the hope that she could wed if only she could hang on until her twenty-fifth birthday.

The Princess shut out the pain of parting with an endless round of nightclubbing with the 'Margaret Set'. She became a familiar face in the gossip pages as she lined up in photographs alongside old friends Billy Wallace, Colin Tennant and Mark Bonham Carter. Meanwhile, Townsend was told his one-year posting would be extended to two years, then to almost three. Every time his return was delayed, it was explained to Margaret that the timing was not propitious. Now and again there were snatched moments of bliss when Townsend would slip back to Britain and the lovers could be in each other's arms for stolen hours. All the while, the Princess firmly believed that one day soon she would receive the blessing of the Church, the State and the monarchy for her marriage to Peter.

Every editor in Fleet Street had marked in his diary the date 21 August 1955. It was the day of Princess Margaret's twenty-fifth birthday, the age when members of the Royal Family can marry without consent. As the date approached, the press correctly speculated that this was exactly what Margaret was planning, although she still hoped to get her sister's blessing.

The Queen and Prince Philip had just undertaken a six-month tour of the Commonwealth, and when they returned they were told by Margaret that she still loved Townsend with all her heart and wanted to marry him. An unprecedented palace conference was held, at which the Queen, Philip and the Queen Mother discussed the constitutional issues and the attitude of the Church. They agreed that if the marriage went ahead Margaret would have to renounce her right to the throne and her income from the Civil List. She would also almost certainly have to live abroad for some years, an effective outcast. The royal 'gang of three' produced a stopgap agreement to allow the lovers to meet again to discuss their feelings. The Queen did not want to force her sister into any unnecessarily final decision. The bond between the sisters was as strong as ever it had been; the difference now was that one of them was the Queen of England and head of its Church.

Peter Townsend was recalled from exile in Brussels. He arrived back in London on Wednesday, 12 October 1955 and was immediately swamped by an army of newspaper reporters and photographers. They followed him as he stopped off at a friend's house to unpack and then went clothes shopping. Margaret arrived in London on a night train from Scotland, where she had been staying at Balmoral, and went straight to Clarence House. There the couple are believed to have been reunited for just two hours. They did not meet again until the following weekend when a house party was arranged at the home of the Queen's cousin, the Hon. Mrs John Lycett, at Allanbay Park, Berkshire. There were too many other guests for the lovers' liking. They returned to London separately on Monday but dined together, alone at last. Fresh hopes arose that they would get the backing they sought for the happy future together they so richly deserved.

There had been two significant changes since the couple were separated. One was the opinion of the Queen Mother who, although still sympathetic to both Townsend and Margaret, now believed that the marriage was a non-starter. The other change was that, with Winston Churchill long retired, the Prime Minister was now Sir Anthony Eden, whom Margaret had known for years as a family friend and regular houseguest of her late father. Eden had been through a divorce himself; only five years earlier he had divorced his wife, Beatrice, and wed Churchill's niece, Clarissa. Surely Eden would back them.

However, on 18 October Eden flew to Balmoral and told the Queen that the cabinet could not support the marriage. One minister had even threatened to resign if it was allowed. Predictably, Prince Philip reinforced Eden's views and *The Times* waded in with a thundering leader condemning the marriage plans as damaging to the Queen's position as the symbol of goodness in family life.

Such humbug seems a moral age away nowadays but it was apparently good enough to convince the couple that they had lost the battle. All the tortured years of waiting had been in vain. Margaret, who had given her sister so much support during her long and diplomatically delicate engagement to the interloper, Philip of Greece, now told her she could put her mind at rest; there would be no marriage. The Princess then visited the Archbishop of Canterbury, Dr Geoffrey Fisher, and told him to fear not. He is said by royal biographer Lady Longford to have responded with the words: 'What a wonderful person the Holy Spirit is.'

The couple themselves reacted in a much less hypocritical manner. That night they met up with friends at a party in London's Knightsbridge and got hopelessly drunk. The following morning they woke up with sore heads and drafted one of the most moving official statements ever released by the palace. An approved version was put out on the agency wires on Monday, 31 October. It read:

I would like it to be known that I have decided not to marry Group Captain Peter Townsend. I have been aware that subject to my renouncing my rights of succession it might have been possible for me to contract a civil marriage. But mindful of the Church's teaching that a Christian marriage is indissoluble and conscious of my duty to the Commonwealth, I have resolved to put these considerations before any others. I have reached the decision entirely alone, and in doing so I have been strengthened by the unfailing support and devotion of Group Captain Peter Townsend. I am grateful for the concern of all those who have constantly prayed for my happiness.

The Times expressed grateful thanks on behalf of the nation. More in touch was the *Guardian*, which said her decision 'will be regarded by the masses of the people as unnecessary and perhaps a great waste. In the long run, it will not redound to the credit or influence of those who have been most persistent in denying the Princess the same liberty as is enjoyed by the rest of her fellow citizens.' That latter sentiment best reflected the views of most of the people of Britain and, indeed, the world. It confirmed that the House of Windsor and the establishment with which it was encumbered had proved itself wholly unsuited to rule the lives of its own members, far less those of its loyal subjects.

Peter Townsend discreetly disappeared from the scene. Ironically, he undertook his own self-imposed exile, starting with an 18-month, round-the-world trip. The group that accompanied him included a young Belgian girl, Marie-Luce, who looked not too dissimilar to his lost love, Margaret. He later married her and bought a country house near Paris where they raised three children.

Margaret, on the other hand, achieved a higher social profile than any royal before her had ever sought. 'PM', as she became known by her partying chums, sought forget-fulness with her high-living and sometimes eccentric set. The Queen began to worry about her carefree image and what the royals might coyly refer to as her 'social excesses'. She was usually photographed at a party – and rarely without a drink in one hand and a cigarette in the other. Margaret briefly became officially engaged to Billy Wallace but when she discovered he had had a fling with a young lady from the Bahamas, she dumped him after a vitriolic slanging match. Colin Tennant was another suitor but they became 'just good friends' and Tennant wed another. It was at this wedding that the Princess first met the up-and-coming photographer who had been commissioned to take the pictures, Anthony Armstrong Jones.

Their brief encounter at the 1956 society wedding was hardly a case of love at first sight. However, they met again at a dinner party at a friend's home the following February and she was charmed by his relaxed patter. The fact that he was a commoner who wholly disregarded her royal status and treated her like the girl next door may have added to the sense of excitement when they agreed to meet again. Soon she was a regular visitor to his scruffy little studio in London's then unfashionable docklands area. They would hide themselves away for entire weekends.

Margaret was happier and more relaxed than she had been for years. Although her official engagement list suffered, for months the Queen remained unaware of the new, controversial liaison her sister had forged.

This time, however, there was to be no scandal. It was as if the world had grown up since the ridiculous impediments placed before Margaret and Townsend. True, the Princess, third in line to the throne, was marrying a commoner. Unlike Philip of Greece, he had not even the faintest historic royal pedigree. Another drawback was that Armstrong Jones's parents had both been divorced and remarried. There was also the question of Tony's unconventional lifestyle, his Bohemian circle and his unorthodox girlfriends. However, when the Queen was eventually told and Prime Minister Harold Macmillan consulted, they gave the match their blessing. The couple were, after all, both 28 years of age and quite able to make their minds up about their own futures. They became unofficially engaged in October 1959 and their betrothal was announced to a stunned but delighted press and public the following February.

There was only one minor hiccup and it was quickly resolved, as can be revealed here for the first time. One of the bridegroom's very best friends was a homosexual. Today the fact would cause less comment but the 'Swinging Sixties' were in their infancy and the permissive society had not yet been invented, so there was much tut-tutting ill-informed innuendo about Tony's chum. A senior executive of a national newspaper felt so fearful that this friendship would blight the big day that he went to the palace and effectively told the Queen's advisers: 'Keep this man out of the wedding arrangements or we will expose him.' Astonishingly, his warning had an immediate effect: the poor man was not only banned from the marriage ceremony but, just to be on the safe side, also banished from the country! He took a diplomatic holiday abroad.

On 6 May, Tony and Margaret had a fairytale wedding at Westminster Abbey, watched by a television audience of 300 million. As a mere photographer Tony was not flush with money, so the newly-weds were supplied with a £10,000-a-year day Caribbean honeymoon aboard the royal yacht *Britannia* and the government authorised a lavish £56,000 refurbishment of a Kensington Palace apartment for their return.

For appearances' sake, plain Tony Armstrong Jones was later given an earldom which entitled him to style himself Lord Snowdon. It also meant that the son born a month later was named Lord Linley, rather than plain David Jones. A daughter, Lady Sarah, followed.

Sadly, the honeymoon period with the British press lasted not much longer than the newly-weds' costly, real-life honeymoon. Newspapers began to turn against them just ten weeks after Lord Linley was born, when Margaret and Tony commandeered an entire first-class airline cabin for a Caribbean holiday. Adding to public anger was the fact that they had left their new baby at home with a nanny. There was also bemused comment as to how 'royal' the former commoner Tony Armstrong Jones had become. He and Margaret travelled in style but often separately. Little work seemed to be done to deserve the ever-increasing Civil List payments being made by the taxpayer. Even the Princess's highly priced *haute couture* wardrobe came under fire. (Cruelly, although Margaret spent lavishly on clothes, she was once on the list of the 'World's Worst Dressed Women'.)

More private rows and public attacks followed for the couple who had such differing temperaments. From the close confines of Kensington Palace, there were constant reports of marital convulsions. One frequent visitor to their home told how he witnessed royal flare-ups on several occasions, one ending with Margaret slamming a mirrored door so violently that it shattered. One massive row began when Tony decided to buy and renovate a country cottage in Sussex. The Princess did not approve. Tony took off for Japan in high dudgeon.

So emotional were the outbursts between them that Margaret actually became ill and went into hospital, presumably suffering from nerves. Once again, the very private, troubled lives of two members of the Royal Family were being played out in the pages of the popular press, to the horror (and sometimes secret delight) of the public.

In a bid to preserve public face, Tony denied anything was wrong with the marriage. Shortly afterwards, they went off for a ten-day holiday to work things out between them, but the cracks in their marriage were already too wide. The couple found it increasingly hard to pay court to the British taxpayers who funded them. No longer were their squabbles confined to their private rooms; they were now becoming very public displays. Several incidents are etched in the memories of the couple's friends.

At a charity ball Margaret watched hawk-eyed as Tony spent most the evening dancing with the same girl. Maintaining her composure, Margaret waited for a break in the music before walking over to the girl and, with no edge to her voice whatsover, asked: 'Are you enjoying youself?'

Snowdon's pretty dancing partner was taken in by the false charm. She replied: 'Very much, thank you, Ma'am'.

Onlookers remember how the smile suddenly left Margaret's face. Her next words were spoken coldly and bluntly: 'That's enough for one evening then. Run along home.' The girl took the hint and left.

Once, when Snowdon accompanied Margaret to a London dinner party, he also took along a portable television set. Placing it on a nearby table, he made no effort to talk to his wife; instead he silently watched the fascinating programme he had not wanted to miss, a dissertation by Prime Minister Harold Wilson on the country's growing financial problems.

On another occasion, a servant reported how Margaret burst into Tony's study while he was discussing work with a colleague. Margaret's face was like thunder as her husband ranted: 'Never come in here again without knocking!'

With Margaret building her own 'palace' on the West Indian isle of Mustique, it was patently obvious the rot had firmly set into their marriage. Despite the house plot being a wedding present from long-time friend Colin Tennant, Tony was never to visit it. Those partying sybarites who accompanied Margaret to this holiday paradise knew that the marriage had been a shell and a sham for some time. If she had not been the Queen's sister and still subject to some sections of the antiquated Royal Marriages Act, Margaret would have separated from Lord Snowdon months, or probably years earlier.

Things could scarcely get worse for the image of the Royal Family. Margaret was being continually slated in the press for doing little to earn her recently increased £55,000 Civil List allowance. Then the focus turned to the company she kept — normally attractive, single men who escorted her to nightspots while her husband was away on photographic assignments. Regulars at this time were Dominic Elliot, an old flame from the fifties, and the sensitive, musical Robin Douglas-Home, until he committed suicide. A year after his death, another of these glitteringly witty and handsome escorts arrived on the scene. At first he was just one of the crowd but, despite a 17-year gap in their ages, he was to become very significant in Margaret's life. The newcomer was blond, social high-flier Roddy Llewellyn.

Roddy's introduction to royalty was accidental. Margaret's oldest chum, Colin Tennant, held a regular September house party on his Scottish estate. In 1973 the party was one short at the last moment and Tennant invited Roddy, an acquaintance of his aunt, to make up the numbers. His friendship with the Princess began within hours of their introduction. They would generally meet at the London homes of friends, but sometimes at more eccentric locations.

One of these was a hippie-style commune at Surrendell

in Wiltshire where upper-crust trendies stayed to get 'closer to nature'. The remote farmhouse, set in 47 acres, must have been the scene of some wild parties. Newspapers later alleged that marijuana had been smoked there; indeed visitors years later spoke of marijuana plants growing in the surrounding fields and hedgerows. Roddy was a regular and he invited Margaret to spend the weekend with him. She joined him and the others in a sing-song after dinner and then stayed the night in less than salubrious conditions. The following morning she was seen wandering around in old clothes and looking for all the world like a poor hill farmer's wife.

It is generally believed that the Princess made only one or two visits to Surrendell but that is far from the case. Margaret became hypnotised by the Bohemian lifestyle and visited regularly but in secret. A friend from that time has told of the astonishing squalor that awaited the Princess when she was driven down to Wiltshire. A servant from an adjoining house was sometimes sent round to Surrendell before the royal visitor's arrival but the cleaning up was no more than cosmetic. There was, for instance, no possibility of bathing, showering or even washing. Seldom can a senior member of a royal house have bedded down in such poor conditions. In fact, there was only one bed in the entire house and that was reserved for Margaret whenever she stayed. She would retire earlier than most of the commune dwellers and Roddy would follow her after a discreet delay.

One night a female member of the group followed the couple and set a tape recorder running outside the bedroom door. 'I'm waiting to hear the royal "squawk",' she explained. Whether the royal 'squawk' was ever recorded for posterity, sadly, is not known.

Sadly for Margaret, the press discovered her Bohemian idyll and descended in force. Commune members cashed in, accepting gifts of large sums of money in brown paper bags – and in one case, in a red velvet purse – to allow photographers to record scenes of Margaret's bare-floor partying. The commune people disappeared as anxious snappers waited at the farm gate to be invited inside!

Margaret's high (and sometimes low) living continued, despite warnings from her sister and royal advisers, and despite fierce press ridicule. A remark she was reported to have made at a charity function in North America caused more of a furore than most. A reporter quoted her as having called the Irish 'pigs'. Hasty denials were not accepted, particularly because of Margaret's natural upset at the recent murder by the IRA of the Royal Family's Uncle Dickie. Margaret's life was threatened. It was said only daily telephone calls from Roddy Llewellyn kept her going. About this time a front-page leader in the *Daily Mirror* even urged her, in the interest of the nation, to give up public life completely. In a way, she already had.

The Princess showed little regard for her public image. The secret love affair with Roddy Llewellyn became stronger. She seemed besotted with this baronet's son who looked to be a younger version of her husband, but without Snowdon's fiery temperament. In March 1974 Margaret escaped with Roddy to her Mustique villa while Tony celebrated his forty-fourth birthday without her at a London restaurant. Newspapers commented on lonely Tony's plight but had no inkling of the seriousness of the Llewellyn affair. Margaret and Tony, probably at the Queen's behest, even made an attempt to patch up their marriage at the end of 1974. Roddy was temporarily given the heave-ho and, desolated, flew to Barbados where he hoped to stay secretly at a house his family owned. He found it empty, collapsed and was flown back to Britain with a doctor at his side.

Meanwhile, Lord Snowdon was making his own waves. He went to Australia to work on a television series. One of the production assistants was industrialist's daughter Lucy Lindsay-Hogg, whose marriage to a film director had ended four years earlier. Snowdon was finding a life, and a love, for himself outside the Royal Family. When he returned from Australia there were scenes of public affection but the marriage was really over.

In early 1976 Margaret cut short a winter stay at Sandringham to seek the sun again in Mustique. This time a journalist managed to breach Colin Tennant's security and stay on the island in the guise of a schoolteacher. One evening he took his camera to a palm-covered bar and captured Margaret in inelegant beach attire sipping a drink. Seated cosily alongside her was Roddy Llewellyn. It was the first time the lovers had been pictured together. The following Sunday the photograph was emblazoned across the front page of the *News of the World* and it sparked a world-wide sensation. It also prompted a phone call from a humiliated Lord Snowdon to the Queen. He wanted out.

Now the Queen had to come to terms with the previously unthinkable: divorce within the Royal Family. Edward VIII's marriage to divorcee Wallis Simpson had been one thing; Margaret's bid to marry divorcee Peter Townsend was another; but this was to be a divorce by the sister of the Queen, the sister of the head of the Church of England. It was to be the first divorce by an immediate member of the Royal Family since the head-chopping days of Henry VIII. It was a constitutional dilemma that recalled for the Queen the agonising she and her family had undergone when the Townsend scandal had broken at around the time of her coronation. It had almost marred that great event. Now Margaret's love life threatened to mar the greatest royal celebrations since the coronation – the Queen's fiftieth birthday and the twenty-fifth anniversary of her succession.

The monarch called in Prime Minister Harold Wilson to square the cabinet and then summoned her personal solicitor, Matthew Farrer (who later represented Princess Anne and Prince Andrew when their marriages failed), to negotiate a legal separation. Snowdon asked for nothing except full access to his children, but he was reportedly offered a personal settlement of £100,000 from the Princess's own investments. He signed on the dotted line and gratefully flew off to Australia on a photographic assignment. He was away again on 19 March when Kensington Palace announced that 'HRH the Princess Margaret, the Countess of Snowdon, and the Earl of Snowdon have mutually agreed to live apart'.

Lord Snowdon appeared on Australian television to make his only public statement on the separation. At times tearful, he said: 'I am naturally desperately sad in every way that this had to come. I would just like to say three things. Firstly, to pray for the understanding of our two children. Secondly, to wish Princess Margaret every happiness. Thirdly, to express with the utmost humility the love, admiration and respect I will always have for her sister, her mother and her entire family.' Afterwards, he answered clamouring reporters by saying only: 'For the last 15 years I have refused to discuss my private life and at the moment I am not going to break that rule.'

Lord Snowdon never again spoke publicly about his marriage break-up. Only months after the split, the Queen 'rehabilitated' him into her family by asking him to use Windsor Castle as the setting for photographs on the occasion of his daughter, Lady Sarah Armstrong Jones's confirmation. The Queen stood and chatted with him as he worked on the snapshots, the entire family wreathed in smiles.

It was the Queen's way of thanking him for the discreet and dignified manner in which he had conducted himself over the most damaging period in royal history since the abdication.

Snowdon retained his royal friendships. His eventual divorce, in 1978, left him free to wed Lucy Lindsay-Hogg in December of that year. His former rival, Roddy Llewellyn, went on to find his own beautiful bride, Tatania Hoskins. Both couples soon had new families to care for.

Princess Maraget remained alone, a sometimes tragic, occasionally sickly, often ignored member of the royal inner circle. The men in her life, Lord Snowdon, Peter Townsend and Roddy Llewellyn, all had new families to enrich their lives and help them forget the past. Princess Margaret had only her memories.

CHAPTER SEVEN

Princess Michael

Prince Michael of Kent was the silent man of the British Royal Family. Often called 'the invisible prince', because he kept a deliberately low profile, compared with his brother, the Duke of Kent, shy Michael was a particular favourite of the Queen. He was 36 years old, unmarried and thought by some royal-watchers to be a confirmed bachelor. Yet this diffident young man was about to provide for the Queen one of the most difficult decisions of her reign – and for the Royal Family as a whole, the sort of constitutional conundrum and sensational scandal that would rock its members to the foundations of their stately homes.

It was 1977 and while the 'Princess Margaret Affair' had been giving the sovereign and her advisers sleepless nights, another delicate family romance had been maturing for nine months or so until it, too, finally had to be brought to the Queen's attention. Her cousin, Prince Michael, had fallen in love with a divorcee!

In any other family, the fact that a young man's bride-to-be was a divorcee would not have presented any problem but for the Queen, head of the Church of England, it was a double blow. For Marie-Christine, Baroness von Reibnitz and lately Mrs Tom Troubridge, was also a Roman Catholic.

It was a problem that, handled wrongly, could have made a laughing stock of the Royal Family. In a sense, it did. At any other stage in history, it would also have prompted a heartbreaking refusal of royal sanction for a marriage. This time, however, the fates were on the side of the young lovers. Ironically, the couple had decided to wed just at the time the Queen's own sister, Margaret, was getting a divorce. Luckily for Michael and Marie-Christine, the Queen had been seen to handle the trauma of her sister's divorce with uncharacteristic leniency. Because she had let Margaret off the hook, it was argued, she could hardly raise strong objections to a liaison between Prince Michael and the divorced Mrs Troubridge. It meant a sovereign's sympathetic ear to what, not many years earlier, would have been ruled out of court as a totally unsuitable royal marriage.

Divorce and Roman Catholicism would, in other times, have been reason enough to prevent a British royal marriage. However, there was a third element of danger that remained hidden at that time from all but her closest friends. It was that her father, Baron Gunther von Reibnitz, had been an officer in the Nazi SS.

At the end of the Second World War, a four-inch-thick dossier on von Reibnitz was on file at the Berlin Documents Centre. It revealed that Gunther had met Marie-Christine's mother, the Countess Marianne Szapary, in 1941. At the time, she was 27, very beautiful and rich and was being questioned by the Gestapo. They had discovered that just before the war she had entertained two Englishmen, one of them being William Douglas-Home, brother of former prime minister Lord Home, who were at the time trying to persuade aristocratic English author and Nazi camp-follower Unity Mitford to return home to England. A postcard written by the Countess, which referred to 'Unity being silly to stay with her boyfriend' [Hitler] had been read by Gestapo censors. Gunther von Reibnitz, 20 years older than the Countess, rescued her from suspicion by divorcing his own wife and marrying her.

Marie-Christine was born in Czechoslovakia in January 1945. Shortly before, her father had been forced to abandon his property and flee from Germany, with his wife, their children and a few possessions on a handcart, to escape from the advancing Russian armies. At the end of the war, von Reibnitz learnt that he was on the Allied wanted list as an SS officer and decided to seek refuge on an inherited estate in Mozambique, south-west Africa, along with numerous fellow expatriates. Countess Marianne did not relish this prospect. She refused to join him and, instead, continued to live with her daughter and young son in Vienna. She divorced Gunther in 1946 and, four years later, joined the flood of Europeans seeking a new life as so-called 'reffos' (the Australian term for refugees) by emigrating to Australia with her daughter.

They settled in Waverley, on the southern shores of Sydney Harbour, where Marianne trained as a hairdresser and eventually ran her own salon. Her daughter became a weekly boarder at Kincoppall convent school in nearby Elizabeth Bay. There she was looked on as athletic, artistic and, by virtue of her background, a bit of a mystery. When Marie-Christine finished school she spent a year with her father in Mozambique before touring Europe studying the history of art. She returned to Sydney to do a course in shorthand and typing before deciding to become a 'Pommie' and move to England to learn interior decorating.

Twenty years after setting foot on Australian soil Marie-Christine arrived on her own in the London of the 'Swinging Sixties'. It was an 'anything goes' age of wild music, outrageous clothes and free love. Marie-Christine decided to give herself a head-start in her new country. Titles meant very little in egalitarian Australia but in London she let it be known that she was a baroness, that her grandmother was 'Her Serene Highness Princess Hedwig-Graetz' and her grandfather had been Australian Ambassador to the Tsar of Russia in St Petersburg. Before long, she met wealthy young banker and Old Etonian Tom Troubridge and they were married in 1971. She was 26.

At the wedding Marie-Christine first came into contact with a member of the British Royal Family. One of her husband's best friends was Prince William of Gloucester; they had been at Eton together. William was the most handsome and extrovert young man in the entire Royal Family. He had returned from business ventures in Tokyo to take over the running of the family estate at Barnwell, Northamptonshire, after his father was paralysed by a stroke.

It may be an illuminating sidelight to royal history that, upon his return to England, William's girlfriend was the startling Zsuzki Starkloff, of Hungarian origin and eight years older than her enamoured prince. They shared an apartment in the late sixties, where they were visited by Princess Margaret. Perhaps she warned Zsuzki of dangers ahead – the exotic lady was also a divorcee. Shortly afterwards, Zsuzki took off to America and never saw William again.

Prince William was overcome by a mixture of anger and sadness. 'In many ways I love being a member of the Royal Family,' he once revealed. 'But there are also many things

I hate. The goldfish bowl ... it's a pain. The Church is forever breathing down your neck. It is a very restrictive life we lead, especially for those of us who actually believe there is life outside the royal circle.'

William was heir to the Duke of Gloucester and would have made a dashing successor, had he lived. In the last few months of his life he saw a lot of Troubridge and his wife, Marie-Christine, to whom he also introduced his cousin, Prince Michael, then a captain in the Royal Hussars. Sometimes they would all go out as a group; on other occasions, William would call in for tea or a drink at the Troubridge home; sometimes they would dine in London. Those close to the young Prince thought that William had fallen in love with his friend's wife.

On 28 August 1972, a bank holiday Monday, Prince William, a keen flier, was taking part in the Goodyear Air Race at Halfpenny Green, near Wolverhampton, when his plane crashed, killing him instantly. After mourning for his cousin, Prince Michael began to visit Marie-Christine, infrequently, until her husband, Tom Troubridge, was posted to Bahrain on business. His wife stayed behind, saying that she did not want to leave England. Shortly afterwards, she was heard to cancel an evening engagement with a girlfriend, giving the excuse that: 'I have a very big fish on the hook at the moment. And I don't want to let him off.'

Prince Michael had fallen in love with Marie-Christine while she was still married to Troubridge. In 1977, anxious to avert a scandal of the proportions of the Princess Margaret affair, Marie-Christine applied to the Roman Catholic

Church to annul her marriage. The grounds were the flimsiest, yet her application was eventually granted, apparently after the intercession of Lord Louis Mountbatten who had mysterious, but none the less valuable, connections in the Vatican. Meanwhile, she and Troubridge also filed for a civil divorce.

Marie-Christine Reibnitz now reverted to her maiden name, just as the Duchess of Windsor had done after obtaining a divorce from Ernest Simpson in 1936. Marie-Christine, who had taken a modest house in Chelsea, was of no great social significance at this stage and her name was not really linked to Prince Michael. Prince Michael felt he ought to discuss the situation with Mountbatten, who had become a sort of 'adopted uncle' since the death of his own father, Prince George, Duke of Kent, in 1942.

Michael took Marie-Christine along with him on his delicate mission. He explained his new-found love to Mountbatten and the two men talked about the problems the Royal Family would face if it should become public. Marie-Christine's later version of the meeting was that Mountbatten said to Michael: 'You'd better marry the girl. She's obviously madly in love with you.' However, the interview was, in reality, far from light-hearted. Nor was Mountbatten in the least frivolous about what he feared might become yet another scandal to shake the royal firmament.

The idea that they would have to involve the Pope in British constitutional matters was almost as fearsome as the alternative option, that the two lovers could live quietly in sin. Marie-Christine pressed the point that they wanted to marry and start a family as soon as possible. Mountbatten knew that the Queen would have to be told.

Mountbatten was quite taken with Marie-Christine. She was a strong and confident girl, he said later, although on at least one occasion her flamboyance became too much for the old man. One night, while she was holding court as his guest, he slid a note across the table to his private secretary, John Barratt, on which he had scribbled: 'If that woman doesn't stop talking I shall scream.'

Despite the occasional shrill earache, Lord Louis became the greatest supporter of young Marie-Christine's marital aspirations. When he realised how determined the couple were and that they would not be dissuaded from their romantic course, he warmed to their plight and did everything possible to help. He offered to speak to the Queen but asked Michael first to write to the sovereign, asking her permission to wed. He also left it to Michael to speak to his brother, the Duke of Kent, and his sister, Princess Alexandra, who both knew that the couple had been seeing one another but who had no idea the love affair had reached such a serious stage.

Then Mountbatten made a suggestion to the couple that went down like a lead balloon. 'One other thing might help,' he told Marie-Christine. 'It might ward off trouble in the Queen's Church if you were to change your religion.' To her credit, Marie-Christine refused point-blank. She and her mother's family had always been devout Roman Catholics and she did not plan to desert her faith, even though her first marriage to Troubridge had taken place in an Anglican church.

Mountbatten then suggested that they should go to see Dr Donald Coggan, Archbishop of Canterbury, and that Marie-Christine should write confidentially to the Pope, seeking his guidance. Unexpectedly, the visit to Dr Coggan was strained. He was understanding but could not give his blessing.

It was hardly a great springtime for the fortunes of the Royal Family. In April the Troubridges' divorce came through. A month later came Princess Margaret's. One week after that the Queen, apparently wishing to dispose of all the adverse publicity generated by these two events, announced that she had granted permission for Prince Michael to marry Marie-Christine. She informed the Prime Minister, James Callaghan, of her decision and on 31 May the Privy Council, which has the power to approve or reject all royal marriages, rubber-stamped the arrangements. As an indication of just how significant to royal standing and protocol this marriage was, the Queen and her Privy Council of advisers attached three conditions to their acceptance, otherwise the permission for the marriage to go ahead would be instantly withdrawn. She stipulated that Michael must forfeit his right of succession to the throne, that he must guarantee that any children would be raised as Anglicans and not Roman Catholics and, thirdly, they must marry abroad.

This final stricture must have cut at the heart of the young Marie-Christine. The haughty woman who was proudly perpetuating a pretence to be a member of a high order of European aristocracy had suddenly been cut down to size by the big guns of the British establishment. Ever conscious of her flimsy standing in British society, Marie-Christine must have felt humiliated. However, the Queen deemed the order necessary to save further royal embarassment. After all, Dr Coggan had already made it clear that the Prince could not marry his divorced bride in the Church of England. Nor was it possible under the Act of Settlement for any member of the Royal Family to be married in a register office or in any form of civil ceremony in Great Britain.

At least, Marie-Christine must have comforted herself, she had her royal catch – Prince Michael – even if she had not gained much royal cachet.

There then followed the most extraordinary change of heart. An unprecedented 'gloss' was put on what the nation was beginning to view as a bit of a royal fiasco. Marie-Christine, who was to be known as Princess Michael of Kent after her marriage, was actually given the one thing she craved most, royal status. The Queen granted her the style and title of Her Royal Highness, a dignity that had been denied to the Duchess of Windsor for the past 41 years!

After that honour, it should all have been plain sailing. Marie-Christine said she wanted to be married in the Vienna Roman Catholic church where her grandmother had wed. Mountbatten offered to make the arrangements personally and telephoned the Apostolic Delegate, Bruno Heim. He assured the couple that there would be no problem over the wedding arrangements. Marie-Christine went ahead with her plans to awe the world as a virginal bride in an elaborate white wedding dress, backed by the young choirsters of the Vienna Boys Choir. It was to be the wedding of the year. What could go wrong?

Back in Britain a cauldron of scandal and resentment was brewing. Reporters returned to their Fleet Street offices after researching 'background' stories in Vienna and told their news editors that there was a lot more to Marie-Christine than ever appeared in Buckingham Palace press officers' briefings. The affairs of Prince Michael and Princess Margaret had disturbed the public's image of the unimpeachable royals. Margaret's lifestyle had filled the newspapers with tittle-tattle for months. The palace and the Church had both been shaken by these explosive romantic events. What was happening to the Royal Family? Was it disintegrating?

The Queen had been bold in making her early announcement about Prince Michael's marriage but she had not realised that it would lead to a confrontation with the Pope himself. In spite of assurances given to mediator Lord Mountbatten, the wedding plans were suddenly shattered. The Pope, now aware of the Queen's anti-Catholic strictures to Michael and his bride-to-be, suddenly decided to retaliate. His Holiness decreed that the baptism and upbringing of any children of this union would be of primary importance. Therefore, he had no alternative but to forbid the marriage taking place in a Roman Catholic church. The fact that the bridegroom happened to be a member of the British Royal Family only exacerbated the row, because of the 'diplomatic pressure' brought on the Roman Catholic Church by the imperious Mountbatten.

Marie-Christine, so used to getting her own way, saw her grandiose wedding plans crumble to dust. Just two days before she was due to walk up the aisle of the ancient Schottenkirche, the Scottish abbey church in Vienna, on 1 July, she was told that the Pope had refused to annul her marriage to Troubridge and sadly had to leave her silk wedding gown in her hotel wardrobe and, instead, settled for a civil, German-language ceremony in Vienna town hall.

Humiliatingly, there was no white dress, no Vienna Boys Choir, no recognition of the wedding by either of the two Churches. The eventual ceremony must have been a crushing blow to Marie-Christine, as she greeted those royals who, out of loyalty to Prince Michael, had taken the trouble to attend. Neither the Queen nor Prince Philip was there. Among the guests were Princess Anne, the Duke of Kent, Princess Alexandra, her husband, Angus Ogilvy, Lady Helen Windsor, Lord Louis Mountbatten and the bride's father, Baron von Reibnitz.

There was one final twist to this first instalment of the Marie-Christine story, which must also have given the Queen and the Queen Mother a touch of heartburn. The newly-styled Princess Michael wrote to the sick, old Duchess of Windsor at her Paris home to introduce herself and to tell her how much she had admired the Duke and Duchess. She added that she now found herself a 'niece by marriage' to 'Aunty Wallis' and said she sympathised with her because of the traumas suffered in common in pursuit of their royal matches. At the end of their honeymoon, which took them to India, Iran and Paris, the newly-weds called on the Duchess at the Bois de Boulogne.

The Duchess's butler, George Sanegre, one of three remaining staff in the empty, decaying house, showed the couple to the old lady's salon. Marie-Christine handed her a bouquet. The Duchess, whose mind by now drifted in and out of lucidity, is reported to have responded with the words: 'Thank you, darling. It is wonderful to have such a beautiful woman in the house again.' Turning to Prince Michael, the Duchess said: 'Your father was David's favourite, you know. He loved him. He was also the only one who showed any sympathy to me.'

Marie-Christine later visited the Duchess twice more on her own and openly paid her this tribute: 'She is a great lady. History will show she was unfairly treated.'

It was hardly a remark likely to endear her to her new royal relatives back in London. The quote was either crass or calculated. Her friends worried that Marie-Christine was beginning to see herself as a second Wallis Simpson. As at several previous turning points in her life, Marie-Christine was beginning to assume a new role. In this case, it was to be a much grander one than even she had ever aspired to before.

At around this time there was a cameo scene that perhaps reveals how fraught feelings were in the Royal Family, and perhaps how sensitive and even fearful the Queen still was towards the scandal that, many years before, had almost seen the fall of the House of Windsor. It occurred when Princess Michael turned up at a family function wearing a pair of earrings given to her by the Duchess of Windsor. The Queen noticed them and questioned her about them. 'Aunt Wallis gave them to me,' was the reply. The Queen made it clear that she would prefer Princess Michael not to wear the earrings in her presence. She never did again.

Prince Michael and his new bride settled down to live in royal apartments at Kensington Palace. They also bought a country home in Gloucestershire. Michael quit the Army and sought directorships of companies in the City of London. After a year of marriage, a son was born; a daughter followed 18 months later. The Princess's father died in Mozambique at the age of 89 but apart from that one tinge of sadness, the couple seemed deliriously happy, the Prince obviously and utterly devoted to his beautiful blonde wife.

Then the careful image that the refugee Princess had cultivated over the years began to crumble. The institution of the British Royal Family was to be seen at its flimsiest. It was as if a corner of the royal red carpet had been turned up and the cleaner had been caught out sweeping the dirt beneath it. The timebomb ticking away beneath the Royal Family finally exploded on Monday, 15 April 1985 when a reporter from the London *Daily Mirror* phoned the palace and gently but firmly inquired whether it was true that Princess Michael's father, at that time supposedly one of the Second World War's innocent sufferers, had in fact been a major in the reviled SS.

The Buckingham Palace press office tried to contact Princess Michael but she was out for the afternoon. They left a message for her. The Princess returned to her apartments at Kensington Palace at 6 p.m. and opened the envelope containing the deferential inquiry. According to James Whitaker, the *Mirror's* renowned royal-watcher, the Princess simply panicked. She said it was 'a wicked lie' and she would do anything to prevent its publication. Her aides attempted to calm her as she threatened injunctions and writs. They implored her to check the story out with her mother before making any response to the press. A phone call was put through to her mother in Sydney and, as she listened to the old lady's hesitant answers, she realised that the awful truth would have to be revealed to the world. Michael Shea, the Queen's ultra-cautious press secretary, was called in to deal with the crisis. After 100 minutes of agonising, the Princess agreed to issue the terse official statment: 'Princess Michael confirmed tonight that it is true that her father was a member of the SS. It came as a total surprise to her when she heard the news from James Whitaker. There will be no further comment or statement from the Princess.'

It was one of those supreme ironies that seem destined regularly to shatter the privileged calm so sought by the Royal Family, that the shy, retiring Prince Michael was now to pay the price for wanting to break with tradition all those years ago and wed his bride with 'no past'. The time-bomb that would shame her family and disgrace her husband's had at last exploded.

The scandal made the front page of half the newspapers of the Western world. Members of both British and European parliaments demanded inquiries. In New York, Jewish militants decried the 'royal cover-up'. Within days, Princess Michael had to break her earlier vow of silence and, as allegations of a cover-up grew ever stronger, took the unprecedented step of going on nationwide television in a bid to curtail the controversy. Her appearance was excruciatingly embarrassing, not only for her but for the entire Royal Family.

Under obvious strain, Princess Michael admitted to viewers that she had known about her father's membership of the Nazi party but not of his membership of the SS. She said: 'It is a deep shame for me. I think it was sufficiently shocking that he had been in the Nazi party but I did not think to look further. It came as a very great blow to me because I always rather hero-worshipped him. When told this report was coming out in the *Daily Mirror* I immediately telephoned my mother and said "Guess what they are trying to pin on me now." And she said "But I'm afraid it is true." I have been in a sort of state of shell-shock ever since but it is something I'll have to come to terms with, and I know that I shall. I don't like it but I have to live with it.'

Princess Michael could have stopped there. She would have been wise to have done so but she then spoke of a document which, she claimed, 'actually exonerates my father; which states quite clearly that his position in the SS was an honorary one'. She added: 'I was brought up to believe that the SS meant one thing – concentration camps for Jews and so on. I have now discovered that he was not involved in anything like that at all.'

Inevitably, such an obvious attempt to excuse her father's past was bound to add fuel to the flames. It certainly fuelled the public's demand for further details of her family's sensational history. Incredibly, these details were not hard to find. While reporters from the national press rushed to London's Heathrow Airport en route to Germany and Austria to hunt down obscure relatives and even more obscure archives, it was discovered that the facts about Baron von Reibnitz had been readily available for years. They were to be found in dusty archives just three miles from Buckingham Palace, in official lists of senior SS officers which had been held in the Imperial War Museum since the early sixties.

Von Reibnitz's military history soon became as well known as that of most members of the British Royal Family. Born on 8 September 1894, he had won an Iron Cross (second-class) and a Front Line Soldiers Cross in the First World War. In 1935 his military rank was that of 'Untersturmführer' (equivalent to the rank of a British second-lieutenant). By October 1944 he had risen to the rank of 'Sturmbannführer' (major). Most sinisterly, one of the honours bestowed on him was the SS 'Death Head' ring. Documents turned up by reporters even revealed a letter from von Reibnitz to Adolf Hitler, asking permission to marry the Countess Marianne Szapary. In the letter he says: 'I was used as a political speaker in the years of the struggle.'

Perhaps most telling was von Reibnitz's Nazi party number: 412855. It revealed the very early stage at which he had joined. Veteran Nazi hunter Simon Wiesenthal said: 'This means that he pledged his loyalty to Hitler and the Hitler ideals and hatreds in the early 1920s.' He added, however, that the Major was not a wanted man. 'He did not, as far as any of our records show, take part in any atrocities.'

According to the *Daily Mirror*, von Reibnitz's Nazi role

was lengthy and active. It even suggested that he may have been planted as a Hitler spy in the early street-fighting stormtroopers, the SA. He switched to the SS at the age of 39, shortly before Hitler wiped out the SA. Von Reibnitz was promoted just four days after the bloodbath. According to the *Mirror*, he was 'the eyes and ears' of no less than Hitler's right-hand man Herman Goering, who gave him a personal recommendation for an army posting.

The SS, under their dreaded leader Heinrich Himmler, was divided into three branches: the front-line Waffen SS, the Leibstandarte and the Allegemeine. The Waffen (or 'Armed') SS comprised many brave fighting men but was also responsible for such atrocities as the Lidice massacre in Poland. The Leibstandarte provided Hitler's bodyguard. The Allegemeine was a more general branch but included the 'Death's Head' brigade, among whom ranked concentration camp guards. Members were moved fairly freely from one section of Himmler's feared legion to another.

It is not likely that von Reibnitz took part in any of the more horrific excesses of the SS. As a captain, he saw action in Poland in September 1939. He told of being in battles at Prezna Rusks and at Pless Nicolai but there is no record of heavy fighting in these areas. It is more likely that he was positioned behind the lines in a desk job. He spent most of the rest of the war removed from active service in Silesia 'at the personal request of Goering'. In 1944 the Baron rejoined the Roman Catholic Church. This was judged a 'character weakness' by the SS and he was forced to resign.

Such a history did not sound like a first-hand involvement in war crimes but, as Simon Wiesenthal pointed out, the SS were responsible for the running of all death camps. Even if he was not personally involved, the Baron must have known what was going on. He inevitably mixed with fellow officers who were helping to massacre millions of innocents. Wiesenthal dismissed as 'absolutely unbeliev-able' Princess Michael's televised claim that her father was merely an honorary member of the SS who never wore its uniform. The Nazi hunter said the Baron had been one of the first people to join the SS in 1933. He added: 'It was impossible that he never wore a uniform. That might have been what her father told her but it is not the truth.'

With daily banner headlines such as 'This Bloody Disgrace' shaming the Royal Family around the world, Princess Michael used her influence to employ the British Ambassador in Bonn, Sir Julian Bullard, in a search for documents that might clear her father. He quickly came up with the findings of a tribunal held in Bavaria in 1948. Von Reibnitz had applied to the tribunal for a rehearing of an earlier court ruling under the post-war Nazi 'declass-ification' programme. This lower court had failed to clear the Baron of Nazi activities but had placed him under the category of 'less incriminated persons'. Von Reibnitz was unhappy about the decision and appealed to the tribunal to have the ruling set aside. This it did, but it still failed to clear him entirely.

The tribunal heard that the Baron joined the Nazi party in 1931 'in the belief that National Socialism would bring about economic recovery' for Germany. Through his post as chief ranger in charge of hunting in his part of Germany, he obtained SS ranking. He had the right to wear the SS uniform but not to issue orders. After conflicts with his superiors, he was dismissed from the SS in 1944 and was threatened with a posting to a punishment battalion. He used his influence in social and military circles to avoid this fate. The tribunal's ruling was: 'The evidence has not adduced references to the effect that the accused should be regarded as a militarist or as having reaped any benefit. He was to be regarded as falling within the category of nominal party member since he took only a nominal part in National Socialism and lent it only insignificant support. The accused was not a member of any organisation condemned as criminal in the Nuremberg judgments.'

Although the tribunal rejected his petition seeking total exoneration, the publication of its findings went far towards defusing the immediate scandal. However, it did not ameliorate the long-term damage done to the institution of the British monarchy. Far from it. Princess Michael had made her new relatives a laughing stock. Few royal-watchers doubted that she had been heavily vetted by Scotland Yard or even MI5 long before her marriage, yet the secret of her past had been ignored, or worse, covered up.

Harold Brooks-Baker, head of royal publishers Debretts, said: 'I did not know this was a secret. I have heard it mentioned many times.' Hugh Peskett, chief researcher at Debretts, said: 'People on the inside must have known. I was told about it in confidence.' Australian author Barry Everingham, who had been writing the Princess's unauthorised biography at the time the scandal broke, said the Baron's SS history had been well known among the royal household. 'The Queen was warned,' he said, 'the Prime Minister was warned and Prince Michael was warned.' Newspapers claimed that Princess Michael had spoken to close friends about her family's past many months before her marriage. She was said to have confided in them her fears that the Queen would refuse permission for them to wed. It was also pointed out that, as a young girl, Marie-Christine had regularly met ex-SS fugitives when she visited her father in the then-Portuguese colony of Mozambique. Von Reibnitz had been something of a hero among them, although not with his indigenous workforce whom, it was said, he treated harshly.

It did not help Princess Michael's standing in the Royal Family that the scandal over her ancestors should have stirred up even muddier waters. The Nazi-hunting press at this time produced the equally unexpected and embarrassing revelations that the Queen's own husband had relatives with strong wartime Nazi connections.

So far, Princess Michael's handling of the scandal had done little to endear her to the rest of the Royal Family, indeed, to the public at large. Now, where denials had failed, tears won. Under obvious deep emotional strain, the Princess made a rare speech at an official function. She spoke sadly of her ordeal, hesitated, then her voice broke. She was reduced to tears. The effect of her sorrow temporarily gained her the sympathy of at least the public. Chameleon-like, she survived again. No one could deny that the woman had guts.

The honeymoon of public affection was to be short-lived. The life of the glamorous royal newcomer was to be blighted with further controversy. She remained the outsider in the family 'Firm'.

Nicknamed 'Princess Pushy' because of her strident approach to her public and private life, she continued to be the subject of newspaper banter over the years. She worked hard to become a 'real royal' but seemed destined always to overplay her role. Equally, she seemed to want not only the approbation of her husband's relatives but also to be loved by the British public. At times it must have seemed heavy going.

In January 1992 the *Daily Express* newspaper commissioned a costly survey into how the nation viewed the principal members of the Royal Family. Asked who their favourite royal was, poor Princess Michael scored only 1 per cent. Asked who had done the Royal Family most harm, she came out second only to the Duchess of York. Asked who among the royals set the best example, she got 5 per cent of the votes. However, she did come top of the poll in one section – 'Who is the most snobbish?' Her 25 per cent of the vote placed her above the next runner, Prince Philip.

Just how snobbish and pushy the Princess had become was revealed when she boarded a British Airways jumbo jet in Los Angeles for a flight to London. The aircraft was delayed for four hours because of a security alarm. Not a particularly pleasant way to waste time but one which most of the first-class passengers, including actor Lord Olivier's widow, Joan Plowright, found a necessary inconvenience. Not Princess Pushy, who threw the most extraordinary tantrum almost as soon as she got on board. She first berated cabin staff for trying to place another passenger in the seat alongside her, furious that she could not have a double seat for herself. Stewardessess were forced to put the Princess firmly in her place by telling her that the other passenger had a fully-paid, valid £3,690 ticket. As the security alarm continued to delay the plane's take-off, Princess Michael, flying under the assumed name of 'Mrs Turner', lost her cool and imperiously rose from her seat. She addressed the other first-class passengers thus: 'You should all sue British Airways. I would if my position did not prevent me.' The incident occurred two weeks before the anniversary of the Pan-Am bomb atrocity above Lockerbie, Scotland. Relatives of some of the Lockerbie victims hit out at the Princess over her impetuous tantrum. An outraged British MP said: 'She should be ashamed of herself. They should have kicked her off the plane. Maybe she wanted to be 20 years early into the next world instead of four hours late in this one.'

Another occasion when her mouth began to motor before her brain was in gear was when she sounded off about the treatment her son, Freddie, then aged 12, was receiving at a boarding school near Paris. The French reacted furiously after she claimed that Freddie had been bullied by a teacher at the school where he had been sent to improve his foreign languages. She said in a television interview: 'I thought he was miserable because of a combination of hay fever and homesickness. It was only when he left that another mother told me that one of the teachers had rather picked on him for being who he was and that the boys had ganged up and protected him. The teacher would mock him and talk in very fast colloquial French which he didn't get in the beginning. He didn't tell me because he knew that his mother would wade in and have the person hung, drawn and quartered.'

In the same programme, she said of her daughter, Gabriella: 'My darling Ella. Ella is the sweet, the sweet child. She has that wonderful smile. She lights up and though she's not at all academic – I don't think I could cope with two academic children, tortured intellectuals – she's a sunny child.'

It was not so much what Princess Michael said on these very public occasions that brought forlorn looks and raised eyebrows to the visages of the Queen's household. It was more the embarrassing novelty of a member of the family publicly discussing such private issues as her daughter's intellect and her son's school bullying. There were greater humiliations to come, however.

Princess Michael became the first member of the Royal Family to be breath-tested. She had been stopped by police in London's busy Kensington High Street and breathalysed in front of hundreds of Christmas shoppers. The test proved negative but the Princess was given a verbal warning not to push her way through the traffic in a buses-only lane!

Another ludicrous piece of newspaper tittle-tattle that year again helped to make the Royal Family a laughing stock. Emblazoned across the front page of Britain's most lurid tabloid newspaper was the news that Princess Michael's brother, Australian civil servant Freddie von Reibnitz, had fathered a secret baby – by a 51-year-old lesbian. It was said that brother Freddie, 48, married and with a daughter of his own, had agreed to do the deed as a favour to the lesbian friend, who wanted to 'complete a family' with her bisexual lover.

'Where would it all end?' asked the Buckingham Palace advisers. The story of the Royal Family in the 1990s was beginning to resemble a coarse West End farce. Princess Michael did not disappoint the royal mickey-takers.

Her next appearance in the headlines was the result of a radio interview, this time about a book she had written. Princess Pushy lived up to her nickname when, confronting verteran broadcaster Michael Parkinson, she made a series of stage whispers, urging him to give her literary master-piece more publicity. As she persisted in pushing her book and pressed Parkinson to mention the name of her pub-lishers, the irritated broadcaster hit the roof. 'Ma'am, I don't tell you how to do your job,' he said.

A further example came in a television interview with top chat-show host Terry Wogan, who quite obviously disliked his guest with some vehemence. Reviewer and columnist Peter Tory reported: 'It was a display which made for both toe-breaking embarrassment and compulsive pillow-in-the-mouth entertainment. She bore herself with the exaggerated poise that suggests the portrayal of an empress by a first-year drama student.'

The subject of the two interviews, and of many others at the time, was Princess Michael's newly-embarked-upon literary career. In this sphere, too, the Princess ran into very serious trouble. In 1986, two writers were paid thous-ands of pounds because parts of her book *Crowned in a*

Far Country, about European royal princesses, were almost identical to their works. With such accusations of plagiarism levelled against her, Princess Michael's new, upmarket occupation of author failed to impress the Royal Family. Neither did it impress the public to any great degree. The Princess pushed the title furiously but, following her attendance at a Foyle's literary lunch in London, one publisher observed: 'It's one of those books where the unsigned copies will be collectors' items.' The Princess's second work came to the bookstands after an equally difficult creative birth. The publishers rejected the manuscript when it was delivered 15 months late and demanded the return of her advance, reputedly £50,000 to £80,000. Eventually the book, *Kings and Courtesans*, about six royal mistresses, was published. It, too, was greeted by a complaint from another author, Christine Sutherland, who said that part of it was heavily based on her own *Marie Walewska, Napoleon's Great Love*. A bewildered Christine Sutherland said: 'Why does she do what she does? You'd need a psychiatrist to understand. It's so sad.'

Author Jilly Cooper, a friend of the Kents, once offered to write an article about the Princess's literary career. The story she published, however, did not limit itself to a literary appraisal, nor was it entirely complimentary. On Miss Cooper's silver wedding anniversary, a short while afterwards, Princess Michael sent her 30 pieces of silver or, to be accurate, 30 shillings.

Away from the glitterati of the book world, Princess Pushy also lives up to her nickname. Upset by the goggle-eyed peasantry who would drive by her Gloucestershire home, she even had the name of her village 'removed from the map'. She ordered all road signs leading to Nether Lypiatt Mansion to be removed in order to rid herself of the curious sightseers. On another occasion she got into trouble when, hunting with her husband in neighbouring Wiltshire, she rode into a private field of valuable mares and foals. Padlocked gates were cut and the couple thundered through, scattering the terrified animals in a panic from which they took days to recover. Owner Joe Hughes said: 'They seem to think they can do whatever they like and ride roughshod over other people's property.'

Life is not always plain sailing at Nether Lypiatt Mansion itself. An applicant for a domestic job there was asked by interviewers about her ability to work under pressure and how she would handle exceptional requests. She was told: 'The Princess does have a reputation for being very off-hand with her staff.' She was warned: 'You must always remember they are "the Royals". Everything has to be perfect.' Staff at the house are instructed to greet the Prince and Princess each morning with a bow or curtsy and a polite 'Good morning Your Highness', although, to be fair to the Princess, it is her husband who is more likely to frown if this courtesy is not followed.

Nether Lypiatt Mansion costs a fortune to maintain and it has not always been easy to pay the bills. When he married, Prince Michael was one of the poorest royals. He lived off his Army pay and the income from an inheritance. His bride yearned for a mansion fit for a princess and rejected the neighbouring Highgrove estate because it was too small. (It was later purchased by Prince Charles.) When they bought Nether Lypiatt Mansion, Prince Michael had to sell many of his investments. Then he had to find a further £100,000 to bring it up to the standard demanded by his wife.

One book that author Princess Michael did not want to see on a sales shelf next to hers was the unsubtly titled *With Great Respect*, by her former private secretary John Barratt. Published in 1991, it claimed that keeping homes in London and the country was a constant drain on Prince Michael's resources and that his wife had even secretly sold some of the family silver to pay the bills. Barratt, who had first met the young Marie-Christine while he was still private secretary to Lord Mountbatten, said: 'Almost from the day I began working for the couple I had to find ways Prince Michael and his big-spending wife could earn extra income.' Barratt, who said he eventually quit because he could not stand the Princess's 'bullying', was the highest-ranking royal aide ever to speak out in public about private palace life. Princess Michael immediately threatened to sue him. Her new secretary, Lieutenant Colonel Sir Christopher Thompson, stuffily defused the situation by saying that his predecessor was 'not the sort of person one would wish to keep in touch with'.

Perhaps the most dangerous headlines the Prince and Princess ever saw drop on their breakfast table came on a Tuesday morning in May 1985, following a holiday Princess Michael had spent at the southern Californian ranch of her friend Princess Esra of Hyderabad. Although Princess Esra was nowhere to be seen, a 44-year-old Texan was. His name was Ward Hunt and he was the cousin of ultra-rich oil mogul Bunker Hunt.

The investigative journalists of the *News of the World* discovered that divorcee Hunt had known Princess Michael for two years and that they had seen each other quite often. She had once visited him at his Dallas apartment after her husband had flown home alone after a US visit. With his mother, Hunt had been a guest at Kensington Palace but on another visit to London he had been booked by Princess Michael's office into London's swish Carlton Hotel. At the last minute the *News of the World* discovered that the Princess and Hunt had had a change of plan. The newspaper believed the pair were planning to stay together for a few days at the exclusive apartment belonging to Princess Esra's brother in Eaton Square. The reporters 'staked out' the area and witnessed Princess Michael arriving at the flat carrying groceries and wearing an ill-fitting red wig. Hunt arrived later. Barring official engagements, the couple stayed at the flat until the Princess was tipped off that she was being watched. Within 24 hours Hunt was on a plane back to the United States and Princess Michael had gone into hospital announcing that she was suffering from exhaustion. Buckingham Palace issued a statement: 'Any suggestion that the Princess and Mr Hunt are other than acquaintances is unfounded.'

Once asked why she thought she received so much criticism from the press, Princess Michael replied: 'They have to have a bad girl, don't they? And I am a pretty obvious target.'

Princess Michael was thought to be pretty bad by the press, the public and the entire Royal Family in June 1991 when she foolishly boasted of her special relationship with the Queen. She told *Paris Match*: 'The Queen has always supported and advised me. Thanks to her I have been able to keep a cool head and show I'm indifferent to criticism. Of course, I'm easy prey because I'm blonde, Austrian and Catholic. But the Queen has said that I am England's most royal princess. This is a great compliment.' That such a compliment had ever entered the Queen's head would, on the evidence, be a surprise. Her further comment would have upset the monarch even more. Princess Michael said the Queen had consoled her over persistent divorce rumours and added: 'The Queen said the press had announced her own forthcoming divorce 17 times.'

Within three months Princess Pushy was putting her foot in it again. She told the magazine *Marie Claire* that she had less German blood in her than the Queen. She said that people expected her to be 'frightfully Germanic' but she said they soon changed their minds when they met her. She admitted: 'If you speak a language, people forget you're not of that country. But I don't think in English, I don't dream in English and my humour isn't English.' Then, in a quote least likely to endear her to her royal relatives, she insisted: 'I've probably got less German blood in me than any single member of the Royal Family.'

So what does the Queen really think of Princess Michael? Do the rest of the Royal Family treat her as a mere embarrassment or as a real danger to the fabric of the family 'Firm'? The only clues lie in the fact that most of the royals have always seemed to distance themselves from the newcomer in their midst at Kensington Palace.

The Queen said tartly of her: 'She is far too grand for

ove: A teenage Lady Diana Spencer on a family holiday

ove: Days of innocence . . . Diana in her holiday chalet

Above: A picture of togetherness, Charles and Diana in 1981

ove: The marriage was already showing signs of strain by 1983

ove: By the end of the 80's the couple were living separate lives

Above: In 1986 Sarah and Diana were still the closest of friends

Top: Sarah's great love was Paddy McNally
Above: Steve Wyatt and young Beatrice in the pages of *Paris Match*

eft: The Duchess of York in *Royal Knockout* style in 1987
bove: The Duke of York on a visit to Canada in 1987

Above: The Royal Family watch the Trooping The Colour fly past in 1992

Above: The Queen is driven to the State Opening of Parliament in 1991

b left: The Duke of Edinburgh, always the action man
b right: Philip's mother, Princess Alice of Battenburg
ove: Humble beginnings . . . Philip (left) dines in Greek style

Above: Mourning the Duke of Windsor...his widow and the Queen Mother

Above: Sad figures in exile . . . the Duke and Duchess of Windsor

Above: The nation's favourite grandmother enters her nineties

Above: A plastic tag marks the pauper's grave of Nerrisa Bowes-Lyon

Right: Princess Margaret and first love Peter Townsend
Below: Margaret with new love Anthony Armstrong-Jones

ove: Princess Anne
Mark Phillips wed on
November 1973
ht: Anne by 1991 tagged
Princess of Toil'

Left: The ever-elegant
Princess and Prince
Michael of Kent
Below: Royal pursuits
by 'Princess Pushy' and
husband
Overleaf: Theatrically
attired Prince Edward
in 1987

Above: Major Ron Ferguson at a River Thames publicity event in 1987

the likes of us.' Prince Charles has been overheard referring to her as 'that bloody woman'. He even told his ex-girl-friend, Anna Wallace: 'Don't bother to curtsy to Princess Michael.' The Queen's nephew, Viscount Linley, has never denied his bitter retort when once asked what he would like to give his worst enemy. 'Dinner with Princess Michael,' was his reply.

Perhaps the most cruel irony about the Princess Michael scandals is that, as an SS officer, her father would automatically have been assigned to Adolf Hitler's great racial experiment to create 'a master race'. Known as the 'Lebensborn' programme, it required SS men to sire strong, healthy children of Aryan stock. Von Reibnitz's most successful progeny was Marie-Christine, who is labelled by the Queen 'Our Val' because of her blue-eyed, blonde, Valkyrie-like, domineering demeanour.

CHAPTER EIGHT

Princess Anne

The privileges of royalty are considerable, although most members of the Royal Family wisely seem to do their best to play them down. The duties that compensate for such power, privilege and wealth can also be considerable. In the case of one member of the family, the workload is astonishing.

Princess Anne originally dedicated herself to her royal duties to heal the heartache of a failing marriage. In the end it won her the respect of the British public, seldom felt in her early years, and the title Princess Royal, conferred upon her by the Queen. In a strange way, it also won her an historic right to the divorce she craved.

The Princess Royal is now the Princess of Toil, highly respected for her courage and energy. Once upon a time, however, the title 'Spoiled Brat' would have been a more likely epithet in the British press. Anne, born on 15 August 1950, was and still is the apple of her father's eye. Educated at Benenden public school in Kent, where she gained six 'O-level' and one 'A-level' examination passes, the Princess not only inherited the Duke of Edinburgh's intelligence, she also inherited his tetchiness. Other traits she got from her father were his capacity for hard work, his love of sport, his acerbic wit, his inability to suffer fools gladly and his short temper.

As with the Duke, there had always been a mutual dislike between the Princess and the so-called 'rat pack' of reporters and photographers who follow the royals everywhere. In 1982 she erupted spectacularly when photographers tried to take a picture of her as she inelegantly fell into a lake at the Badminton Horse Trials. 'Naff off!' she screeched at them. On an Australian tour a photographer made the mistake of urging her: 'Look this way, my love.'

With a withering glare, Anne rounded on the poor man and curtly told him: 'I am not your love.'

Anne acknowledges this tetchy trait but says: 'It's too late to do anything about it now.' What she did do, however, was to turn the tables on the critical newspaper editors by winning the admiration of their readers, the public at large, for her astonishing record of public service. Such dedication to duty earned her the respect of the press whom she so disdainfully dismissed. At first this respect was given grudgingly but nowadays it is proffered fulsomely by her multitude of admirers, from the Queen downwards.

The story of how the 'Spoiled Brat' princess became the Princess Royal and then 'Princess Toil' is a fascinating one, for it is not so much a story about palace duties, itineraries and work schedules as a saga of very real, human emotions – love, jealousy, heartache and ultimate joy. It also holds a moral for the future wellbeing of the entire Royal Family, but essentially it is the chronicle of a marriage. Tragically for Princess Anne, it was a marriage that went hideously wrong.

Anne married on the rebound from her first love, commodity broker Sandy Harper, the man thought by many at Buckingham Palace to be the partner she would devote her life to. Whether sharing candle-lit dinners or escorting her to the theatre, Sandy Harper, the polo-playing son of a lieutenant-colonel, was frequently at the young Princess's side in 1969, and she rapidly fell for him.

However, perhaps frightened by the trappings of the

royal circus, Harper broke off the relationship without warning and instead married (and later divorced) model Peta Secombe.

The rift from Harper deeply saddened Anne and prepared the ground for her engagement to army officer Captain Mark Phillips, to whom she had been introduced a year earlier while still in love with Sandy Harper. Until officially announced, Anne's engagement created the most intense press speculation world-wide, for which the Princess herself was largely to blame. She was insistent on keeping her romance with Mark a secret as long as possible and their friends went to extraordinary lengths to help them.

The penny eventually dropped when Anne was discovered out fox-hunting with Mark in December 1972. She was a guest at his family house at Great Somerford, Wiltshire. His mother, Anne Phillips, recalled how they had only six weeks of calm from the time Anne first visited their Wiltshire home until all hell broke loose. Mark and Anne denied the relationship publicly and played a cat-and-mouse game for months. 'At that time we were very friendly but I had no intention of getting married – I was a confirmed bachelor,' Mark recalled later.

The Princess added: 'He kept telling me he was a confirmed bachelor and I thought at least one knows where one stands. I mean I wasn't even thinking about it.'

It was only after the Badminton Horse Trials in April the following year that the couple privately agreed that marriage was a good idea. The engagement was announced on 29 May 1973. Mark had flown home from his regiment in Germany on the Easter bank holiday weekend to ask Prince Philip formally for his daughter's hand. He was 'petrified' at the thought of performing that duty but was put at his ease by his prospective father-in-law. Prince Philip was not, however, totally satisfied with Anne's choice of husband. He considered Mark to be dull and only capable of talking about horses or the army.

Mark Phillips's background was unexceptional; he was the type of man to be found anywhere among the middle-class families of England's shires. Neither of his parents had royal ancestry, although Mrs Phillips was the daughter of Brigadier John Tiarks, at one time aide-de-camp to King George VI.

Following his schooling at Marlborough College, Mark found his academic qualifications insufficient to get him into Sandhurst as an officer, so he enlisted in the ranks of the Royal Green Jackets and for six months served as a private soldier. He was good-looking, smartly but dowdily dressed and an agreeable companion, although he earned the nicknames 'Foggy' and 'Mud' because he was deemed to be thick and wet! He was a keen sportsman and an outstanding horseman. He had been in the British Olympic 1968 contingent in Mexico at the age of 20 and it was as part of the British equestrian team that he first met Anne.

In contrast to Prince Philip's fears of his future son-in-law's shortcomings, the Queen Mother was more positive about the relationship. She remarked that if Anne and Mark's particulars had been put through a computer dating service it was likely they would have matched up.

Although seemingly reserved, like Anne Mark was

strong-willed and at times quite stubborn. It was Mark's wish that he remain master of his own household. Both were aware of the problems that might confront them; perhaps like the husband of a film star, his wife's achievements might totally overshadow those of her husband. This is why Mark never took a title – whether as a soldier, farmer or professional horseman, he wanted to control his own destiny.

The big day arrived with all the pomp and pageantry that the British throne could muster and on 14 November 1973 the marriage took place at Westminster Abbey, watched by a television audience of 500 million. Afterwards, Anne, aged 23, guided her 25-year-old husband in the art of public relations. As they reached the west door of the abbey, she said: 'Get ready to acknowledge the crowds on the way back.' Later, on the balcony of Buckingham Palace, she told him: 'Come on, wave.'

Already there was criticism. Barbed questions were asked about the cost of the honeymoon on the royal yacht *Britannia* and Mark's allocation of Oak Grove House, traditionally occupied by Sandhurst's Director of Studies, where he was to take up a post as an instructor.

What was in store? Would Mark be forever the quiet man at his wife's side? There were already clues. Their lifestyle was being likened to *The Taming of the Shrew*, but it was far from being a comedy, at least at that early stage. Anne had been attracted to Mark in the first place because he was strong-willed enough to disregard her autocratic and wilful manner. He could tame her temper but he knew that at times Anne would have to rule the roost, when it would be barely credible for him to expect her to serve and obey. On the other hand, Anne herself was sensible enough to realise that both must have well-defined areas of their lives and that on occasions he must lead.

The first two years of married life were centred at Sandhurst where Oak Grove had been refurbished. From an early stage, it was difficult for Anne to adopt the role of loving housewife. Sometimes Buckingham Palace would book her for three or four engagements in a single day. She was all over the country and Mark sometimes had to attend as well; the pressures were enormous, as Mark was just discovering.

Princess Margaret's overcoming of the 'no divorce' rule within her family would put greater pressure on Anne and Mark. This was the greatest crisis the Royal Family had faced since the abdication. It signalled the start of a gloves-off approach by the popular press which Anne would have to endure whenever her own marriage came into the spotlight. The Queen would not want another divorce in her close family circle in the near future.

By 1976, Anne had decided that she and Mark would move into a new house and start a family. They visited an especially expensive and magnificent mansion. This was it, Anne said to the estate agent. They would take it, she decided without throwing a glance towards her husband. Mark intervened. What Princess Anne really meant, he said, ushering her towards the door, is that they would go away and think about it. They did, and they didn't buy it.

Mark, more than most husbands perhaps, over-compensated by refusing to be the one to back down in an argument. He would always remember the advice of his brother-in-law, Charles, who told him 'not to let Anne get away with too much'. They eventually moved into Gatcombe Park, Gloucestershire – a £5,000,000 present from the Queen – where a son, Peter, and a daughter, Zara, helped to create an aura of domestic bliss. In 1978 Mark went to the Royal Agricultural College in nearby Cirencester to study farming for a year.

As she reached 30 Princess Anne began to change her image. It didn't happen overnight and it seems to have been a deliberate and planned move towards a more acceptable public face. She has never admitted she embarked on such a course, but a certain mellower and softer approach was noticed and she was not on quite such a short fuse. Yet, as her list of public engagements grew, and with it the approval of the public and press, she was also having to adapt to a certain loneliness. At times she would rely heavily for support upon members of her staff.

By 1983 there was at last a new mood of congratulatory respect for Princess Anne. Following an African tour and a visit to Pakistan, the headlines were favourable. At home she had given 21 official audiences of top-level importance; she had attended 36 receptions, lunches or banquets; she had officiated at four meetings; and had carried out a further 107 official visits up and down the country.

The newspaper *The Mail on Sunday* made an interesting observation when, in 1983, she joined her husband on a private visit to Australia. Writer Richard Shears asked:

Is Princess Anne's character that of a chameleon, changing only when she flies abroad? Does she have to escape the Establishment restrictions of Britain... to show she is warm, brave and caring? Must she go to the opposite side of the earth to prove on Australian TV and radio that she has a brain which flashes as quickly as a dragonfly, a droll turn of self-mockery and a sense of humour that makes professional comics happy to fall about?

On a television chat show in Australia, these attributes came over to the home-viewing public for the first time. The result was a relaxed, witty and intelligent encounter in which even the monosyllabic Mark Phillips came over sensibly. During the Australia trip, the couple had dinner with entertainer Victor Borge. Anne sang along to some music, but Mark yawned – only to receive a prod in the ribs from his wife who said: 'Wake up. Or go and join that man over there who's nodding off.'

However, by the middle of 1984 it seemed that all the good things to say about Princess Anne had, sadly, been exhausted. Princess Diana was temporarily out of the spotlight awaiting the birth of her second child, and the focus was once again turned on Anne and Mark and that old chestnut, the state of their marriage. The public interest couldn't have come at a worse time for either of them.

Anne had been up to her eyes in engagements; Mark was busy with his horses and a ripening harvest on the farm. It was reported that the Queen and Prince Philip were deeply concerned about the gulf in the couple's marriage and the way they were now leading separate lives. Later that month Anne and Mark slept in different rooms when both attended the Olympics in Los Angeles.

Mark reacted angrily to the scandal-mongering. He said he and his wife had separate busy schedules. He blamed the Olympic arrangements, even the traffic, and added that it was 'absolute nonsense' to talk of a marriage split. Rumours that the Queen herself had ordered the couple to put on a show of togetherness were followed by Mark's appearance at his wife's side for her next three engagements. The effect suffered, however, when Mark got lost in the crowd at the Berkeley Square Ball and was treated to a show of tetchiness by Anne. She asked him: 'Where the hell have you been?' She did not dance with her husband once, and on leaving, at 1 a.m., she returned to her apartment in Buckingham Palace, while he made the long drive back to Gatcombe Park.

The sensitive matter of the loyalty of members of the royal household hit the headlines in spectacular fashion in late 1985. Out into the open for the first time were allegations that Anne's former bodyguard and ex-sergeant in the Royal Protection Squad, Peter Cross, had been touting around for the previous three years. Cross, aged 37, was asking £600,000 for his story, claiming he had enjoyed a 'special relationship' with the Princess. He and his employer would sit on Gatcombe's back stairs while she poured out her heart. He said she frequently telephoned him and they had clandestine meetings. One of Peter Cross's most incredible claims would be that Princess Anne rang him on the night of the birth of her second child, Zara, in May 1981.

Anne and Mark were deeply hurt. Buckingham Palace refused to comment. Mark expressed his anger over the 'hurtful stories and fantasies' but the scandal was up and running worldwide. Anne, like many other royals, had perhaps trusted her detective and constant companion rather more than she should have done. Sergeant Cross, who had been with her for almost a year, was often the only person with whom she could speak immediately after a tense public engagement, and all at a time when her husband was not by her side.

Peter Cross was gradually exposed as a vain man who had indulged in several extra-marital affairs and who boasted that Anne was in love with him. Condemnation was widespread but for Anne it was one of the most galling and potentially embarrassing situations of her life. Interestingly, she emerged as a vulnerable woman, drained and tired by the constant strain of a three-week press battering.

Anne had always been seen as overwhelmingly self-assured, but perhaps not too sure about herself as a woman. Her sex appeal was not something of which she was especially confident – although she is strikingly attractive, with delicate skin and a good figure. As a result of the publicity surrounding the Cross affair, she began to experiment with new fashions and hairstyles for her public appearances, successfully fighting off self-consciousness as she went about her engagements.

A family skiing holiday in the French Alps the following year was seen as a second honeymoon and Mark talked afterwards of having had a 'wonderful time – we haven't had a holiday like it for nine years'. Then he spoilt it by referring to the cost of the skiing trip, which he had had to pay for himself.

The constant references to money and to his need to earn a living were an embarrassing whine to the ears of the Royal Family. His obvious nervous withdrawal at public events was also seen to be letting the side down but Mark has always found public life daunting. His Army nickname of 'Foggy' was perpetuated by some of the Royal Family who also thought Mark was 'thick and wet'.

After the skiing holiday, Anne and Mark once again headed off in separate directions. She had eight trips overseas marked in her diary, and Mark was pencilled in to join her on only one of them. It was to be the mixture as before.

By the summer of 1986, the public had been treated to another royal wedding, with Sarah Ferguson, now Duchess of York, joining the Royal Family. In that climate of high romance, Princess Anne's name was linked to the happily married film and television star Anthony Andrews, who had dined with the Princess while her husband was away from Gatcombe. The rumours angered Andrews and his heiress wife, Georgina, who got fed up with having to dismiss them as rubbish.

From the mid-eighties Anne and Mark's marriage, once billed as the egalitarian fairytale of the princess and the commoner, became a marriage of total indifference. They shared a love of horses, two beautiful children and the vast country mansion bought for them by the Queen. In the end, however, it was a marriage the Princess Royal just didn't want.

She was tough, headstrong and used to getting her own way. He was made of softer metal, less tough, less ambitious. He made up for these supposed shortcomings by becoming a workaholic. He spent an average of four months a year travelling and when back at Gatcombe he routinely worked a 16-hour day. He said: 'I appreciate it is rather trying for my wife and family but at the moment it is a necessity.' It was true, they really did need the money at the time. As his business enterprises flourished in an 'un-royal' pursuit of wealth, his family life suffered. The couple spent seven wedding anniversaries apart.

What began as a classic case of the husband going out to work while the little woman stayed at home to look after the kids ended with this little woman rebelling. Like her husband, the Princess took on a punishing public workload, which, in the end, became almost addictive. She also found her own friends to share her off-duty hours. Mark, who has never been short of girlfriends himself, became jealous of his wife's companions. It was Mark who caused the fuss that got rid of Anne's 'over-familiar' detective Peter Cross. It was Mark who objected to her friendships with actor Anthony Andrews and Major Hugh Lindsay, who was killed in a Klosters avalanche while skiing with Prince Charles.

In 1986, a tall, austerely handsome Naval officer went to work for the Queen as her new equerry. His name was Timothy Laurence. He moved comfortably in and out of the royal circle and, whereas Mark Phillips always appeared awkward and ill at ease in the confined goldfish-bowl atmosphere of the palace, Tim Laurence effortlessly smoothed everybody's path. It was inevitable that he and Princess Anne should meet; it was not surprising that they should fall for each other.

In April 1989 Buckingham Palace named Commander Laurence as the writer of four personal letters stolen from the Princess Royal's briefcase and sent to a newspaper. Their contents were never revealed but they were said to be 'affectionate'. The ever-discreet officer behaved with dignity and silence when the story of his stolen letters broke in the world's press. They were obviously love letters from himself to the Princess Royal.

Four months later it was announced that Anne and Mark were to separate. It was said that there were no plans for divorce – the Queen was still haunted by the 1978 divorce of her sister, Princess Margaret, and Lord Snowdon.

Anne and Tim remained close but their meetings were secretive and seldom. For two years Commander Laurence remained at the helm of his frigate HMS *Boxer*, his brief leave periods allowing them only snatched moments together. They enjoyed candle-lit dinners aboard the ship at Portland naval base in Dorset. It was no coincidence that while Tim's ship was being refitted in Plymouth in 1990, Anne's official engagements in the area increased. The couple were also seen strolling in the grounds of Balmoral during stolen Scottish weekends.

When Princess Anne and Captain Mark Phillips went their separate ways, their love of their children and their love of horses somehow kept them genuinely good friends. Remarkably so, as Mark had often been mentioned in the gossip columns because of his many female friends and close business partners. Writers presented the dedicated equestrian as a bit of a dark horse himself.

Way back in the summer of 1988 his name was linked with Canadian Kathy Birks, who was advising him on public relations. The lady was forced to sue (successfully) when newspapers failed to heed her denials that the two of them were anything but business partners. Stories about them were rightly dismissed as total rubbish, but they did not help the Phillipses' shaky marriage at the time.

Other of Mark's female friends who have sympathised with him over his marital troubles have included champion horsewoman Ginny Leng, American rider Karen Lende and British television news presenter Angela Rippon. Long after the marriage break-up, in January 1992, Mark's name was for the first time linked with 29-year-old Jane Thornton after they spent a skiing holiday together. Travel executive Jane, described as a 'Princess Anne lookalike', danced the night away with Mark at the French resort of Val d'Isere. Only a month or two later, their friends confirmed that they were 'deeply in love'. Mark appeared at last to have found the perfect partner.

However, long before that welcome romance blossomed, there was one, less fortunate, liaison that rocked the royals and cast Mark Phillips out for ever.

In March 1991 a 40-year-old New Zealand art teacher named Heather Tonkin named Captain Mark Phillips as the father of her six-year-old love child and lodged a paternity suit against him. She claimed the child had been conceived during a night spent with Mark at an Auckland hotel in November 1984 when she was 31 and Captain

Phillips was 35. It was a week before his eleventh wedding anniversary. She said they got together at a party following an equestrian event.

She said: 'We were in awe of him. I was anxious to please him and I wanted to make the most of it. On the last evening of the course there was a party. I knew he was showing some interest in me, possibly because I was sensible and mature and not the type to be indiscreet. I suppose I was infatuated by Mark. No man I have ever met seems to match up to him.' At the party Captain Phillips asked for her telephone number then rang her at home at 10 p.m., getting her out of bed. He asked her to drive to his hotel in town and when she asked how she would find his room he told her he would leave his riding boots outside the door!

The child, named Felicity, but known as 'Bunny', was born on 10 August 1985. Miss Tonkin said that Mark had made regular payments to her, perhaps of up to £40,000, described as 'fees' for acting as an equestrian consultant. In 1991 she read varying newspaper reports quoting figures of up to £1 million as being the settlement Captain Phillips was to receive following his separation from the Princess Royal. Heather Tonkin was said to have given Mark a £300,000 pay-or-tell ultimatum but is believed to have agreed on an out-of-court payment.

Although Mark never accepted that he was Bunny's father, he is believed to have set up a trust fund for the youngster in a deal that gags Miss Tonkin from ever publicly linking him with her pretty daughter. During the early negotiations, Heather Tonkin is believed to have made anguished phone calls to Gatcombe Park, so it is hard to believe that Anne did not know of the scandalous secret. However, private knowledge and public shame are two different things. Even though separated, the story of his love child infuriated and embarrassed the Princess.

Buckingham Palace retaliated in the normal way and threw Mark Phillips to the wolves. Although he contested the paternity allegations, Mark was ostracised by the Royal Family in a way not witnessed since the Duchess of Windsor. He was an outsider, a royal 'non-person' – to everybody, that is, except the loyal royal, his wife the charitable Princess Anne. She forgave her errant husband but divorce became inevitable. Anne set about making it an amicable one.

When it came, it was all very 'gentlemanly'. Indeed the announcement was delayed so that it would not clash with the 1992 general election and with the seedy break-up of the marriage of the Duke and Duchess of York. The divorce was the result of long and careful planning, with the happiness of their two children, Peter, then aged 14, and Zara, 10, being top priority. It was agreed that they would continue to live with their mother at Gatcombe while Mark, just down the road at Aston Farm, would have unlimited access to them. Anne and Mark met regularly to discuss the welfare of the children and even turned up together at social events. He continued, jointly with Anne, to run a series of three-day events at Gatcombe. It seemed that their love of riding, as much as their love for the children, had saved the pair from further animosity and scandal.

It was a full two and a half years after their separation that Princess Anne actually instituted divorce proceedings against her husband. On 13 April 1992 an historic but typically terse statement from Buckingham Palace signalled the end of the 18-year marriage: 'Her Royal Highness is starting the necessary legal proceedings.' The Princess wasted no time. Her petition was presented to the Divorce Registry the very same day. Anne laid low as the announcement was made; Mark carried on working behind the gates of Aston Farm, the house on the Gatcombe Park estate where he had lived ever since the separation. Commander Tim Laurence was also nowhere to be seen. He was believed to be taking a sailing holiday away from the desk job which he had recently been given at the Ministry of Defence, a stone's throw from Buckingham Palace.

It just could not have happened that way a generation before, as poor Princess Margaret bitterly remembered. Upon hearing the announcement of the Anne–Mark split, royal expert Harold Brooks Baker said: 'Divorce among the Royal Family is no longer a tragedy. And because the Princess Royal has served her country so well she will be the first royal to remarry with her parents' approval. The public also approve because they respect her so much.'

Anne had successfully worked her way through the hostility she had met with from the world's press, particularly the British newspapers. Today it seems almost impossible that the young woman doing such a sterling job for the Royal Family deliberately cold-shouldered public attention and had such a hatred of the royal photographers and reporters she called the 'rat pack'.

She leads a quiet life, determined not to have the eyes of a critical world upon her. She no longer takes part in equestrian events on such a regular basis as she did a few years ago. Instead, when not at home being a down-to-earth mum to Zara and Peter, the only time she is seen in public is carrying out her royal duties diligently and with dignity. Her dedication as patron of the Save the Children Fund earned her the honoured title Princess Royal on 13 June 1987, bestowed upon her by the Queen after a particularly gruelling series of visits to highlight Third World aid problems. She was photographed showing genuine concern for the young children she met. Even the most critical royal-watcher could not fault her for her determination not to stand on ceremony. The Princess roughed it with the rest of her party. This was no glittering publicity stunt, she seemed to want to tell the press she had previously snubbed. This was the *real* Anne doing what was closest to her heart, working.

The *Daily Mirror* newspaper revealed in a leading article just how attitudes to the Princess had changed. It said: 'She is the one who greatly helps the world's sick and suffering children and Britain's neglected and disabled. She is a royal grafter, the Workaholic Princess.' Those close to her in the royal circle sometimes wondered at the workload she increasingly inflicted upon herself.

Some said she became a workaholic with the aim of healing her double heartache, the sadness of her failed marriage to Mark Phillips and the suffering for the love of a man who couldn't, at that time, be hers. Royal protocol dictated that Tim Laurence had to remain in the background for the three years between their romance blossoming and her divorce coming through. So Anne, the royal with the real stiff upper lip, threw herself into a harsh schedule of visits and public engagements to take her mind off the hurt.

Her workload began to worry her secretaries in 1991. It seemed that Anne had sunk to a depth of personal sadness and was filling as many hours of the day as possible. One day alone in July 1991, she flew from Gatcombe Park to Cornwall to christen with pride a new lifeboat RNLB *The Princess Royal*. From there she flew to Glasgow as a VIP guest at a reception dinner for the Save the Children Fund of which she is president. It was early the next day before she returned home where her children were tucked up in bed. After just a few hours' sleep, Anne was up again the next day to ensure she could make the most of nearly a full day with Zara and Peter. Then, after an early tea, she kissed them goodbye again before heading to London for the Royal Tournament of which she is patron . . . and so it went on for the Princess of Toil.

As if carrying out some spiritual cleansing, Anne would attend engagements for the Riding for the Disabled Association, the British Academy of Film and Television Arts, the Windsor Horse Trials and the Missions to Seamen, just some of the organisations to which she is attached. Then, of course, there is all that hand-shaking, and the hours of painstaking boredom when she would rather be at home at Gatcombe Park 'doing real work' such as supervising the stables or grooming her much-loved horses.

As undisputedly the busiest member of the Royal Family, no two days are the same, despite Anne's sometimes desperate attempts to provide a continued secure atmosphere for her children. Much of her time is spent travelling between Gatcombe Park and Buckingham Palace, her 'office'. She tries to spend as few overnight stays in London as possible, even if it means a crack-of-dawn start or midnight finish. A typical day for Anne starts early with a short ride, necessary she says, because 'often it is the only challenging thing I have to do most days'. Many would argue with that too-modest statement. On a day she isn't flying or driving directly to an official engagement, she makes straight for Buckingham Palace around 7.30 a.m. She puts on her own make-up, something she really can't be fussed with, and chooses from her wardrobe – sparse by royal standards – before going through the day's itinerary with her ladies in waiting and private secretary, Lieutenant Colonel Peter Gibbs.

Always pushing herself, sometimes against her advisers' counsel, she can often carry out five or six engagements in one day, travelling hundreds of miles and taking in all sorts of places from factories and schools to fund-raising events and evening gala shows. She once said: 'There is no room for complacency. The need is always there.'

Now, for the first time in years, there are compensations. By being the first of the Queen's children to get a divorce (a four-minute 'quickie' in dingy Court Three of Somerset House on 23 April 1992), Anne is able to add a further fulfilment to her emancipated lifestyle as a thoroughly modern, unattached, hard-working woman. She is free to choose her own companions. As a royal aide confided at the time: 'The Princess adores the company of men and is unlikely to remain single for very long.'

What a difference a decree makes! Princess Anne revelled

in her new, free spirit by taking off her wedding ring. Her first official engagement after the divorce was to christen a new boat. The bottle of champagne she smashed against the bows of the *Pride of Teeside* was a symbolic moment for the Princess: the smashing of an old life and the celebration of her new one. Love glowed from her when she took to the floor with Commander Laurence at the Caledonian Ball in May of that year. It was the first time the deliriously happy couple had 'gone public'.

Religious, constitutional and legal problems were hastily overriden so that Anne could plan an early remarriage to Commander Laurence. Of all the royals, she was the first to have earned the right to decide her own destiny.

There was also a lesson for the monarchy itself in the way the British public took to the newly liberated Princess Royal. In the eyes of the nation, she had 'earned her stripes' by setting a shining example of good sense, good humour and sheer hard graft to the rest of her family. Princess Anne's perceptive biographer, John Parker, said on the day of the divorce announcement:

She has patently made an effort during the past few years to stand above the pop image of royalty, the sort that has brought some of her close relatives into disrepute. And those who take the constitutional monarchy seriously and believe there is a future for it beyond the soap-opera-style sagas into which it has sunk would recommend that, in spite of her divorce, the Princess Royal's style is the right course for its salvation. That is, if it is not already too late.

CHAPTER NINE

Prince Andrew

He was once the world's most eligible bachelor. Prince Andrew, spoiled rotten by his mother and father, grew up dashing, handsome and carefree. He became a playboy and a war hero. Although his elder brother and his two nephews are before him in the line of accession, it would be Andrew who would be called upon to act as regent if anything happened to Charles and Diana. Such power, such prestige, so many opportunities were handed on a plate to the lucky young man the popular press fondly labelled 'Randy Andy', and then he threw it all away.

Why did the playboy Prince, who fought with distinction in the Falklands conflict and returned home to a hero's welcome with a rose in his teeth, why did such a man turn inwards and become a lonely, reclusive husband and father, lacking the ability to communicate even with his own family? The first clues to Prince Andrew's psyche came at an early age when he found life in the nursery at Buckingham Palace to be character-forming in a less than pleasant way. 'He was not always a ray of sunshine,' his mother once observed. The tiny Andrew took delight in shouting abuse at the palace servants. One footman was so tormented that he gave the little Prince a great slap that sent him flying across a corridor. The poor servant immediately offered the Queen his resignation; she refused to accept it.

Evening visits from his mother and father were the highlight of Andrew's days at the palace, divorced as he was from common humanity. On one occasion he revealed his apalling early arrogance when the Queen and the Duke of Edinburgh put their heads round the nursery door as

Andrew and his nanny watched the television soap opera
Coronation Street. Startled, Andrew tried to disguise his
embarrassment at being caught out as a fan of Britain's
favourite downmarket saga. 'Oh God,' he exclaimed. 'Look
at these common people.' His father immediately rounded
on the young clever-dick and told him: 'If it were not for
people like that you would not be sitting here.'

Of Prince Philip's three sons, only Andrew seemed
to have enjoyed his father's rough, tough, old school,
Gordonstoun, and to have felt the benefit of retaining links
with it as an 'old boy'. It is significant, however, that he
was the only one of the Queen's sons to be passed over
for the position of head boy. He did make it to 'head of
house' (it would have been unthinkable for him not to
have done so) but the terrible snub of the headmaster
finding him unsuitable for the top title annoyed him ever
after. Andrew was not popular at the Scottish school,
where he was known as 'the Great I Am'. A contemporary
said: 'He was a boy with a big bottom who laughed at
his own jokes.' However, the military-style regime at
Gordonstoun obviously prepared him well for his career
as a Naval officer, one that his father had been forced to
curtail. (Philip no doubt envied Andrew the freedom that
he himself was denied when he married Princess Elizabeth.)

Just as at school, Andrew used his position to gain
unfair advantage over his fellow Naval officers. He often
got it wrong. One evening in the mess he graciously
informed a senior officer: 'You can call me Andy.'

Icily, the man replied: 'And you can call me sir!'

A colleague who trained with him at Dartford Naval

College in Devon said: 'He played "the Great I Am" all the time.' However, part of this seeming Teutonic bombast was put down to his enthusiasm for service life. Lacking any real self-motivation, drive or ambition, the discipline suited him. 'When I'm at sea I feel six inches taller,' he once said. 'One can ignore all that is going on in the rest of the world and get on with one's job.'

In the Royal Navy the Prince is known as 'H', short for His Royal Highness. His finest hour came when, for once, he stood up to his mother and threatened to resign from the Senior Service if she prevented him from seeing action in the Falklands War. In the South Atlantic, Andrew valiantly flew his Sea King helicopter to act as a decoy for the Argentinians' feared Exocet missiles aimed at his mother ship HMS *Invincible*. He rescued from death the crew of the supply ship *Atlantic Conveyor* when it was sunk by the enemy. No one can ever take such feats of heroism away from him.

A humbler Andrew emerged briefly from the heat of battle. 'It was,' he said with candour, 'horrific.' Asked what he most missed while at war, he replied: 'Silence and the smell of grass – and milk, that's what I wanted. I haven't had any real milk for five and a half months.' Humility also in this quote: 'I was just one of the pilots. We were all doing it; I guess I had to mature after seeing what I saw and feeling what I felt.'

His popularity, both among his colleagues in the Navy and with the press and public outside, peaked after the Falklands. He again began to reveal the arrogant, selfish streak that had originally set many against him. Despite his modest alcoholic intake, he has always preferred to hold court in the mess or in the pub rather than return home to his family. Even in the company of high-ranking fellow officers, he can display the worst excesses of boorishness and coarseness, more suited to the football terraces or to a school changing room than to the Senior Service. His artificial *bonhomie* has failed to endear him to the very people he seems determined to impress with his 'hail fellow well met' brand of conviviality.

A former shipmate has revealed a particularly unpleasant way in which one of them got his own back on the royal for displaying too much of his Hanoverian ancestors' arrogance. So unpopular was Andrew with the lower ranks, not to say his more humble fellow officers, that helpings of food being prepared for him in the galley sometimes received an extra ingredient not on the menu. On more than one occasion, said the informant, a crewman undid his fly and dipped his private part in the Prince's food before serving it to him.

Had uppity Andrew known, he would (quite understandably) have failed to see the funny side of such a coarse prank. Fond of playing practical jokes on others, he is nevertheless deeply offended when anyone tries the same tricks on him. His unsubtle humour and boorish behaviour were clearly displayed on an official visit to California in 1984. The Prince held court at a 'photo opportunity' in the Los Angeles black ghetto of Watts – and sprayed white paint over the press corps of photographers. 'I enjoyed that,' was his only comment on the embarrassing incident.

Respected CBS television commentator Bill Stout was

more voluble: 'It was the most unpleasant royal visit since they burnt the White House in 1812. When you recall that royalty used to have fun ravishing village maidens or chopping off people's heads, maybe we've been lucky with Prince Andrew. He settled for simply displaying his gross bad manners for everyone to see during his visit here. He reminded us that spoilt, rich kids are much the same the world over, no matter what their titles.'

The paint-spraying incident earned the Prince the title 'Duke of Yob' in the British press but he was quite proud of his jolly jape and boasted about it afterwards. No doubt he thought it helped his carefully honed devil-may-care image. For Prince Andrew nurtures a vision of himself as a 'real man's man', possibly because, as the Queen's favourite son, he is often seen as a bit of a 'mummy's boy'. Both views are a measure removed from the truth. Andy is nobody's boy but his own. 'I have lived a life quite happily on my own and I make friends as and when they come along,' he once said. A virtual teetotaller, he can sometimes appear almost prissy, only able to be 'one of the lads' when surrounded by his close, carefully chosen, respectful chums. Respectful is the operative word; astonishingly prickly about his royal position, he insists even today that his closest friends address him as 'Sir'.

Strangely for one so utterly conscious of his own eminent position, Prince Andrew has generally sought female companionship outside his class and social circle, even outside his own country.

His first love was Canadian Sandi Jones, a willowy blonde whom he met at the Montreal Olympics in 1976 when they were both 16. The colonel's daughter visited him regularly when he spent two terms studying at Lakefield College in Ontario. They spent blissful nights at a remote log cabin in northern Ontario, but young Sandi was stunned when the Prince proposed to her in the moonlight. She turned him down, knowing that it was all an impossible teenage dream. Sandi later confessed that she bitterly regretted rejecting him, and they continued to correspond regularly when Andrew returned to Britain. On visits to London she would see the Prince at Buckingham Palace and even attended his twenty-first birthday at Windsor Castle. When Andrew was in California on his infamous paint-spraying visit, he called in to see Sandi at the home she by then had in Beverly Hills.

Other girlfriends followed as Andrew tried to recapture the intensity of his first love affair. His romantic efforts soon earned him the soubriquet 'Randy Andy'. Former James Bond actress Carolyn Seward was just 17 years of age when she met Andrew at a Naval reception. 'We were immediately attracted,' she said. The ex-Miss UK beauty contestant was once spotted by a Buckingham Palace footman leaving Andrew's quarters at dawn. Carolyn was reportedly jealous when Andy invited another girl to the lavish party marking Princess Margaret's fiftieth birthday in 1980. His guest was model Gemma Curry, who was two years older than the 19-year-old playboy Prince.

Another actress and dancer, Finola Hughes, 32, dated Andy in 1983 before moving to America to find parts in the John Travolta movie *Staying Alive* and in the television soap *General Hospital*. Yet another actress, 31-year-old blonde Katie Rabett, dated Andy through most of 1984. She fell from favour when nude photographs of her were published in a Sunday newspaper; she went on to marry Kit Hesketh Harvey, a left-wing comedian with a transvestite act.

Stunningly beautiful Catherine Oxenburg, a star of the American television series *Dynasty*, was the last in a long line of actresses to be romantically linked with Prince Andrew. Catherine was 24 when they had their fling. However, even though she could claim royal blood (her grandparents were the deposed rulers of Yugoslavia and she is a third cousin to Prince Andrew) the romance quickly fizzled out.

The Queen must have breathed a sigh of relief in 1984 when she thought Andrew had found a suitable match at long last. The girl in question was Carolyn Herbert, an amazing Princess Diana 'lookalike', with whom the Prince spent several weekends. As the daughter of the Queen's racing manager, the Duke of Porchester, Carolyn seemed ideal material as an addition to the Royal Family. However, it was not to be, and only a year later she married bloodstock agent John Warren.

Once again, the Queen must have wished her son would settle down and wed after hearing of his Caribbean escapades that same year. Extrovert topless model Vicki Hodge couldn't wait to tell the world what had transpired when Andrew's ship HMS *Invincible* docked in Barbados. Indiscreet Vicki, who had a home on the island, earned £40,000 from a Sunday newspaper for revealing how Andy made love among the tropical flowers. The 37-year-old baronet's daughter introduced him to her friend, Tracie

Lamb, with whom Andy flirted, kissed and posed for pictures before vainly exhorting her not to talk to the press. But it was Vicki for whom the dashing Naval officer really fell.

Andrew's affair with Miss Hodge lasted for more than a week. Only much later did she confide that she had found the young prince immature; he had been lots of fun but 'just a little bit thick'. Vicki also revealed that when she first fell into bed with Andrew, she found one of his habits somewhat eccentric. It transpired that the lover-boy's brief encounters with previous girlfriends had been exactly that – all too brief. So one of his old flames had taught the young Prince the art of making their lovemaking interludes last longer. The method employed by Andrew during lovemaking was to count, as if he were counting sheep. However, what Miss Hodge found most disconcerting was that the Prince counted *out loud*!

Over the days and nights in the Caribbean, worldly-wise Vicki further tutored her royal lover in the art of making their passionate interludes more like marathons than sprints. After eight amazing days, the grateful Prince sailed off into the blue, presumably with a smile on his face.

However, the real love of Andrew's life was Kathryn 'Koo' Stark. A former soft-porn movie star, Koo captivated the playboy Prince. He fell desperately in love with her. The doyens of the British gossip columns, Nigel Dempster of the *Daily Mail* and rival Ross Benson of the *Daily Express*, both have a high regard for this American actress-turned-photographer with all the charm, femininity, sophistication and intelligence that Andrew so sadly lacks. Dempster has always claimed that Prince Andrew first met

Koo in a group of mutual friends at the writer's own house in February 1982. Koo and Andy wrote to each other during the Falklands War, then holidayed together at Princess Margaret's villa on the island of Mustique.

Koo was wonderful for Andrew. She understood the 'little boy' trying to get out of the carefully nurtured macho exterior. His affair with Koo, two years his senior, brought out a more sensitive side to his nature. She gave him the love he was lacking, the companionship he craved and the sophistication and style he so desperately needed. She deferred to him and allowed him to keep centre stage while still being ready to nurse his bruised honour and ego at every turn. The Royal Family liked Koo and entertained her at Balmoral. The Queen was impressed by her unexpected, demure demeanor. The Duke of Edinburgh found her entrancing. The Queen Mother was enchanted by her obvious love for her wayward grandson – but they were all horrified at the thought that Andrew might be considering marriage to her.

Their intense, 18-month relationship ended in 1983 when the Queen and the Duke of Edinburgh became alarmed at the continuing furore over her soft-porn cinematic credits. Loyal at least to his mother, Andrew cut the poor girl stone dead. Without having the decency even to telephone her, he ordered the Buckingham Palace switchboard not to put her calls through. It was a callous, though perhaps royally predictable, way of ending what had been an amazingly passionate love affair with a hugely loving and supportive young lady. A year later Koo married Green Shield Stamp heir Tim Jefferies, six years her junior.

They separated after only 15 months – less time than she spent with Andrew – and they divorced in 1989. *The People* newspaper alleged that she had continued her affair with the Prince after her marriage but she successfully sued them for libel and won damages of £300,000.

Prince Andrew's life story up to this time had been amazing enough but the events of the following decade could never be dreamed up by a movie scriptwriter, never mind predicted by the Royal Family, as they closed ranks and set about mapping out a safe, secure and hopefully scandal-free future for the Duke of York.

In hindsight, it is quite clear that both Prince Andrew and Sarah Ferguson married on the rebound. The love of Andrew's life was still Koo Stark; the love of Sarah's was still Paddy McNally. Andrew had been forced to drop Koo because of her unsuitability as a royal bride and new girlfriend, Sarah, arrived on the scene only a few months after the break-up of the great love of his life. Likewise, Sarah had decided to drop Paddy only after her failure to persuade him to marry her. The depth of her feelings towards him can be gauged by the fact that it was a full three months after meeting Andrew that she confronted McNally at the Italian Grand Prix in the autumn of 1985 and gave him the ultimatum: 'Marry me or I go.'

It was Fergie's pal, Princess Diana, who played cupid to the Prince and the Titian-haired Sloane Ranger. She engineered an invitation for Sarah to join the Royal Family for dinner at Windsor. Paddy McNally actually dropped her off at the gates! Later Diana asked Fergie to join her on an official tour of Andrew's frigate, HMS *Brazen*, when it visited the Port of London. The Queen also actively encouraged the blossoming affair between her son and the highly suitable Sarah. Prince Charles, too, was keen on a match between his boisterous brother and the daughter of his polo manager, Major Ron Ferguson.

Besotted, Andrew invited Fergie to join him at Floors Castle, home of his friends the Duke and Duchess of Roxburghe, and got down on one knee to propose. On 19 March 1986 he stood proudly by as his fiancée showed off an oval ruby surrounded by a cluster of ten diamonds on a yellow and white gold band. Andrew declared that he was 'over the moon' but after catching a stern glance from his fiancée he amended his considered comment on the engagement to: 'We are over the moon.'

Sarah, asked what had attracted her to the Prince, replied: 'It was his wit, charm and good looks.'

In turn, Andrew said: 'It was her red hair.' Asked whether he still thought that falling for Fergie had hit him like a thunderbolt, the sage young romancer riposted: 'I am at a loss really about what to say. I don't think Sarah is a thunderbolt.'

Quick as a flash, witty Sarah added: 'Nor am I a streak of lightning; nor is he.' And so on.

On 23 July, Prince Andrew led his radiant bride up the aisle of Westminster Abbey and later displayed his love to an estimated 500 million television spectators world-wide with a lingering kiss on the balcony of Buckingham Palace. Five days later the couple boarded the royal yacht *Britannia* for a honeymoon cruise to the Azores. He declared that 'married life is wonderful' and added that his decision to wed Sarah 'was and always will be' the best he would ever make.

In the early months of their marriage the Duke and Duchess of York could barely keep their hands off one another. Andrew would take every opportunity to touch his new wife. They would link arms when walking up stairs. He would fondle her when pinning on a brooch. On a skiing holiday at Klosters in February 1987 she snuggled up to a proudly grinning Andrew and said: 'Save your energy for later, darling. You'll need it!' They would kiss quite openly in public. His nickname for her was 'Fergie chops'. During an interview she patted his knee, saying 'I'm so proud of my boy'. Indeed, their body language was amazing; their movements mirrored one another, a sure sign of a compatible physical relationship, according to psychologists. In the couple's interview with *Hello* magazine, Fergie said: 'The most important thing I felt, and now looking back I know this definitely, is his amazing ability to make one feel like a lady, like a woman.'

The trouble with Andrew and Sarah was that, although matched physically, they soon found that this was the only way they had of communicating with each other and that a physical relationship alone was not sufficiently strong as a rock upon which to found an entire marriage. Fergie is irrepressibly bright but neither she nor Andrew is particularly articulate. When he attempted to express his feelings to one interviewer, he came out with: 'I think the simplest way to put it is that I still don't know why I love my wife. It's rather complicated to put across. I love her; that's the end of the story.'

Author and 'agony uncle' Phillip Hodson commented: 'Fergie and Andrew are emotionally illiterate. They don't seem able to communicate to one another how they feel.'

In November 1987 Andrew, who had been doing roughly a nine-to-five job as a flying instructor, decided to go back to sea. Keen to relaunch his career in the Navy, he joined the crew of the destroyer HMS *Edinburgh*. Fergie was upset but threw herself into what she saw as the royal round of duties, rewarding herself with many a freebie jollification, sometimes with her husband, sometimes without.

The following May saw the first cooling of their passion. Andrew, somewhat hypocritically in view of his own juicy past, was horrified when a newspaper revealed that Major Ron Ferguson had been frequenting a notorious London massage parlour euphemistically entitled the Wigmore Club. The Royal Family rallied round in an obvious show of support for Sarah's disgraced father. Secretly, however, Andrew was furious at this indiscretion which he saw as reflecting badly on his family. Fergie was pregnant at the time of the scandal and, happily, the birth of their first child, Princess Beatrice, served both to cause the public to forgive and forget Major Ron and also to pull the young couple closer together again.

Foreign tours to Australia and Canada followed, along with a liberal sprinkling of unofficial junketing. Andrew celebrated his thirtieth birthday dancing with a very pregnant Fergie at a London nightspot. Two months later, in March 1990, Andrew rushed home on 48 hours' leave to share a romantic dinner in a swish Mayfair restaurant. Only a week later he was the father of a second baby girl,

Princess Eugenie. However, even this fresh addition to the family was not enough to rekindle their early bliss.

Showing off their children in a much-criticised article in *Hello* magazine, the wide smiles barely hid the underlying trouble. Fergie was quoted as saying: 'Andrew and I don't really have any hobbies together; there isn't the time. I find weekending the worst. When he goes away for a long period of time you know you're not going to see him for six or eight weeks and then we'll see him at the end. Fine. But weekends are difficult because he's working Monday through Friday. He comes back tired on Friday night.'

By then Andrew's marriage had begun to totter as he spent longer and longer periods away from home with the Navy. It was in 1990 that the Duchess let slip: 'We've only spent 42 nights together.'

There had been no shoulder for Fergie to lean on for most of her marriage. Andrew went away a hot-blooded hero and came back to a life less glamorous than he had expected. Despite his wife's emotional welcomes and her constant flattery (she was the one who insisted on including the word 'obey' in their wedding service) Andrew was cold and surly. She placated him, cajoled him and in the end pandered to his every selfish whim. It was obviously a thankless task.

His wife was fanatical about her support for him and about fulfilling her domestic role – the role she thought her seagoing Prince would appreciate. She was wrong. The Duchess of York gave up her job, gave up smoking, lost an amazing amount of weight, even went to deportment classes. She left her baby at home to follow her husband to Australia but it was all to no avail. When she turned to him for support under a welter of criticism, he was nowhere to be seen.

Fergie used to be a heavy smoker. She has been photographed at the Verbier home she shared with Paddy McNally, seated at a table surrounded by empty bottles and cigarette packets, looking for all the world as if she was trying to roll her own fag! Strong-willed as ever, Fergie managed to give up the habit but then she started having the odd cigarette when she went skiing with Beatrice in Klosters in 1991. Friends said her crumbling marriage was to blame for the return to the weed.

Andrew's reputation for not being too bright, particularly in his taste and approach to women, became increasingly obvious as the marriage went from rickety to ragged. His wife was tormented by press attacks upon her. She pretended not to read the newspapers but she sometimes devoured them and ended up in tears. She once told Ingrid Seward, editor of *Majesty* magazine: 'I am tough on the outside but I'm marshmallow on the inside,' adding ominously: 'Andrew doesn't understand.'

At that time, her husband, then a lieutenant commander, was safely away at sea and had unsympathetically told his wife to 'take no notice'. 'Taking no notice' was what Andrew was good at. At the time Ingrid Seward was interviewing Fergie, the Duchess had just adopted a dramatically new bobbed hairstyle. When asked what Andrew thought of it, she replied that he had not mentioned it, not even once. 'He didn't say whether he liked it or not,' she said sadly, 'so it probably means he doesn't like it.' Neither did Andrew take much notice of his wife's career. Even though she wrote him in as a character in her Budgie books and sent him a first copy of every one, he did no more than flick through them. 'I thought it was good to include him,' said Fergie. 'His ship was called *Campbelltown* and I changed it in the book to 'Camballtown'. Andrew didn't notice.

Asked about her husband's attitude to his family, the Duchess of York said shruggingly: 'It's what I'm used to, from the moment I married a Naval officer. He's happy as long as his wife and children are happy.' Warm-hearted Fergie, in stark contrast, describes her children as 'my world – they are the only thing in my life that I know is 100 per cent safe and loving and wonderful'.

What came across at the time his marriage was beginning to falter was the arrogant, unfeeling behaviour of the Duke. In the whole of 1990 he spent only 42 days with his wife and family. During those fraught 42 days his wife was desperate for his support as she came under an endless barrage of criticism. He displayed a regal indifference to his wife's suffering, peppered only with long moods that she could not break into. Friends have revealed that he would spend his leave periods slumped in front of a video at his bad-taste home, Sunninghill, in Berkshire. Now and again he would rouse himself to play a game of golf with his rent-a-chums.

Prince Andrew's obsession with golf has also been blamed for driving his marriage off course. Although he had toyed with golf at school, the Prince took his first lesson in 1989 and soon his wife was left to find her own entertainment as he spent more and more of his home leave playing the private courses at Windsor and Sandringham. His handicap came down to 15. When they moved into their new home at Sunninghill, Fergie found that Swinley Forest golf course, at Ascot, was far too close for her liking. Worse was to come.

In the summer of 1991 he joined Edinburgh's Royal Burgess Golfing Society, one of the country's most élite golf clubs and one that allows only male members. Women are allowed in the clubhouse only as guests. If they wished to play they would have to change in the car park. According to Jack Lamport Mitchell, a top sports psychologist: 'It may seem strange but some golf widows would rather their husbands find another woman, because that would be a foe they could understand, rather than playing second fiddle to a game.'

Fergie's feelings were summed up in the comment she made to a friend: 'The only way I shall see my husband is if he takes me on as a caddie.' On another occasion she told *Majesty* magazine: 'I spend a huge amount of time on my own and I don't like playing golf. Maybe when I'm 50 I will but at the moment it's not my scene.'

The portents of the scandal that was to shake the Royal Family and shatter his marriage could, perhaps, have been forecast by Andrew, had he been a more perceptive character, way back in 1990. It was then that his wife flew off to North Africa without him on the private family jet of Texan Steve Wyatt. They vacationed with a small group of friends at a Moroccan hotel before Fergie again flew off on the Wyatt jet to continue her holiday in the South of France. Sometime later she shredded all of Andrew's love letters, with the excuse that they might one day be stolen.

In July 1991 Andrew attended his last official public engagement with his wife. The less-than-musical couple seemed to suffer rather than enjoy a performance of *Don Giovanni* at a Sheffield theatre. Their own act, however, still fooled the British public. A magazine poll in September revealed that, whereas only 8 per cent believed that Charles and Diana were in love, a whopping 75 per cent believed that Andrew and Sarah were. It was far from the truth, as Fergie's gaunt looks and Andrew's gloomy ones revealed. Andrew began spending more time enjoying country pursuits with his parents, while Fergie spent more time at Buckingham Palace and less at the family home, Sunninghill.

The slow-fused timebomb eventually went off in January 1992 when 120 photographs were found in a London flat once occupied by playboy Steve Wyatt. Confused and bitter, Prince Andrew withdrew into his shell. He was horrified when he saw the snapshots of his wife laughing and joking, cheek by jowl, with a handsome young playboy – just like himself in earlier, happier days. A picture of Wyatt with his arm around Princess Beatrice was the last straw.

Predictably, Andrew went straight to Mummy. The Queen desperately tried to save the marriage of her favourite son but in March Fergie asked her permission for a divorce. The Duchess called in her lawyer, Charles Doughty, and recalled her closest pal, Lulu Blacker, from a Swiss skiing holiday to spend long, tearful hours mapping out her plans. At Andrew's behest, the Queen summoned royal lawyer Sir Matthew Farrer.

As the story of their split began to leak out, anxious Andrew kept in touch with the press-fuelled inferno by having early copies of newspapers faxed to his private study. He still breakfasted with his wife and children at Sunninghill before leaving for work but, according to a member of staff, they were 'pretty cold, formal meals without much chatting'. On 19 March the pretence was ended. A formal separation was announced by Buckingham Palace.

True to form, when his marriage collapsed, Andrew sought old friends for comfort. He contacted the former love of his life, Koo Stark, despite the fact that he had so cruelly dumped her when his mother became upset at her unfortunate movie-star past. Koo, who lived in a Kensington flat purchased with part of her £300,000 libel award, had avoided association with the Prince since his marriage six years earlier but she had bumped into Andrew at least once, at a party given in 1990 by Michael Pearson, heir to the fabulously wealthy Viscount Cowdray. Shamefully, the Duke of York cut her dead. However, according to one newspaper report, when Andrew realised that his marriage was at an end he telephoned Koo and received the sympathy he expected from a loyal old flame.

Andrew also sought out another old friend at this stressful time, the Duchess of Roxburghe, who, with her husband, Guy, had been host to the couple when Andrew proposed to Sarah at their magnificent Georgian home Floors Castle, in the Scottish Borders. In Andrew, Jane Roxburghe had found a shoulder to cry on when she ditched the

Duke in 1990, accusing him of womanising. Now she returned the favour. Her home was within an hour's drive of Andrew's frigate HMS *Campbelltown* when it docked at Rosyth. According to royal insiders, Prince Andrew made frequent visits to the 38-year-old divorcee during the final months leading up to his split with Fergie in March 1992.

There were few other people Andrew could turn to, apart from his mother and father. Despite the camaraderie of service life and the queue of fawning followers who would like his patronage, he has no one with whom to share his private thoughts. His few close friends include his Gordonstoun contemporary Charlie Young and his shipmate and golfing partner Wayne Sheridan, but without them he is insecure. He is ill at ease in large groups; he hates nightclubs; he is most at home slouched like a couch potato watching a video. He is no conversationalist. Unlike his brother, Charles, who has a voracious thirst for knowledge, Andrew barely reads a book. He enjoys gossip but has little to say for himself. He is regularly described as 'oafish' by acquaintances who ill-disguise their annoyance at his boorish behaviour and coarse manners.

At the end of the day, Andrew is probably a bachelor at heart. A loner. Even lonely. He is no 'mummy's boy' but he does seem to prefer the company of his close family – with a few liaisons on the side – to any serious domestic responsibilities. When he married the Duchess of York, Prince Andrew insisted that their rooms at Buckingham Palace remain unchanged, even after the birth of his two daughters. The rooms were his old bachelor quarters. The boy had never grown up.

CHAPTER TEN

Fergie

At first she was jolly old Fergie, the girl next door who blew away the cobwebs and breathed fresh air through the corridors of the 'old Firm'. Sarah Ferguson, brought up on a farm in Hampshire, not only *looked* the jolly hockey sticks sort, she whooped and yelled her way into the Royal Family as though she *was* on a hockey field.

Exactly six years on from the announcement of her engagement to Prince Andrew, it was a very bitter and sad young woman who retreated from the royal circle in circumstances utterly unprecedented in the history of the British monarchy. In publicity that reached every corner of the globe, and a scandal that blew the country's mighty monarchy apart, Sarah Ferguson, mother of two little princesses, wife of the Queen's second son and daughter-in-law to the world's most established figurehead, had quite simply given the Royal Family up.

Not since the abdication of Edward had so much been written about such a royal uproar. The split between Sarah, Duchess of York, and Andrew, Duke of York, the ensuing press coverage, public speculation and opinion, together with the most vitriolic of palace reactions, made it, in the words of royal-watchers 'a blockbuster'.

What made the events of March 1992 so riveting was their suddenness. Royal followers realised that their eyes, which had been so firmly focused on the marital discord of Princess Diana and Prince Charles, had completely missed the very real and desperate turmoil between Fergie and her dashing Naval officer husband. No one had even contemplated that anything was amiss. Yes, Fergie had just emerged from some of the most highly publicised and stressful few months of her life, but it was never considered that her sometimes bizarre behaviour of late 1991 and early 1992 was hiding a very tragic secret, that she had fallen out of love with her husband and was soon to fall out of favour with the Royal Family.

The exclusive newspaper report that served up the shock revelation was in the *Daily Mail* on Wednesday, 19 March 1992. The headline, which swept news of the forthcoming general election from the front page, said simply: 'Andrew and Fergie to part'. Every other paper had seen the *Mail's* front page late the night before and followed suit. What made the news even more convincing for editors was the lack of a vehement denial from the Buckingham Palace press office. In fact there was no denial at all, just a very uneasy silence. To hardened reporters, used to dealing with the most difficult of media manipulators, this was virtually a confirmation.

It came as no surprise when, mid-morning the next day, the most terse of official royal statements was made. Tellingly omitting the normal address of Her Royal Highness in relation to a female member of the Royal Family, the Queen had carefully worded as much as she wanted to reveal to the world. The announcement said:

> In view of the media speculation which the Queen finds especially undesirable during the general election campaign, Her Majesty is issuing the following statement. Last week lawyers acting for the Duchess of York initiated discussions about a formal separation for the Duke and Duchess. These dis-

cussions are not yet completed and nothing will be said until they are. The Queen hopes that the media will spare the Duke and Duchess of York and their children any intrusion.

It was strange that the Queen had seemingly used the words 'last week' quite unnecessarily. There had been no substantial hint of marriage problems between Sarah and Andrew until the *Daily Mail*'s story just 24 hours before. Missing were the oft-used words of royal statements issued in similar circumstances – 'sadness' and 'regret'. Within moments of the announcement, the palace went out of its way to stress that, with immediate effect, the Duchess would no longer be undertaking royal engagements. Within an hour, Sarah left her Sunninghill Park home near Windsor in a Vauxhall Carlton estate car piled with bags and cases.

Rumoured comments by Sarah were rife. She was 'fed up' with the lack of support she had received from 'the Firm', she could 'no longer stand it' and her marriage was 'past saving'. The palace hit back. It froze her out and claimed that Sarah had hired her own public-relations expert to stage-manage her separation from Andrew. The expert in question was Sir Tim Bell, who strongly denied any involvement.

The battle royal got bloodier. On the day of the statement, radio listeners heard BBC diplomatic and court correspondent Paul Reynolds report: 'The knives are out for Fergie in the palace.' He went on the BBC's *World at One* programme after a briefing at Buckingham Palace to reveal:

They are claiming she has been employing a public-relations firm to brief the *Daily Mail* which is the source of the story. They even name the firm and the gentleman concerned and they are getting their briefing in now in retaliation. I have rarely heard palace officials speak in such terms about someone. They are talking about her unsuitability for public life, royal life, her behaviour in being photographed in *Hello* magazine, fooling around putting paper bags on her head on an aircraft while she was being watched by reporters.

Reynolds was referring to Fergie's behaviour of the last couple of years, and most recently on a flight she had made from Miami to Heathrow that January. He also made reference to the fact that the *Daily Mail* had reported a private lunch the Duchess had had with the Queen, adding that the palace believed the only person who could be responsible for talking about this meeting was the Duchess herself. The BBC man also said that the palace blamed the Duchess for initiating proceedings to bring her marriage to an end and that she had deliberately organised a media leak so that there was no alternative to the separation becoming official.

Where had Reynolds got all this information? It was to transpire that he had gleaned it during a conversation with the Queen's press secretary, Charles Anson, in a quiet moment *after* an official press briefing. Ending what had been 72 hours of one of the most dramatic royal sagas ever witnessed, Mr Anson was forced to make a public apology to the Duchess for his attack which, reported the *Daily Mail*, 'bordered on personal abuse'. Anson had even offered his resignation to the Queen but had been allowed to stay.

In his apology he said:

Yesterday I gave to the media a short statement concerning the marriage of the Duke and Duchess of York in terms authorised by the Queen. It was that statement alone, and factual answers to questions as to future arrangements, that were authorised by Her Majesty. As head of the Buckingham Palace press office, I accept full responsibility for anything said beyond that, and I very much regret that what was said should have been interpreted by the media to the detriment of the Duchess of York, to whom I have offered my personal apologies. I have also apologised to the Queen and both Her Majesty and Her Royal Highness have been kind enough to accept these apologies.

While the announcements and the presses thumping out the latest twist in this tantalising royal saga rolled on, Sarah and Andrew grimly tried to carry on as normally as possible. A pinched-faced Sarah stuck to the family routine of dropping her eldest daughter, Princess Beatrice, off at school. A grim-jawed Andrew still drove the 20-minute journey from Sunninghill Park to Camberley where he was on a training course. On the Friday of the crisis, he was spotted walking in the bleak cold with the Queen in the grounds of Windsor Castle. Both Andrew and Fergie determinedly ignored the packs of reporters that greeted them everywhere they went. The couple locked themselves away in their home that weekend, desperate to retain some family unity for the sake of the younger daughter, Eugenie, who was to celebrate her second birthday the following Monday. As one royal insider said: 'The semblance of normality must be maintained at all costs. The Queen expects nothing less.'

Quietly, Sarah and Andrew were making their own plans; he to return home to his mother and his former bachelor rooms at Windsor Castle and Buckingham Palace; she to retire from royal life for ever.

It was a tragic end to what had been one of the most exciting romances of the century. The love between a dashingly handsome young Naval officer and a vibrantly attractive girl from the country would have been captivating enough in itself. Adding the royal ingredient made it headline material around the world.

Everybody wanted to know every detail of the story of this amazing young lady who had captured the heart of a prince. It was reported that Sarah Ferguson, born on 15 October 1959, had been, predictably, 'bright but naughty' at school (she had once glued her teacher to a chair).

She had first gone to Daneshill School, near Basingstoke, Hampshire, where she excelled at sport. At her next school, Hurst Lodge, at Sunningdale, Berkshire, she gained six 'O-level' examination passes (six more than her good chum and royal mentor Princess Diana). After school came a period at a 'crammer' before she took a secretarial course so that, according to her family, she could 'get a job anywhere in the world'. In fact, she ended up joint bottom of the class and her first job was as a secretary in a London public-relations firm. She soon landed a £20,000-a-year job helping to run the London office of fine-art publishers Richard Burton. Even in these early days, young, free and single, Sarah wangled extended time off for holidays. One of these was a trip to Argentina to visit her mother, Susan.

Her mother had left Sarah's father, Major Ron Ferguson, and run off with handsome Argentinian polo player Hector Barrantes. Major Ron was left to run the family farm at Dummer, Hampshire. He divorced his wife in 1974 and set about bringing up his two daughters, Jane and Sarah. Sarah was a great support to her father when her mother bolted. She acted as a little mop-haired 'mother' herself, cooking, cleaning and helping muck out down on the farm. She was once quoted as saying: 'It would have been awful for them to go on living together if they were at each other's throats all day.'

Sarah Ferguson was always extremely proud of her father, particularly after his appointment as Prince Charles's polo manager. When her father remarried – to farmer's daughter Susan Deptford who, at 28, was 15 years his junior – teenage Fergie remained diplomatically friendly with both her absent mother and her new stepmum. (She was equally supportive when, 13 years later, her father was caught visiting a London massage parlour where sexual services were offered. Sarah was about to give birth to her first baby at the time and celebrations were not noticeably marred by her dad's sexual indiscretions.)

Quite apart from Major Ron's mixed marital fortunes, the press were able, in the early days of 'Fergiemania', to dig up some interesting vignettes in daughter Sarah's short romantic history. Two men had particularly influenced Fergie's early years. The first was Kim Smith-Bingham, tall, handsome, two years her senior, with a job in the City. When Sarah was 19 he wooed her with flowers and squired her to the Ritz and to nightspots like Annabel's. Smith-Bingham said later that the relationship had been a casual affair. 'We were too young for people to have thought of us as a long-term couple,' he said. However, Fergie thought differently. He had been her first real boyfriend and his apparent dismissal of their young love hurt her.

It was Smith-Bingham who introduced Sarah Ferguson to her next boyfriend, former racing driver Paddy McNally. Both Smith-Bingham and McNally had homes in the Swiss resort of Verbier, one of Fergie's favourite ski haunts.

Impressionable Sarah was awed by worldly-wise McNally's social contacts and by the way he knew his way around. Despite an amazing age difference of 22 years, they became lovers; they lived together on and off for about four years. She was very good with his two sons from a previous marriage, Sean and Rollo, but Paddy never saw her as a potential wife.

During a rather on-off period with McNally Sarah became the specific friend and confidante of Princess Diana. The two women had first been introduced to one another at a Cowdray Park polo match during Diana's courtship by the Prince of Wales. Fergie became a frequent visitor to Buckingham Palace and took tea with Di, the Queen and the Queen Mother. It was inevitable that she should meet Diana's dashing young brother-in-law, Prince Andrew, and it was inevitable that Andrew, lonesome after having to give up his sexy actress girlfriend Koo Stark, should be attracted to the flame-haired temptress, Sarah.

One morning in the summer of 1985 Paddy McNally drove Sarah down the M4 to Windsor Castle so that she could take up an invitation to join the Queen's house party during the week of Royal Ascot races. Paddy dropped her off at the castle's private side entrance, little realising that he himself would soon be 'dropped' in fickle Fergie's romantic affections. As Sarah unpacked she saw on her bedside table a card showing the seating plan for luncheon. She was placed next to Prince Andrew. The layout was no coincidence, for her chum Princess Diana had decided to try a little match-making. It obviously worked, because Andrew and Sarah were virtually inseparable throughout the day's racing and beyond. Her former flatmate Carolyn Cotterell recalls: 'When she came back from Ascot she had stars in her eyes. She had been bowled over.'

Paddy came a loser in love following that day at the races, although ever after he has loyally refused all blandishments to reveal any details of his long love affair with Miss Ferguson.

Sarah herself was pretty good at keeping a secret. At the time she lived in a modest terrace house in Clapham, south-west London, with flatmate Carolyn Beckwith-Smith. The phone ran hot with calls from the Prince but Carolyn helped to keep their relationship quiet for about six months during which even Sarah was still unaware of where it would all lead. The turning point came when Sarah told Paddy McNally, with whom she had still kept in close contact, that since he was obviously not the marrying kind they could no longer see each other. On 23 February 1986, at Floors Castle in Scotland, Andrew asked Sarah to be his wife. He went down on bended knee to pop the question. She said: 'When you wake up tomorrow morning you can tell me it's a joke.' The following day she realised that the Prince was deadly earnest and confirmed her acceptance, although they still had to wait for the Queen's permission before an official engagement could be announced.

The secret courtship continued. There were regular meetings when Andrew docked with his ship, HMS *Brazen*, for brief but romantic periods of shore leave. One of those reunions clinched what the press had suspected all along. Wearing a check dress and coat, Sarah met Andrew at the quayside and there was something, just something, about the way they greeted each other that meant the two were very close. The secret was out.

The first time Sarah spoke about her friendship with Prince Andrew was a tale of how the two had hurled bread rolls at each other over lunch. That was when she realised she loved him, Sarah told a world agog at such very unroyal behaviour. It hadn't been like that with Diana Spencer and Prince Charles, newsmen mused; their love had blossomed on a polo field. However, press and public alike still found the openness of royal newcomer, Fergie, endearing.

If the Queen had reservations about the freckled redhead who had captured the heart of her second son, she uncharacteristically kept them to herself. Perhaps Sarah was just what the Royal Family needed at a time when it was increasingly coming under fire for its élitist, out-of-touch image with the British people.

By the time Andrew and Sarah's engagement was officially announced, on 19 March 1986, the Queen had already deliberated long and hard about such a match. She had meetings with the Queen Mother, a professional at dealing with the young royals and the problems they brought into the family. The Queen and her mother once talked long into the night about whether their agreement to the relationship was right. Would Sarah be a blessing to the Royal Family or would her wild ways and common touch be an embarrassment? Sarah was despatched to see the Queen Mother at Clarence House before the engagement was approved. The Queen Mother offered the somewhat intimidated Sarah a gin and tonic. She smiled when the nervous girl accepted. From that moment on the Queen Mother had a soft spot for Miss Ferguson, a patronage that held Sarah in good stead as her behaviour deteriorated over the years.

The Queen and other senior members of her family, position and tradition instilled in them since birth, may have tut-tutted under their breath when Sarah not only beamed broadly as she waltzed down the aisle with her handsome prince in July 1986 but also pulled the goggle-eyed face that was to become her trademark and then actually *winked*. The Queen Mother just smiled indulgently.

The first sign that this was to be no ordinary royal

marriage came when journalists began digging up young Sarah's high life in Verbier and her love life with Paddy McNally. The couple's frantic socialising at Paddy's Verbier chalet, 'The Castle', was recalled. It amounted to a string of wild dinner parties for the rich, famous, bizarre and exotic. It was reported that as well as vast quantities of alcohol, other diversions were sometimes enjoyed at these functions. Newspapers got hold of old snapshots of Fergie surrounded by empty bottles and cigarette packets and one of her riding a bicycle into a swimming pool!

Such stories did, if anything, enhance Sarah Ferguson's standing in the public esteem. She was a wild child of the eighties who might just put a bit of much-needed pizazz into the moribund image of the Royal Family. Despite her four-year affair with McNally, people seemed to find it intriguing rather than scandalous that the Duchess of York was the first royal bride in a long time to go to the altar in a state less than virginal.

It did not take long, however, for the fickle, critical public to turn. In flame-haired Sarah's case, that point was reached less than two months after the birth of her first daughter in August 1988. In fact, the birth was at 8.18 on the eighth day of the eighth month of 1988, said in some Oriental cultures to be an omen of good fortune ahead.

Up until then her love of fun as the wife of a Royal Navy husband was thought endearing by those who had become Fergie fans. Many appreciated her excellent good sense at being determined to carry on a career. Here at last, they all thought, was a high-spirited girl who would bring the Royal Family closer in touch with the people. She was certainly breaking the mould of traditional marriages within the monarchy.

Fergie kept her old job with London-based company BCK Graphics. Her rumoured salary of £24,000 was for seeking out new projects in the publishing world. However, treacle-sweet press reports about the new royal refusing to abandon her career failed to mention that her working hours were, to say the least, flexible. One of her publishing bosses was quoted as saying: 'Fergie has a job with a salary. She is a working girl like the rest of us, except that her office is in Buckingham Palace.' Another gushed to a magazine: 'Every day you see her it's a great joy.' Deep down, however, most of her colleagues knew that Fergie's commitment to her work was waning.

When she took a job with the auction house Sothebys, it was thought that some of the fine arts she was dealing with might rub off on her. But the only thing that was off was Fergie; she was never there! Despite a denial that she was paid £24,000 a year for her services (a moot point — in fact she was paid £28,000), her colleagues were perplexed that the Duchess was never to be seen earning even a penny of it. She turned up one evening to pass royally along a line of other staff, including a very bemused black lady with an armful of lavatory rolls, and inquired of a highly respected, extremely talented art historian: 'Aren't you awfully young?'

Fergie's interest in her job seemed to wane in inverse proportion to the anger of her colleagues. When a depression in the art market forced Sothebys to announce redundancies, the board asked senior staff for suggestions as to cost savings. The response was clear: 'Sack Fergie!' So, without a fuss, without any announcement to the press or even to the poor staff, Fergie departed to continue her ride on the royal bandwagon towards fresher, even greener pastures!

It had seemed a great idea at the time for the Royal Family sweetheart to cram into her life a career, charity appearances, formal dinners, less formal nightclubbing, a host of sporting hobbies, hours of flying lessons to earn her wings (and the nickname 'Chatterbox') plus a generous smattering of holidays (she had already had three by the height of Fergiemania in mid-1987 and two more were planned). What suffered, of course, were her official engagements and her children.

Little was heard about Sarah's last days as a career girl. Much was heard, however, when just seven weeks after giving birth to Princess Beatrice she left her behind for a tour of Australia. Whereas the public seemed willing to accept her gadabout lifestyle as a single girl and as a young bride, they did not take kindly to the way she ignored the responsibilities of motherhood. Her visit to Australia brought all her other trips and free holidays sharply into focus and the Duchess of York's popularity suddenly began to slide.

On that Australian tour of 1988 the Duchess came in for an astonishing salvo of vicious, personal criticism. One newspaper commented on her 'waddle'. Another said her husband wore the expression of a man 'making a slow recovery from a kick in the soft extremities'. The *Sydney*

Morning Herald added further insult to the Duchess by stating: 'Her general aura of awkwardness was exacerbated by her choice of clothes – a pale suit of matronly cut, topped by a hat resembling an ocean swell at Bondi.' The newspaper said Andrew lived up to his reputation of being rather wooden and dull and complained that Fergie showed scarcely a sign of the rugged individualism, let alone the high spirits, that had sometimes incurred the Queen's displeasure.

The papers also reported on the question a little girl put to the Duchess during a visit to Canberra's Child Therapy Centre. It was the question no one else had dared ask. The waiting press held its breath when tiny Melissa Webster held Fergie's hand and whispered: 'Where's your baby?' After thinking for just a moment, the Duchess replied: 'She's at home. She needs to sleep at home. She loves her bed.'

Fergie was away in Australia for seven weeks. She had broken new ground, even by recent royal standards, in leaving her baby behind for such a long period (although the Queen once left Charles and Anne for six months). For although there had always been the tradition that royal children are not taken on tours, they have almost always been left in the loving care of grandparents. Fergie had left her baby with nanny Alison Wardley. The talk was that by the time Fergie made her return on 2 November 1988, Princess Beatrice believed that Alison was her mother.

In all ways, 1988 was not a good year for the Duchess, who was finding it more and more of a strain to conform with royal tradition and discipline and with the ideals of a critical public. There had been her visit to Meribel in the French Alps in February that year. The Duchess had been visiting the top resort to appear at a ski championship organised by the Combined Services Winter Sports Association, of which she was patron. She had only four hours' work to do but arrived three days early! She was then accused of grossly unladylike behaviour.

The story of Fergie's behaviour on the trip somehow seemed so much worse when it was revealed that her chalet was lent free of charge for the week by its owner, Lady Lorna Cooper Kay, and that the Duchess had used a free aeroplane from the Royal Flight to get her there and back. The trip and accommodation were worth around £55,000. Fergie also had a convoy of free Range Rovers at her beck and call. Said one aide: 'It's embarrassing. She'll do any-thing to scrounge a week's skiing.'

By the start of 1989, the Duchess of York had earned herself a new title: Her Royal Idleness. A poll revealed that more than a third of the country now believed she represented the worst value for taxpayers' money among the royals. One in five questions said their opinion of the whole Royal Family had fallen.

The timing of the poll by a Sunday newspaper was deliberate. The Royal Family was already in the firing line for its lack of public compassion over the horrific bombing of a Pan-Am jumbo jet over Lockerbie, when no royal volunteered to break his or her Christmas–New Year holiday to mourn the 270 dead, and for their display of unconcern for the victims of London's Clapham rail dis-aster, in January 1989, when none of the royals, it seemed, could be bothered to attend a memorial service for the 35 dead; they already had other plans. In the end, it was only Fergie who made an appearance and even then it was by the skin of her teeth. The press counted down the hours as she made her way to the service at Winchester Cathedral after flying back from yet another skiing holiday. Although picked up by limousine at Heathrow Airport, she insisted on switching to a soft-top Jaguar sports car to continue her journey to the cathedral. Fergie had got it wrong again.

In that same 1989 poll, the questions asked were not simply to judge Fergie's popularity (although 34 per cent asked said she had done the most damage to the Royal Family). The public also lashed out at holiday-mad Fergie returning to the Klosters ski slopes where Prince Charles's close pal, Major Hugh Lindsay, had died in an avalanche the year before. Fergie was also criticised for 'not giving a damn about public opinion' and for not listening to her advisers.

In July 1989, Fergie was off again, this time for a 12-day tour of Canada. Royal aides said the tour schedule was too hectic to enable baby Beatrice to go along too. Now 21 months old, Princess Beatrice was again left in the hands of her nanny. By the end of that year, Fergie had enjoyed eight holidays, including an 11-day visit to see her sister, Jane Makim, in Australia. The Duchess was unable to keep secret the fact that she stayed at a £250-a-night hotel on Bedarra Island off Australia's Great Barrier Reef. In fact, Fergie was helping her elder sister, Jane, aged 34, to get over her split with her Queensland cattle farmer husband, Alex Makim. Jane was caught up in a nightmare divorce-court battle for the custody of her children, Seamus, ten, and Ayesha, five.

The effect of the criticism must have hit home to Fergie. Back in Britain she told an onlooker during a visit to a new community centre in Stapenhill, Staffordshire: 'The reporters have got it all wrong about me. They say people don't like me but look at how many people are standing here in the cold today. This is the best welcome I have ever had.'

The Duchess of York's public image altered little in 1990. In October she was packing for her seventh holiday of the season, in Australia, the third trip there in as many years. Her holidays in 1990 had already included Switzerland in January, Morocco in May, America in June, Argentina and the South of France in July and Balmoral in August. There were the odd, additional holiday weekends, and an eighth vacation before the year was out. She was recalled from that one by the Queen, who thought the gadfly of the ski slopes was safer spending Christmas with the rest of the royals rather than with the fun folk of St Moritz!

In 1991 the roving redhead took seven holidays. In November she was the only senior royal not to attend either the Festival of Remembrance at the Albert Hall or the Remembrance Service at the Cenotaph. She was 3,500 miles away, staying with friends in Toronto. The British public was particularly baffled by her absence as her husband was a serving Naval officer and veteran of the Falklands War. Labour MP Peter Snape, an ex-corporal in the Royal Engineers, was prompted to protest: 'People are starting to ask whether or not they are getting value for money, particularly from her.'

Newspapers began totting up Fergie's freebies. They included air fares of £22,000 for herself and five friends to start the Whitbread Round-the-World Yacht Race in South America. There were fur coats worth £3,000 on one of her Canadian visits. Gifts worth £17,000 were collected by her and Andy during the couple's visit to Venice. On a visit to a Los Angeles shop she hinted that she fancied some of the items on display; she was given a £300 rose bowl and a suede jacket worth thousands. Just one private holiday down under cost the Australian government £100,000.

She even got a lavatory seat free on one of her trans-Atlantic trips. Her schoolgirl sense of humour was revealed when, during a visit to a store, she spotted a toilet seat which played the 'Star Spangled Banner' whenever anyone sat on it. She immediately asked if she could have one that played 'God Save the Queen' as a homecoming gift for Andrew. Much to her chagrin, they did not have such an item, so Fergie had to make do with the American tune instead. It is intriguing to imagine what might have happened if she had been successful – and had installed such a plaything in time for a teatime visit from the Queen. It is probable that her mother-in-law would not have been amused!

Money, free holidays and gifts had always been three of the main subjects of controversy dogging Fergie, cruelly nicknamed the Material Girl of the Monarchy. In 1989 she had launched herself on a new career in her own right, as author of children's books about Budgie the Helicopter.

Far from earning her the critical praise she had expected, Fergie landed herself in further trouble – accused of being not as charity-minded as she could, or indeed should, be.

Her publishers, Simon and Schuster, set about publicising her first books with great gusto. One of these promotional activities was a TV interview with presenter Sue Lawley. The Duchess claimed that all profits from the book would go to sick children. It was later discovered that only 10 per cent of the royalties went to charity. The rest was kept by the Duchess herself. Calculations were soon made about just what that amount could be. She was thought to have accrued £10,000 from the book sales, £80,000 from American serial rights and £20,000 from her original advance. (That, it later transpired, was only the tip of a very large iceberg!)

Adding it all up became a particularly bitter task for royal critics because on top of all that was the £120,000 the Duchess had demanded to give a newspaper interview to publicise her Budgie books. It was a lot of money for royal hype. The newspaper concerned, the *Daily Express*, could not believe the Duchess's underhand way of going about things. For that amount of money, she had not thought it worth mentioning during the course of the inter-view that she was pregnant with her second child, even though she had been asked about having more children. The announcement about her pregnancy was made by Buckingham Palace in the normal official way the very next day.

Controversy over the Budgie books would not die down. The Duchess's secretary, Lieutenant Colonel Sam O'Dwyer, quit because of rows over money. He was understood to have disputed the handling of the royalties of her Budgie books, believing it would be 'unseemly' of her to pocket the money.

Criticism from an unexpected quarter came when Fergie was accused of stealing the idea for her books from another author. It was claimed that a 1964 book titled *Hector the Helicopter*, by Arthur W. Baldwin, bore a remarkable similarity to the Budgie stories. In Baldwin's tale, Hector the Helicopter feels unwanted and forgotten, twiddling his thumbs in a hangar while all the other planes go off to exciting places. In Fergie's tales, Budgie feels dejected sitting in a hangar twiddling his thumbs while all the other planes appear at an air show. The duchess's publishers, Simon and Schuster, said the similarities were 100 per cent coincidence.

Fergie's literary career advanced when, in 1991, she set about writing her first adult book, a biography of Queen Victoria and Prince Albert, with whom, she modestly announced, she and Andrew had considerable affinity! Palace officials were at pains to make it clear that, this time, profits would all go to charity.

Apart from her too-obvious avarice, there was another important aspect of royal etiquette that Fergie constantly failed to come to terms with: that the privacy of the Royal Family is deemed by its members to be sacrosanct. It is not cheap entertainment.

The Queen, an old hand at dealing with approaches from the media to cover fly-on-the-wall moments of her leadership of 'the Firm', is always very cautious about sharing the family's private lives with the outside world.

Although realising the public-relations value of such coverage, she is rightly wary about what should and should not become material for public consumption. The Queen was therefore consulted when Fergie was offered the chance to put the record straight about being a wayward mum who took off from her daughters and home to fly abroad at the drop of a hat.

The sugary-sweet magazine *Hello*, with its reputation for waxing lyrical about everybody and anybody with enough money and enough social standing, decided it wanted to show the Duke and Duchess of York at home. The Queen was dubious about the merits of the project but she reluctantly agreed, believing that more good than harm could come out of informal pictures of a son and daughter-in-law who needed all the good press they could get. She laid down certain provisos. The young married couple could not be photographed being too intimate (in royal terms that means kissing) and that a sense of decorum should be maintained throughout the photographic session. Finally, the couple should not allow themselves to be coerced into pictures they did not feel happy about.

The photo shoot should have been problem-free as it was set up by a close friend of the Duchess, working on behalf of the magazine. However, what resulted from the 1990 picture portfolio was page after page of what professional photographers called 'amateur snaps'. They were poorly constructed pictures of such moments as the Duchess changing her baby's nappy. The whole episode became an over-hyped PR exercise that did nothing for the Duke and Duchess of York. Salt was rubbed into the wounds when it became clear that money had changed hands for the photographic session. The price quoted was around £250,000. The palace denied the Duchess was actually 'paid' for her *Hello* appearance. The magazine itself was vague, too, admitting only that some money was involved but it wouldn't say whom it was paid to or why. Rumours had it that the payment found its way discreetly to the bank balance of a trusted recipient.

The Queen Machine – the palace officials who believe they are the secret power behind the throne – were becoming distinctly edgy about the Duchess's indiscretions and insensitivity. Their relations with her were icy. She constantly badgered them with what they saw as unreasonable demands. Sometimes they got their own back. When Fergie demanded that two rooms at Buckingham Palace be converted into a nursery for occasional use by Bea and Eugenie, they told her: 'Quite impossible; this is a *working* palace!'

Freeloading Fergie, the Material Girl, giggled her way through the criticism both inside and outside the palace. The least one could say for her was that she had the ability to ride unperturbed over the welter of humiliating copy being written about her in almost every media organ (apart, of course, from *Hello* magazine). Her money-grabbing, her vacationing, her lack of maternal instinct, her exotic show-business friends, her clothes, her figure, even her deportment came under fire. She must have cringed when she read the unflattering advice of one magazine editor, that Sarah 'should consult a plastic surgeon to correct one of her most annoying habits, face-pulling'. Her cheeks, the magazine advised, 'should undergo surgical stapling to prevent that open-mouth, pop-eyed look'.

Harsh criticism over the Duchess's general lack of good taste also centred around the home she and Andrew shared just a short hop away from Windsor Castle. The fact that their architect-designed house was a £5 million gift from the Queen was galling enough, especially as its construction coincided with the start of the British recession when ordinary folk were losing the roofs over their heads that they had worked hard all their lives for. In the four years or so that it took to build the high-tech, ultra-modern, red-brick house, critics observed that the leafy environment of Berkshire was giving birth to a monster. When the outside of the house was finished, no one could ignore the fact that it looked remarkably like an ASDA supermarket.

Other nicknames were coined for the ranch-like home, including Dallas Palace and Southyork (the latter a play on 'Southfork' from the American TV soap series *Dallas*). Blame for the blight on the Berkshire landscape could not entirely be laid at the feet of architects Law and Dunbar-Nasmith. The Duchess had taken a liking to the style of country home she had seen during a visit to Connecticut. That same American visit had sparked off Fergie's interest in a mix-and-match approach to interior design. The result was that, in contrast with the Royal Family's more trad-itional values, Southyork abounded with novelty furniture, mixed styles and poor taste. The house boasted a 35-foot entrance hall that swept up into a glass dome in the ceiling. There was a ministrel's gallery with rustic beams and natural stone floors. The rooms were enormous, of course. The master bedroom was 35 feet long, the kitchen huge. There were 12 bedrooms, an office each for Sarah and Andrew, a billiards room, cinema, stables and a swimming pool.

Set in five acres, the cost of the 50-room mansion kept going up because its completion took so long. Instead of quietly settling in her new home, which would have been the only way to avoid further public and press wrath over the escalating cost of providing a poor-taste home for a rich girl who didn't deserve it, Fergie decided a house-warming party was in order. It was no low-profile event. The party cost £60,000 and neighbours such as pop star Elton John and Scottish comedian Billy Connolly and his wife, Pamela Stephenson, popped in to help the celebrations along.

Sarah couldn't defend the bad-taste decor but she did defend herself against criticism of the cost. 'I'm many things, but I'm not materialistic,' she said. 'That's why Andrew did most of Sunninghill. It's mostly his hard work. I think Andrew wanted to build. That was him and his mother and I wasn't fussy.'

It seemed to be open season on poor Fergie from the critics. Yet she seemed to be weathering it well. On 26 September 1991 she told the prestigious magazine *Majesty*: 'Five years ago I was living in Clapham. Now here I am with two lovely girls and a great husband. To be part of such history is just extraordinary.' Sadly for the Duchess of York, the lessons of history are often unlearned, even by a newly-launched historical author. Fergie, like many a high-flier before her, had failed to heed the warning signs.

Years of gross royal misconduct came to a head early in

1992. Headlines screamed about the girl next door who was now the harridan you wouldn't want to live next door to.

Six years after signing up as a royal, Sarah was failing badly. She was voted 'the person thought to have done most harm to the reputation of the royals'.

The January 1992 newspaper survey had just 4 per cent of those polled naming her as their favourite royal. She was described as setting the worst example, being the least intelligent, one of the most snobbish, one of the rudest members of the Royal Family ever. She was quite simply, the royal who got it all wrong.

Fergie did come high in one area, however. She was unsurprisingly voted second in the 'most fun' stakes. However, 'most fun' was the last escription the Queen would have attached to the name of the Duchess of York, in a week when her daughter-in-law had caused the biggest furore the Royal Family had suffered for years. She had been accused of behaving outrageously on a trans-Atlantic flight, more details of that year's run of 'free' holidays had been emerging in the press and, worst of all, her name had just been linked to that of a young Texan millionaire.

Fun-loving Fergie, the practical joker of the Royal Family, now had to face a few, practical, old-fashioned facts. Playing with her daughters at their home in Sunninghill, Berkshire, Fergie received a phone call telling her in no uncertain terms that whatever she was doing was not as important as what she was now expected to do: get over to see the Queen at Sandringham. Andrew was summoned too. The couple arrived at Sandringham early that Wednesday evening.

Neither was given the courtesy of a welcoming drink. Nor was supper offered. It wasn't just the look on servants' faces that made Fergie and Andrew fear what was to come.

They already knew, as word spread throughout the Sandringham estate, that the Queen and Prince Philip were in one of the angriest moods ever witnessed. Indeed it proved so when the couple were summoned to Philip's presence. It is the Duke of Edinburgh who hands out the dressings-down in the royal household, and this one was one of his fiercest. Andrew was dismissed from the room while Fergie was read the riot act.

First on her father-in-law's 'crime sheet' list was Fergie's friendship with Texan oil tycoon Steven Wyatt. The rumours about the two were so strong that they were making news on American TV. Fergie was lambasted by the Duke of Edinburgh over the discovery of 120 photographs, including some of her and 36-year-old Wyatt, found by a cleaner at a London flat he once rented. The snapshots had been passed on to a newspaper which courteously declined to publish them but the embarrassing familiarity displayed in the snaps was reported upon. The Queen feared that more photographs of her daughter-in-law might be circulated and become public property.

Gradually, some pictures did appear in British newspapers. Some of the offending photographs showed Fergie and Wyatt together while on a trip to Morocco via the South of France in 1990. One revealed Wyatt sitting at the feet of the 32-year-old Duchess. Another snap was of Sarah and the Texan riding together in the French countryside, again both wearing sunny smiles. But the one photograph that really infuriated the Royal Family – and Andrew in particular – showed Wyatt crouched down beside the naked tot Beatrice; both were beaming into the camera lens, with all the appearance of a father and daughter.

Other snaps were taken in the early morning on the steps of Constable Burton Hall in Bedale, Yorkshire, that same year. The Duchess was then five months pregnant with her second daughter, Eugenie. She had suddenly decided to turn a day visit to Constable Burton Hall into an overnight stay when fog made travelling difficult.

Such shenanigans provoked royal expert Harold Brooks Baker, publisher of *Burke's Peerage*, to tell a newspaper in the most censorious terms: 'Incidents involving the Duchess pose tremendous dangers to the future of the monarchy. The world showed itself willing to forget Miss Ferguson's past when she became the Duchess of York. It is surely her duty to make sure that the present and the future appear in perfect and pristine shape.'

The Duke of Edinburgh undoubtedly agreed with him. 'Appalled' was his comment on the pictures. His manner at that Sandringham meeting with Fergie was chilling. He had dismissed Andrew after a curt greeting. Now he waded into his daughter-in-law. He never shouted. That was what was so unnerving for the Duchess. He spat his words out with venom but remained always in control.

The Duchess stood there as Philip sent a newspaper skimming across the table. It contained yet another damning report about her. It said that back in 1991, when her closeness to Wyatt had begun to embarrass the Royal Family, the

Queen had ordered Sarah never to see the Texan again but Fergie had ignored the order. According to the newspaper report, she had secretly visited his London flat in Cadogan Square at least twice.

Sarah hung her head, knowing that to interrupt or attempt to make any excuses would only prolong her ordeal and make it a million times worse. Fergie had been down this road before. This was a meeting ordered by the Queen of England between her consort and a disgraced member of her family. Gone was any hint of warmth or understanding. This encounter was as formal as when plain Sarah Ferguson had met the Duke of Edinburgh for the very first time.

The Duchess picked at the edge of her skirt as the Duke turned to her latest foreign trip, to Florida. It was the most recent of what the world had come to know as Freeloading Fergie's Freebies. Her only engagement there had been to attend a charity polo match with her father.

Earlier that month, Fergie had decided to go skiing in Switzerland without her husband. While she took off with her daughters, Prince Andrew stayed at home at Sandringham. The trip couldn't have been a worse move for the Duchess. Still smarting at speculation over constant separation from her husband, she became the target for sniping news reports throughout the world. Then the cameramen at Klosters zoomed in on the pale face of her elder daughter, Princess Beatrice. Lots of bright pink spots could be seen and were later confirmed as chicken pox in pictures that newspapers and magazines worldwide rushed into print. Thoughtless and incompetent, was just one criticism made of the Duchess for taking her sick daughter on to the slopes. One British doctor roared: 'Fergie is to motherhood what husband Andrew is to nuclear physics. I do not believe any normal, caring mother would have taken her child abroad.'

What got under the skin of an increasingly irritated public was that this £5,000 Swiss holiday, like many before it, had cost Fergie virtually nothing. It was paid for by town officials at Klosters who were only too happy to have royalty as guests. However, it was the Florida trip, flying first class back from Miami on American Airlines, that convinced the Queen her daughter-in-law was in serious need of royal counselling.

The press had a field day, describing in great detail how Sarah's father, Major Ron Ferguson, sat mortified with embarrassment as Sarah, two hours into the flight, threw paper and packets of sugar at him and airline staff. How she put a paper bag over her head before poking her tongue out through a hole she had made in it. She also made bird noises and chirruped like a telephone. Napkins went flying. Her secretary joined in the 'fun' by throwing sugar packets back at Fergie. She then ignored no-smoking regulations and lit up two cigarettes before the effect of two glasses of champagne apparently took hold and the Duchess slept soundly until the plane landed. Pushed to the limit of understanding, even for the daughter he loved, Major Ferguson calmly answered press questions. 'She has been working very hard,' he said. 'It is just her way of letting off a little bit of steam.'

The Queen and Prince Philip were less charitable. It was this behaviour that made them wonder if something was seriously wrong with their daughter-in-law. How could she behave like this in the midst of newspaper speculation over her extra-marital friendship? Had she got what educational psychologists would call 'behavioural problems'?

The Duchess of York had the law laid down to her by the Duke of Edinburgh that night at Sandringham. She was told exactly how things would be from now on. Only after an hour of tongue-lashing was Andy allowed to return to the drawing room, and his father talked further about the public obligations both were expected to fulfil.

Fergie later told friends that her father-in-law 'had gone potty'. She was scared stiff throughout the angry dressing-down. Only afterwards did she become angry herself at her humiliating treatment. She knew then that the confrontation was the final straw – she and the Royal Family would be parting company. The next day Sarah arrived at daughter Beatrice's school in Windsor looking pale and drawn, her seemingly unwashed hair pulled back by a black band. She was dressed in dowdy, baggy, green pants and a long sweatshirt. It looked as if she had not slept that night.

News later broke that Fergie was not, after all, going to take her next freebie trip in quick succession – a visit to Austria for four days on the piste to indulge her passion for skiing. The Duchess had been due at the annual Combined Services Winter Sports Association championship a week later, but the icy blast from the Duke had warned her off. She had been told never to bring the family into disrepute again.

Then came the announcement that the Duchess's next

few months of engagements were to be cut. She was to maintain a much lower profile in public and concentrate instead on her personal and family life. The Duchess's press spokesman, Geoffrey Crawford, confirmed the new line being taken. He said: 'The Duchess is spending more time at home with her family at the moment, by her own choice. But there are other things in the pipeline. There will be some engagements.' One scheduled public outing that was quite firmly knocked on the head was that week's opening of London's swankiest new hotel, the Lanesborough. The fact that Steve Wyatt was rumoured to be on the guest list with other Texan dignitaries was enough to have her attendance banned.

More revelations followed. As well as having an empty official diary for the summer, it was stated that Fergie would not be accompanying Prince Andrew on any of the 12 visits he had agreed to fit in between his full-time Naval duties. The Duchess of York made her last official appearance for a long time at the Sports Aid Foundation dinner at London's Guildhall on 11 February 1992. For the immediate future, fun-loving Fergie's lifestyle was reduced to that of a surburban housewife. It was, a tearful Duchess of York confided to close friends, 'the worst week I've ever had in my whole life'.

It was no wonder that Fergie was feeling fretful. She was suffering the greatest stress she had ever experienced since becoming a member of the royal club. It was also not surprising that she should seek help, not only for tension, but also for the aches and pains that now accompanied it. Unfortunately, even this most private of actions was witnessed by eagle-eyed reporters. Equally unfortunately, Sarah had chosen not an orthodox doctor for treatment, or indeed one by royal appointment, but a Greek clairvoyant named Madame Vasso, who lived in a basement flat in north London.

During one visit to Madame Vasso, the clairvoyant spent three hours and 20 minutes 'healing' the Duchess. The bizarre session involved Sarah sitting under a large pyramid construction. The idea was that Sarah was transported back to the time of the pharaohs and received spiritual guidance from an Egyptian god of healing, Imenhotep. Long-suffering detectives, on standby to drive the Duchess home, discreetly turned their backs as Madame Vasso hugged Fergie outside the flat. Obviously, this had not, by any means, been the Duchess's first visit for treatment.

The idea of the Duchess of York sitting for hours under a pyramid captured the imagination of the British press. Reams were written on the significance of the pyramid in healing and all other walks of life. Its history was marvelled at. Pyramids were given away as prizes in newspaper competitions. Reporters were despatched to Madame Vasso's modest bedroom, with its polkadot wallpaper and blue curtains, to undergo the same alternative treatment. Audiences in bars were later regaled in great detail about the wooden stool that sat below a blue perspex pyramid, raised up from the floor on a wooden support. Madame Vasso was chivvied into giving interviews about her very important client. It soon came out that the mystic ran a fortune-telling stall at weekends at nearby Chapel Market, using tarot cards and palm-reading.

Warming to her subject, Madame Vasso, also known as Mrs Kortese, hit out at rumours that the Yorks' marriage was going through a rocky patch. 'She loves him very much and he loves her,' she said. 'They are very happy together and Sarah is very happy now. She is such a lovely person, I can't begin to tell you. I think the press have been very unfair to her. If they really knew what she was like they would never say such things.'

Madame Vasso's foresight was not entirely accurate at that stage; nor did she foresee that the Duchess was about to become involved in one of the biggest scandals to hit the Royal Family for decades.

The tongue-in-cheek coverage of Fergie's obviously sincerely-held belief in the power of the pyramid prompted the Duchess to complain to friends that she had become a 'moving target' for press photographers. 'There's something very wrong in being tailed like a criminal,' she said. 'I now feel I can't make a move without being followed. It's a horrid feeling. I want something done about it.'

The Duchess of York concentrated on spending time with Princesses Beatrice and Eugenie. Pictures of mother and daughters acting like an ordinary family started to appear by design in the newspapers. Buckingham Palace remained tight-lipped about rumours that Fergie herself had announced she was 'going on strike' and stopping official duties but newspapers kept a closer watch whenever she went out privately. A lot had been learned from the saga of the power of the pyramid.

So what did Fergie do? She did what came naturally – she went on holiday. Fergie led the press a merry dance as she island-hopped during an extended exotic trip, accompanied by her daughters, nanny Alison Wardley and the man described as her 'financial adviser', John Bryan. Mr Bryan, it was soon revealed, was a close friend of Steve Wyatt. An instant audience of fascinated royal observers tut-tutted at this flaunting of established royal behaviour, but wasn't the soap opera fun to watch!

On 19 April 1992, Fergie and her entourage flew to their first holiday destination, the exclusive resort of Phuket in Thailand. After being photographed by a fellow guest at the £150-a-night Amanpuri Hotel, Fergie begged Bryan to get her away. He hired a £3 million Lear jet to whisk the group to the Indonesian Moluccas Islands. Again they were discovered and again they were on the move. Fergie ended up on Bali but she did not have to pay the high hotel prices like other visitors. She was a guest of the hotel's owner. Exactly what the whole trip cost was the subject of speculation. The hotel bill in Phuket alone came to £13,000, paid for with an American Express charge card. Whose card it was was not revealed.

Andrew, deeply embarrassed back at home, could only wait to see what Fergie planned to do next. The Duke of York, suffering the total humiliation of being labelled by the tabloid press a cuckolded husband, didn't have to wait long. Johnny Bryan, on instructions from Fergie, was despatched back to Britain to discuss exactly what financial terms the Duke might offer his wandering wife. Fergie was away from home for a month. When she eventually returned with her daughters, she resumed the role of the young mum. Smiling broadly, she drove into Windsor to deliver Princess Beatrice to school.

It required only one other player to complete the over-theatrical farce. True to form, Fergie's type-cast father arrived centre-stage to play the buffoon. Major Ron Ferguson hit the headlines again through his close relationship with glamorous, polo-playing Lesley Player, 26 years his junior. The 59-year-old Major was said to have written passionate notes to her. 'Ron has always been a sucker for a pretty girl,' said a friend. The Major's long-suffering wife, Sue, 45, refused to comment.

Fergie, meanwhile, was confirming her new-found independence in a very positive way. She moved lock, stock and barrel from the marital home at Sunninghill to a new house on the nearby exclusive Wentworth estate. The rent was £4,000 a month for the six-bedroom property, complete with heated swimming pool and annexe for nanny Alison. The Duchess had chosen the new, grand location (owned by a millionaire African chief) because she was determined that she would only move to a home grand enough for a duchess. Hence 'Romenda Lodge' with its leopard-skin furniture.

Andrew and Sarah still met regularly. On a couple of occasions the Duke and Duchess of York baffled onlookers when they dined at local restaurants, looking for all the world like a loving couple. Yet the direction of Fergie's life had by now been set. A reconciliation with Andrew was out of the question. The two met regularly but only for the children's sake and sometimes to discuss financial arrangements for their and their mother's future. As well as support for the two Princesses, 'hush money' would have to be paid, an agreeable amount that would ensure the former Miss Sarah Ferguson would never, ever reveal the secrets of her life within the Royal Family. 'The Firm' think of everything.

The astonishing irony is that flashy Fergie could probably live out her life in luxury without spending a penny of the Royal Family's carefully withheld coffers. Blessed with a stroke of amazing good fortune, she looked set to become a multi-millionairess in her own right after Johnny Bryan sold the film and merchandising rights to her Budgie books to a television cartoon company. The world-wide deal with Sleepy Kids plc meant that at last Fergie would always be financially independent from the Royal Family. Not, perhaps, what they themselves would have wished!

The remarkable chapter on Fergie and her brush with royalty was coming to an end but she still had a few surprises up her sleeve. During Ascot week in 1992, she behaved in an extraordinary fashion. Obviously no longer entitled to take her place in the royal carriage parade that heralds the start of the day's racing, Fergie was still determined to join in. For whatever reason, be it arrogance, mischief or simply to let her tiny daughters witness royal pageantry at close quarters for the last time, she organised a picnic with friends on the parade route. As the Royal Family rode by, she waved a white hanky, encouraging her daughters to do the same. The group all squealed with delight, shouting 'Hello' as the Queen passed.

Fergie later confided to a friend that she had gone to Ascot out of sheer devilment – but had been infuriated when she overheard a minor courtier criticising her flamboyant picnic as 'shameful'. She decided to do one better, and the following day persuaded Prince Andrew to join the group. Together they all waved at the Queen!

Yet again, the world was astonished at Fergie's antics. Such behaviour from a disgraced royal was simply out-rageous, but then Sarah Ferguson was no ordinary royal. She was the girl who achieved the impossible. She captured her handsome prince and joined Britain's most exclusive 'club'. She was loved by him – and by the nation for her natural exuberance and for daring to be different. The royal straitjacket, however, did not suit her. She grew to hate the Royal Family with a vengeance, particularly after the humiliating, Christmas dressing-down given her by Prince Philip at Sandringham.

However, if she was going to go, it would not be quietly. First, there was the question of a suitably royal pay-off. If the deal was not to her liking, the Duchess always had the option of using her publishing contacts to write a book on her life and times with the Royal Family. It would be worth at least £4 million to her – but it would also change the British monarchy's standing for ever.

The man negotiating the settlement for Fergie was, of course, her 'financial adviser', but it was the self-same man who also helped her towards her greatest shame. After constant denials of a romance with Fergie, after threats to newspapers and threats to the palace ('I'll have them by the b***s,' he said) he blew their 'platonic' cover in the most farcical manner. Bryan and the Duchess of York were photographed on holiday together in August 1992, kissing and cuddling.

The photographs showed Fergie having her toe sucked

by Bryan as the couple lounged around a pool at a hide-away villa in St Tropez on the French Riviera. They were photographed in an embrace as Fergie stretched out on a sunbed. There were pictures, too, of Bryan rubbing oil on her and gently tucking her hair behind her ear. There were also pictures of Fergie walking around topless, all in the company of her two little daughters – and two male bodyguards.

The photographs were taken by paparazzi photographer Daniel Angelli, crouched furtively among thick bushes surrounding the villa belonging to businessman Charles Smallbone. The pictures appeared in magazines in Europe, but much worse was their appearance in British news-papers. Some reached saturation coverage, with page after page of Fergie and her 'financial adviser'. The *Daily Mirror* reputedly paid £70,000 to secure exclusive rights for British publication. On one day alone, the *Mirror* ran 20 pages of 50 frolicking Fergie pictures. Deals were struck world-wide for further publication and, throughout, Fergie and her Texan were lampooned in cheeky captions, in barbed cartoons and in newspaper headlines. She was labelled a 'tramp'.

The scandal far exceeded any other Fergie had caused before and provided positive proof that any reconciliation with her husband was inconceivable. Andrew was humili-ated, a proven cuckold. The Duchess's estrangement from Prince Andrew and his entire family was beyond repair.

The pictures were released as the Royal Family gathered at Balmoral for its annual Scottish holiday. Andrew and Fergie had been there for only two days when the story broke. Headlines screamed: 'Fergie's Final Boob', 'Can Andy Still Love Her?', 'Strip Her of Her Title' and 'Shamed Fergie Faces Exile'. Newspapers said Fergie had done more to drag the monarchy through the mud than Wallis Simpson. 'This silly strumpet has behaved in a way which would disgrace a council house, let alone a palace,' said the *Daily Star* in a leading article.

Quietly, shame-faced, the Duchess of York packed her bags and left the Scottish Highlands – and the family whose wealth and prestige she had drawn on. It was reckoned that since her marriage she had benefited by more than £10 million from the public purse.

In the end, it was Fergie who decided to leave the fold and only when she had left did Andrew, like a spoilt brat, realise what he had missed out on during his selfish marriage. The Duke wanted his Duchess back again. But although Fergie could now twist him around her little finger (she still called him 'My Super Honeypot') she was having none of it. Extraordinarily, she had given up the royal life as a bad job.

Sarah Ferguson's brief visitation upon the Royal Family, however, had not lost her half as much as it had lost them.

CHAPTER ELEVEN

Edward

Not so long ago it would have been unimaginable that any royal offspring should find a role in life making tea for a company of actors. Yet such was the chosen path of shy, awkward Edward, the Queen's youngest son, when he entered the effete world of stage performers by eagerly accepting humble, paid employment in millionaire composer Andrew Lloyd Webber's Really Useful Theatre Company.

Prince Edward met Lloyd Webber's ambitious producer, Bridget 'Biddy' Hayward, at the Queen's sixtieth birthday celebrations at Windsor Castle. Biddy, who was impressed with his passion for the theatre, gave him a £15,000-a-year job as a trainee production assistant. Self-effacing Edward arrived for his first day clutching a packet of PG Tips tea, jokingly acknowledging the PA's main task of chief tea boy and bottle-washer.

Two years later Edward was on the move again within the theatre world when Lloyd Webber decided to rationalise his business in order to bring it back wholly under his ownership. Jobs had to go and, royal or not, Edward was one of the first to leave, hot on the heels of Biddy. His career as a glorified tea boy had come to an abrupt end. A royal insider was quoted at the time as saying: 'If Lloyd Webber really is squeezing the Prince out, that won't cost him a knighthood – if anything, the reverse. The Queen never approved of Edward's spurious theatrical job.'

Edward wasn't out in the wilderness for long. Biddy had decided to set up shop herself and Theatre Division was born, with Edward joining the seven-strong team as technical administrator. Soon the jinxed Prince was once again out of work when the company failed within a year and a major backer dropped out. Edward's own inexperience had not helped – his personal recommendation that they stage the play *Same Old Moon* resulted in the company losing its entire production costs of £250,000. With disastrous ticket sales, the play closed after only a month.

Prince Edward's bumbling attempts to master the theatrical craft (he was also president of the National Youth Music Theatre) not only made the Royal Family even more of a laughing stock, it also gave rise to unprecedented personal insult. The Prince's association with his trendy thespian friends prompted outrageous allegations about his sexuality.

Edward was cornered at a New York party in 1990 by an eager British journalist who boldly demanded of the Prince: 'Are you gay?' His silent but shocked response was seen as a denial and attracted world-wide headlines. Two years later, international playboy Taki Theodoracopoulos went on the prime-time American television programme *A Current Affair* and described the Prince as 'very gay'. He told viewers: 'In Europe we have young Prince Edward who has to deny the fact that he is gay, very gay. He can't admit it because it will cause uproar.' On the same programme, Una Mary Parker, author of the book *The Palace Affair*, confirmed: 'There are rumours of a rather limp-wristed prince in the palace.' A Buckingham Palace spokesman at the time refused to give credence to the story, saying: 'The programme is not worth commenting on. Enough has been said on the subject already.'

Such slurs on the unmarried Prince have cut to the royal quick. Edward has had a string of occasional girl companions but has seemingly never been involved in a serious romance.

An early sweetheart was Romy Adlington, who was dated by the Prince when he was 20 and she was just 17 years of age. Seven years on, just as the gay slurs began appearing, Romy decided to spill the beans on her year-long 'romance'. She talked about an uneventful holiday at Balmoral during which they went for long walks on the estate. She recalled: 'It was the most wonderful time for us. We began to talk about what we felt for each other, what our emotions really were. We were both young so nobody thought about marriage or anything like that. It was all just good fun.'

In a further clue to his character, Romy also described the great lengths to which Edward went to avoid being recognised when they were out together for a candle-lit dinner. 'Edward was paranoid about being spotted out on the town with me,' she said. 'Because of this I hit on the idea of dressing him up in disguise.' She enlisted the help of a make-up artist friend and together they set about transforming the Prince. 'We built up his nose, greased back his hair, added sideburns and gave him a wonderful moustache. The evening passed without event until Edward set his moustache on fire leaning across the table.'

Romy went on: 'When we were together the transformation in Edward was remarkable. He was a totally different person. He could really unwind. He was able to be a human being rather than someone constantly aware of himself. Far from being the tense and stressed boy at public functions, he was able to smile and be normal.'

Cynical royal-watchers have subsequently wondered whether Romy was involved in a palace propaganda exercise aimed at establishing beyond doubt Edward's masculinity, but the truth is that the 'romance' was platonic. The couple drifted apart after a year and he had no other serious liaisons. Nevertheless, 'first love' Romy Adlington clearly retained a deep affection for the young royal, saying: 'He is warm and giving. I consider myself highly privileged to know someone like Edward and we remain strong, close friends. He deserves to be treated fairly and sensitively, not criticised at every opportunity.'

To a very large degree, Romy is right. Poor Edward, once tea boy with the Extremely Useful Company, has ever since been considered the Extremely Useless Prince.

It didn't always look that way. At Gordonstoun School Edward was seen as the very opposite of his elder brother, Andrew. Young Edward was well liked. He became head boy, was good at rugby and amateur dramatics but made no major impact on school life. He was remembered as being 'bright but not outstanding' and a bit of a loner. After leaving school he worked as a trainee teacher at a school in Wanganui, New Zealand, for two years. When he finally went up to Cambridge University in October 1983, some students objected to his admission because his A-level results were inadequate. Nevertheless, the Prince briefly blossomed in those hallowed halls of learning. He enjoyed the company of a tight but jolly circle of friends, including a particular chum, graduate Anwen Ground, nicknamed 'Blodwen Nipples Filofax'.

However, his Cambridge degree in archaeology,

anthropology and history did not help find him a career. Cruelly, in 1991 *The Sun* newspaper, using the name 'Edward Buckingham' and listing his qualifications and work experience, wrote off on his behalf for jobs with several major companies. They all turned him down.

It was Prince Edward's unsuitability for any job that caused him to suffer his greatest, most desperate, public humiliation. Prior to his ill-fated foray into theatreland, he stunned the nation, and especially his strict father, in 1987 by quitting the Royal Marines before even completing his 34-week training course as an officer cadet. The very idea of his own son paying £10,000 to buy himself out – or, in some eyes, to chicken out – must have been absolute anathema to Philip.

Edward had announced that he was to join the élite fighting force as an £8,000-a-year trainee officer when he finished his three-year degree at Jesus College, Cambridge. Prince Philip, being honorary Captain-General of the Royal Marines, was delighted. So were the Marines themselves, desperate for a member of the Royal Family within their ranks at a time when they were faced with Ministry of Defence cuts. However, joining the Marines was a disastrous mistake from the start. The gentle 22-year-old was not cut out for the rough and tumble of life as a commando. Marine training is tough and Edward was expected to pull his weight as well as any other officer. Within four months Edward found he could not cope with the gruelling regime. His university degree was no qualification for this tough life.

His misery was once compounded when a lowly corporal delivered the ultimate put-down. Edward had appeared on the parade ground sporting a new dress hat. He asked the NCO: 'How do I look?'

To which he got the sarcastic answer: 'You look lovely, darling.' And the NCO planted a smacking great kiss on his cheek. Edward was mortified.

On another occasion, when his group were on a particularly exhausting exercise on Dartmoor, he set himself up for yet another fall. While everyone lay exhausted on the grass their NCO, not giving an inch, demanded: 'Who's the Captain-General of the Royal Marines?' A single hand shot up. The NCO ignored it and asked if anyone else knew the answer but no one had the interest or the energy to rack their brains for it. The NCO turned slowly to the still-raised hand and said sarcastically: 'Yes, it's Daddy isn't it.'

Edward very quickly earned his Marines nickname of 'Smartarse' after a few such episodes. Once, when he was duty officer, he rubbed his colleagues up the wrong way by behaving like an officious school prefect and treating them as children. They got their own back when his entire group turned on him and stuffed muck into his eyes, ears, nose and mouth. It was army humour but Edward could not take it. He found that sort of behaviour barbaric and coarse, not quite the genteel way of life to which he was accustomed.

When he went home to Sandringham for Christmas 1986, he had already made up his mind that he would never return to his Devon training course, but he had not yet confided his determination to a single soul. On the long, night-time car journey from the West Country to meet up with his family for their traditional seasonal holiday, the wretched Prince broke down. He wept pathetically as he told his personal detective his secret shame. It revealed much about the harsh nature of the Duke of Edinburgh that his frightened son could confide to his detective what he dared not reveal to his own father.

When he had dried his eyes and composed himself, Edward faced an ordeal he must have thought far worse than any training exercise: breaking the news to Prince Philip that he would not be coming home with the coveted Green Beret, worn only by those who had completed the strenuous 34-week training course. Philip was horrified by his youngest son's lack of staying power. Both he and the Queen begged him to return to finish the initial training that would have made him a competent troop commander.

Throughout the holiday and right up until the time that Edward failed to return to Lympstone Commando Training Centre on 5 January, his superiors remained unaware of his decision. The revelation that he was leaving came as a thunderbolt to his training officers and colleagues at the camp. They thought his absence was due to a bout of 'flu and that he would be back in uniform by the end of the week. The palace made the formal announcement five days later in a statement that read: 'Prince Edward is leaving the Marines with great regret but has concluded that he does not want to make the service his long-term career.' It went on to say that the Prince made his decision 'after much consideration'.

The intention had been that Edward should spend nine years in the Marines. He couldn't even complete basic training. While some wished him well for the future and even admired him for his guts in admitting he had made a wrong choice, others were not so impressed. A commando sergeant was quoted as saying: 'Forget all the bull. He just couldn't hack it. When the going got tough he buckled and ran. That's not what the Marines are made of. Nice bloke – too soft.' A Falklands veteran added: 'It's a pity his sister didn't come on the course instead. She would have walked it.'

Prince Edward has repaired his life since then, but following his shaming Marines experience he has worn a sullen, petulant air. His existence is seemingly aimless, despite theatrical and charitable ventures.

Royal advisers were unable to dissuade the Queen from giving her permission for one particular theatrical event masterminded by her youngest son. The only virtue of the televised royal *It's a Knockout Tournament* at Alton Towers theme park, Staffordshire, was that it raised funds for charity. However, the sight of young members of the Royal Family, including the new Duchess of York, dressed in medieval costume and cavorting with stars from showbusiness and the pop world, made for embarrassing TV. Teams, each containing a royal member, competed against each other in silly games against the backdrop of a castle.

The spectacle was unseemly. In the eyes of those who firmly believe a sense of dignity should always be upheld by the royals, it reduced the Queen's children to court jesters. Even before the tournament was screened, it made headline news. Prince Edward threw a tantrum and flounced out of a marquee during a press conference when asked if he thought the show trivialised the royals. He sulkily accused the media of not showing enough enthusiasm

for his venture. His reaction was likened to that of some foppish, over-sensitive actor.

At the height of anti-royal feeling during the Gulf War in 1991, Edward did little to endear himself. The Royal Family was criticised for not taking time out to visit troops in the Gulf and for not meeting the wives of servicemen involved in the war. Eventually, certain members re-arranged their itineraries to acknowledge the war and show support for both the serving men and their families. All except Edward, the ex-Marine. Ten days after the first Iraqi Scud missiles were fired, Edward attended the London Mozart Players concert and dinner. Two days later he gave a dinner for the National Youth Music Theatre. Everyone knew that Edward preferred the roar of the crowd to the sound of the gun, following the Marines fiasco, but it was now apparent that he had turned a deaf ear to the roar of public disapproval. It was suggested that the Prince should at least go to the Gulf to *entertain* the troops on stage. It was also pointed out that Edward is the only member of the immediate Royal Family not to hold an honorary position with a serving regiment.

It is hardly all his fault but he does still suffer the same gibes as the more senior royals, and the same serious criticisms about his role as a member of 'the Firm'. In August 1990 the newly-announced Civil List guaranteed Prince Edward £1 million over the following ten years. Not bad for a 26-year-old, but most young men on that sort of money either have a particular talent or work amazingly hard to earn it. In the year of this massive pay award, Edward had only 100 engagements, and few of those could be classed as arduous; most were evening theatrical appointments that most of the world would think of as 'freebies'. His 90-year-old grandmother carried out as many, and his sister, the Princess Royal, undertook 450.

While criticism was heaped on the Royal Family in 1991 and 1992, Edward continued to pocket his £100,000 a year of taxpayers' money while doing little to show the country that he was earning it by standing on his own two feet. Even when he took over the chairmanship of the Duke of Edinburgh Awards Special Projects Group, he was simply following in his father's footsteps.

Prince Edward still lives in a virtual timewarp, oblivious and probably unable to help mould a new course for his illustrious relatives. The Prince still lives in the same north-west wing of Buckingham Palace, in the very same rooms that he shared with Prince Andrew as a child. At night a cold meal is left out for him; Edward being teetotal, it is accompanied only by mineral water or soft drinks. Before going to bed he enjoys practising conjuring tricks (he receives lessons from television magician Paul Daniels and hopes one day to join the Magic Circle). It is an unreal world for a grown man. In the private quarters he grew up in, with his old housekeeper, Miss Colebrook, to make his bed and with his personal valet, Michael Perry, to dress him, he remains tied to the household of his childhood.

CHAPTER TWELVE

The Young Royals

They are royal by name, but human by nature. The young royals might bear the responsibility of being linked by birth to the House of Windsor but they also bear the problems, the passions and the pressures of the girl or boy next door. They use royal residences Sandringham or Windsor as weekend retreats but they live a life far removed from the crowns and coronets of the great state occasions.

Their parents were royal and were expected to do their duty; indeed, they did it blindly. Now, changing times have meant changing attitudes. Today the young royals carry the title of prince, lady or earl but live modern lives in the modern world and it's sometimes a life that shocks.

Twenty years ago it was inconceivable that a young cousin of the Queen, the daughter of a princess, would talk of her love of kinky black leather. That she would pose for photographs mocking the monarchy. Let alone that she would be proudly pregnant before she married. Marina Ogilvy, daughter of Princess Alexandra and Sir Angus Ogilvy, did all that and more. In some ways, even more shocking to the Queen and the establishment was the fact that she talked openly about her behaviour and the problems it caused the highest family in the land.

The man in her life is photographer Paul Mowatt. When they met he wasn't a photographer in the mould of Lords Snowdon or Lichfield. He was a 24-year-old, ordinary middle-class boy from a mock-Tudor semi in Kingston, Surrey. Said an editor of *Tatler*, the top people's magazine: 'His low ranking is salting the wound. As any divorce lawyer would say, the best thing to do is to marry someone of similar social status. The royals believe the same.'

Paul Mowatt and Marina Ogilvy started going out together after meeting at a dinner party. He had no idea who she was. Later he told *Today* newspaper: 'Once we got stuck in the rain in the middle of London and Marina said, "My dad has a flat nearby." We drove into St James's Palace and I though "Ooh, this is an odd place" and then I remember I said "Who's your old man then?" The name Ogilvy rang a bell and I said: "Does your mum live in Richmond Park? She's Princess Alexandra isn't she?" Then it dawned on me of course. But it didn't bother me.'

However, the relationship would soon bother Marina's parents a great deal. Twenty-three-year-old Marina, then twenty-fourth in line to the throne, began living with the boy educated at a comprehensive school. It wasn't long before she discovered that she was pregnant. It would be the first illegitimate royal baby for 90 years.

Marina was appalled by her mother's reaction to the news. She said later: 'Mother has this public image of being serene, composed and completely in charge of things. But I know she was desperate for this not to come out and to see the whole image she has tried to build up shattered. We had no option but to do this and to shatter everything. We had to either break out of this family regime or not.'

The choice that the royal rebel was given was stark and simple, even coldblooded. Princess Alexandra announced icily: 'You have got two options — either you get it aborted straight away in Harley Street on Monday or we arrange for you to get married this week by special licence.'

Sir Angus Ogilvy's reply to Marina's next question also showed clearly the different attitudes between the new breed of blue-bloods and the old traditional royals. Marina asked her father: 'What comes first, Queen and country or your own daughter?'

'Queen and country,' came the stiff-lipped reply. The generation gap could never have been better displayed. Paul and Marina, a talented pianist also known as Mo, were stunned but they were equally shocked when they visited a Harley Street doctor's surgery to confirm the pregnancy. They discovered, they said, that an abortion had already been laid on. The young couple did, indeed, want to marry but Alexandra and Ogilvy preferred a quiet, hole-in-the-wall affair before the birth of the baby. They simply could not tolerate the idea of their daughter staying single and pregnant. Marina and Paul also made it clear. They *would* get married, but only after the birth of their child.

Said Marina: 'Paul and I said very calmly that we did very much want to get married but that I didn't want to jump to the altar with a big, fat tummy.' Her father was furious and the usually sweet-natured Alexandra snarled in anger. According to their daughter, they gave her a final ultimatum: 'Either take one of the two options or we want nothing more to do with you.' Her strait-laced father told her if she had the baby without getting married it would change history and bring disgrace on the monarchy. The rebellious daughter commented a few days later: 'My father loves being married to a royal. He has always gloried in it. It's a bit weird really.' She also described her parents' reactions as the 'Dark side of the Royal Family', adding: 'The other side of the postcard is for the tourists.'

Talking about the planned abortion, Marina revealed

how Princess Alexandra had gestured with her finger and thumb in front of Marina's face and told her: 'It will only be that big. You are a healthy young girl and you will conceive easily again.' It was difficult for the attractive young royal to believe that her mother could talk so coldly about the baby, her own grandchild.

Marina continued her series of interviews to the newspaper about how her pregnancy had shaken her family and her love for them. She told how Princess Alexandra and Sir Angus Ogilvy had banned her from their home. 'We know about all the pressure we will be under as a result of what's happened,' said Marina. 'But we would rather have ten years of hardship and pressure than endure the thought that we have been forced into having the baby aborted. We couldn't live with that.'

Marina even confided that she had sent a six-page letter to the Queen, who was travelling on the royal yacht *Britannia* to the Far East on an official visit. The Queen was reported to be 'upset' at the newspaper revelations and worried about the effect they would have on Princess Alexandra.

Sensationally, her parents issued a statement of their own to the press. It read: 'Princess Alexandra and Sir Angus Ogilvy are very disturbed to read the story which has been published in the *Today* newspaper. They are concerned about the number of inaccuracies. In particular, they have not cut off their daughter. Marina is always welcome at her home. They love her very much and feel deeply for her at this difficult time. No further statement will be made.'

Marina hit back: 'All this statement has proved is yet

again my parents cannot get through this barrier between the duty they say they have to Queen, Church and country.'

Her words could be the anthem of the new young royals but Marina has been the only one to express these views so publicly. Others may have the same thoughts in mind but never before has the royal straitjacket been so clearly cast off.

To Princess Alexandra, her daughter's actions meant only one thing: betrayal. She had betrayed her family, her upbringing and the monarchy. Forgiveness was not easy. Matters were not helped when the *Sunday People* came out with a shocking headline just a day or so later. 'Marina had sex with a painter in Palace' it screamed. It told of claims made by painter and decorator Phil Filton that Marina had picked him out in a pub and invited him back to St James's Palace for sex sessions. The affair lasted six days, he said, while her parents were away.

Marina hit the news again four months later, when she finally walked down the aisle at the nineteenth-century St Andrew's Parish Church in Ham, Surrey. She had special permission from the Queen to marry and remained twenty-fourth in line to the throne because her new husband agreed to renounce his Roman Catholic faith. However, it was still not a normal royal wedding by any standards. Despite curt lawyers' letters warning them to stay away, the press were there in force; they even outnumbered the wedding guests. Fewer than 30 close relatives and friends arrived for the ceremony; noticeably missing were Marina's godparents Prince Charles, Princess Margaret and the Duke of Kent.

Marina's parents no doubt gritted their teeth when they saw what she had decided to wear for the ceremony — a tight-fitting, black, crushed-velvet dress and a wide-brimmed black hat. The best man had a pony tail and a silver earring. However, at last the bride's mother and father were rising above it all. Their main concern was that what had to be done was *being* done. Marina even publicly kissed her father outside the church as she arrived and Princess Alexandra smiled in satisfaction throughout it all. It was a strange scenario for two royal parents who had been prepared to sacrifice their unborn grandchild for the sake of appearances.

That should have been the end to it all. As far as Princess Alexandra and Sir Angus Ogilvy were concerned, everything had been neatly tied up. Like many a parent, each was guilty of wishful thinking. It was not long before Marina's name again made the news when she was photographed wearing thigh-high kinky boots and carrying a gun. Then came another picture, this time on the cover of a magazine, when she chose to be photographed wearing skin-tight leather trousers and jacket, with 'royal' corgis at her feet and a cheap crown on her head! It was considered to be the height of bad taste and a gross insult to the Queen.

A few months later, Marina was blabbing to the press again. This time she was complaining about the lack of interest her parents had shown in their grandchild, now a year old and bearing the bizarre name of Zenouska. Marina complained that she was now estranged from her parents. She said there had been no visits from them, no cards at Christmas and that they had slammed the front door of their Richmond Park home on her.

She said: 'Sadly, they have missed a whole year of Zenouska's life. Those moments can never be recaptured... every day is so precious in a child's life. We are just like other married couples with a child and we would just like them to see Zen from time to time.'

Paul added: 'We have actually lied on occasions to protect Marina's parents because it's embarrassing having to say they haven't seen Zenouska.' This time around, the Ogilvys elected not to comment.

Just under a month later, Marina was in the news again. This time it was over her attendance at a party in a zoo in Amsterdam. It was alleged that drugs were taken and wild sex took place at the party. Marina's choice of rubber clothing was also highlighted because it was bought at a London shop that had a 'kinky' collection in the basement. 'There's absolutely nothing kinky about rubber,' Marina stormed. She denied there was drug-taking or sex at the party. Answering the newspaper report, Marina said: 'I'm just an ordinary person living my life. It wasn't me who called myself a royal rebel but I suppose if that's what they want me to be, then OK I'll be that. I don't believe for one moment that I've embarrassed the Queen or my parents. I'm just an ordinary woman trying to live my life with my husband and daughter and trying to pay the mortgage.'

In a bid to support Marina, her husband inadvertently drew attention to the whacky and wild partying of another of the young generation of royals, Princess Margaret's son, David Linley. Said Paul: 'David wears lipstick. So what? No one remarks about that.'

It was indeed true that David, Lord Linley had been photographed on a couple of occasions wearing lipstick. Once was during the celebrations of his twenty-ninth birthday in 1991, for which he painted his lips bright red and wore a glittering kaftan. Despite the presence of Susannah Constantine, his long-term, on-off girlfriend, together with another of Linley's female escorts, Nicola Formby, he preferred the company of others and danced with transvestite waiters from the outrageous Soho club Madam Jo Jo's. Linley was also celebrating the opening of his second restaurant of the same name in Chelsea Harbour. After the bizarre birthday evening was over, Linley slipped away through a back door still wearing his lipstick.

'Everyone had a great time and Viscount Linley really enjoyed himself,' said a fellow party-goer. 'I have seen him at other parties and he loves dressing up and wearing make-up. He also likes a bit of lippy and kept asking people if it suited him.'

At another party, Linley donned a blond wig, sunflower-patterned Bermuda shorts and a large-brimmed hat. This time he opted for pale pink lipstick.

It was not surprising that Linley once got involved in a battle over the return of a missing roll of film that had been taken at a private party. He took out a High Court injunction against three men over pictures taken with his own camera. The photographs were shot at a late-night party which he had attended in Chelsea. He also success-fully brought cases over two news stories. One was about him supposedly gatecrashing a party in Hampstead and being rude to the guests and then getting punched in the face; the other wrongly alleged that he had been thrown out of a Chelsea pub after pouring beer over people. He received a small apology for the first and £35,000 damages for the second.

Described as a 'hard worker with a fat Filofax', Linley has managed to carve out a career of sorts for himself. He made a success of his furniture shop in the New Kings Road, suffering only a slight setback when fire gutted the premises early in 1992, and has developed the reputation of someone whose aim in life is to make money (he receives not a penny from the Civil List).

Having earned money, Linley also likes to spend it. Once, despite objection from his advisers, he bought a £65,000 BMW motor car. This was not a good idea, as he already had the worst motoring record of the entire Royal Family. He was given three driving bans for speeding in two years and faced nine driving offences over a short period. Each time, his motor insurance increased until it was well over £5,000 a year.

*　　*　　*

There are two young royals who have been an adornment and a credit to their family. One of these is Linley's younger sister, Lady Sarah Armstrong Jones. The most natural, unspoiled member of the Royal Family, Sarah has always been determined to lead her life her way. She would never dream of doing anything to bring her name or those of her close family into disrepute. She is the most unroyal of royals, and is like a breath of fresh air in what is becoming a sullied, scandal-ridden dynasty.

Even here, however, among the happy-go-lucky clique of West London's trendy young royals, the stifling influence of the senior Royal Family prevails – and harms – with its fuddy-duddy thinking. An issue was made out of Sarah's relationship with actor Daniel Chatto. It was claimed that Chatto was the illegitimate half-brother of screen star Edward Fox and his brothers James and Robert. Their father, the late theatre impresario Robin Fox, had a long affair with Daniel's mother Ros Chatto. Robin's widow, Angela Fox, scotched these claims of illegitimacy. 'It's just not true,' she said. 'His mother, Ros, was married to a delightful man called Tom Chatto and he was the father. The only people who can be hurt by scandal like this are Danny and Sarah.' True or not, they have possibly been hurt, as was evidenced by a gathering of friends of Sarah's father. On a country-house weekend Lord Snowdon appeared furious as he confided that Sarah and her boyfriend were being discouraged from marrying because of doubts over Daniel's parentage.

Snowdon said the pair were 'blissfully happy' and yet the Queen had opposed marriage. Fellow guests were shocked but Snowdon told them that his daughter 'respected her family' and would toe the line.

Such thinking is astonishing, not only in its injustice but also in what it reveals about the far-from-reality attitudes of the Queen and the antique array of out-of-touch 'yes men' who act as courtiers and advisers. The contrived controversy was swiftly passed over in the press, who generally had to admit: 'Sarah has almost single-handedly rescued an increasingly tarnished royal image.' No one could find anything nasty to say about the jean-wearing, fresh-faced, bicycling young girl. As Princess Margaret once put it: 'My children are not royal. They just happen to have an aunt who is the Queen.'

'Hard luck for them' would probably be the opinion of the public at large.

Lady Helen Windsor, daughter of the Duke and Duchess of Kent, has not been treated unkindly at the hands of the critics either. Like Sarah, she manages to conduct her life with dignity and charm, presenting no threat to the image of the 'Old Firm'. Even when lurid novelist Sean Thomas made claims in a Sunday newspaper that he was dating Lady Helen, no one took his revelations seriously.

Only trivial naughtiness has been connected to Lady Helen. When she was 16 she was photographed smoking. At 17 she was pictured dancing wildly and semi-clad in a nightclub. When she was 18 she was caught leaning out of a boyfriend's bedroom window at dawn. After leaving school she entered a fun-loving world of parties and boyfriends, which included moving from the sedate family home to a bachelor flat in Pimlico, London. The only time Lady Helen suffered personal press comment was when her shapely body earned her the nickname 'Melons'. The name was dropped when Helen shed weight and became a size 10 instead of a size 14.

Her stunning blonde hair and blue eyes have attracted many admirers including old Etonian disc jockey John Benson, Ghanaian Isaac Ayer-Kumi, old Etonian Nigel Oakes and Gerard Faggionato, whom Helen was accused of stealing from Lady Sarah Armstrong Jones. Helen's most publicised relationship was with advertising whizzkid David Flint Wood, who was usurped by Helen's new beau, art dealer Tim Taylor.

Publicity-shy Lady Helen strode through it all. So desperate is she not to be in the public eye that she refused to give evidence in court against a man who was alleged to have harassed her continually. Freelance television cameraman Simon Reynolds, 36, denied using abusive or threatening words and behaviour towards the Queen's cousin in February 1992. The first incident was said to have happened at the Mayfair art gallery, Karsten Schubert, of which Lady Helen is a director.

One columnist noted that, despite her love of partying and high living, Sarah retained her popularity 'partly because she looks like Grace Kelly and has the same composure... Her English-rose charm is a powerful asset.' It was that English charm that bowled over Tim Taylor. 'By the time Tim walked into her life,' commented one newspaper, 'Helen was already on the road back to respectability.' In January 1992, the couple officially announced their engagement.

The 18 July wedding of the 'English Rose' at St George's Chapel, Windsor, was just what the more senior, older and supposedly wiser members of the Royal Family needed in the middle of, for them, a nightmare year. Within the previous six months they had seen the separation of the Duke and Duchess of York and the divorce of Princess Anne and Mark Phillips, as well as frightening revelations about the sham marriage of the Prince and Princess of Wales.

Perhaps the youngsters had something to teach them after all.

CHAPTER THIRTEEN

The Prince of Wales

To the outside world, he is an heir apparently forever lost in a world of his own. Prince Charles, king-in-waiting, talks to his plants, embarks on voyages of deep self-discovery in far-flung places and seems sadly remote from the family he longs to lead as a sovereign. Future subjects are baffled by the Prince of Wales, his headline-making quirks and his almost embarrassing efforts to understand ordinary folk, their humble aims and aspirations.

Charles Philip Arthur George Windsor, future king, was born on a clear, crisp day on 14 November 1948. He came into the world at a time when Britain was struggling to recover from the Second World War and ration books were still in use.

Weighing in at 7 pounds 6 ounces, baby Charles was born in Buckingham Palace itself. The forty-fourth heir to the throne, he is the first male in direct succession for more than 80 years. Accession to the throne would make him King Charles III.

Prince Charles was the first royal to be sent to day school: Hill House in London. Then, like his father, Prince Philip, he went on to attend boarding schools, Cheam and Gordonstoun. It was during his time at Cheam that Charles showed the beginnings of his talent for art. While there, he did hundreds of drawings and paintings. He kept his parents amused with the little pictures he sent home every term.

He was a perfect son, gentle and loving, writing assiduously to his parents every week he was away, but the Prince also had a mischievous streak which revealed itself in the many pranks he indulged in as a pupil at Cheam. This was to be the start of the joker trait that was to stay with him throughout his life.

At 14 his parents sent him to Gordonstoun, the tough Scottish boarding school his father had attended as a teenager. Gordonstoun was founded by Dr Kurt Hahn, a Jew who set up the school when he was hounded out of Germany by Hitler in 1933. The sons of royalty mixed with the sons of ordinary folk, all of whom, in Charles's time, paid an average £519 a year.

Life was Spartan at the school where a pupil's day started at 7 a.m. with a brisk run around the grounds, come hail or shine, followed by a cold bath before breakfast. The day's solid studies were interrupted only by afternoons on the playing fields or on various adventure courses. The only time a pupil had to himself was an hour after supper when he was allowed to listen to radio or watch certain television programmes.

Charles flourished under the strict regime, making friends he was to keep for life. Although he was only a middle-stream pupil, he proved himself artistic and musical.

During this time the Goons, the famous comedy foursome, were introducing a zany new brand of British humour. Charles was instantly addicted and mastered all of their accents. He even insisted to friends that, should he mimic 'Seagoon', then the person he spoke to had to answer back as 'Bluebottle'. His powers of mimicry stood him in good stead in later years when he trod the boards at Cambridge.

His love of the Goons lasted and he struck up friendships with all four members: Spike Milligan, Harry Secombe, Peter Sellers and Michael Bentine. He became, in effect, the fifth Goon and spent hours volleying jokes back and forth with them. Even when he was away, they exchanged cabled gags.

Meanwhile, back at Gordonstoun, Prince Charles was involved in what was considered to be a huge scandal at the time. The hapless Prince was caught drinking cherry brandy while on a school trip! The press went wild. Charles described the episode years later in a radio interview:

At the time I thought it was the end of the earth. I was all set to pack my bags and leave for Siberia. What really happened was this. I was on a cruise from Gordonstoun in the school yacht and we went to Stornoway... I suddenly thought 'I can't bear this any more' and decided to go off somewhere else. The only other place I could find was the bar.

Having never been in a bar before, the first thing I thought I ought to do was to have a drink. I was terrified and asked for the first drink that came into my head. It just happened to be cherry brandy. I had drunk it before when it was cold and I was out shooting. I had hardly taken a sip when the whole world exploded around my ears. It caused a terrific uproar. Anyway I was severely punished by my parents and I think that's why they packed me off to Australia and Geelong Grammar School.

Charles's need of solitude was to put him on the front pages time and time again in the coming years. But the Prince didn't have long to wait until his next press appearance. A copybook full of his school essays was stolen and sold to a national newspaper. It was dubbed the 'Exercise Book Affair'. An investigation carried out by the school failed to reveal the culprit who had sold the Prince's golden words, which included an essay on his parents.

Not long after, the 17-year-old Prince was on his way to Australia and for three months he lived a life out of the public eye. The tough-nut Aussies took to him immediately. He raised a laugh among fellow pupils at the outback bush school Timbertop when he wore a classic City of London suit, a bowler hat and carried an umbrella. He was nicknamed 'the Pommie Bastard'. Privately, he found Timbertop, the bush annexe of Geelong Grammar School, every bit as tough as Gordonstoun.

Back home in England, he went straight on to Trinity College, Cambridge, where his studies were interspersed with much larking about. The student Prince also threw himself into acting, starring in several student revues. He left Trinity with a not-too-impressive class two, division two degree. He also left with a highly tuned sense of humour and wit, finely honed by such comedy greats as Peter Cook, Dudley Moore and David Frost, former students whom he later befriended.

The title Prince of Wales does not come automatically and its bestowal is at the discretion of the sovereign. Charles was created Prince of Wales in 1958 at the age of ten. When he was invested at Caernarfon Castle on 1 July 1969, he made his maiden speech in Welsh, a language he had studied at the University of Aberystwyth. He even managed to make a reference to his comic hero, Welshman Harry Secombe.

Of the 21 English Princes of Wales, Charles is considered to be the best Wales has ever had. Until his investiture, his ancestors took little interest in the place but Charles is a firm believer in the Prince of Wales motto, 'I serve' and always does his bit to promote Wales in his travels.

Once again he followed in his father's footsteps when he took the 'royal route' and joined the Navy. There the real adventurer started to surface. Royal Navy lieutenant Charles Windsor gave rein to his daredevil streak, often with potentially dangerous results. Action-man at heart, he went on to excel as a deep-sea diver, sailor, helicopter pilot and parachutist, although some felt his antics were downright reckless, exposing the heir to the throne to unnecessary risk. Throughout his life in the services he was an ad-man's dream; his image proved to be a real recruit-puller.

It wasn't long, however, before the prankster in Charles reared its head again. While at Cranwell RAF College in 1971, he noticed that fellow student officers all wore the same expensive hand-sewn shoes. The Prince announced on the Tannoy system that all of the shoes were faulty and the manufacturers were withdrawing them to replace them with brand-new ones. More than half the cadets complied with the request that they hand their shoes over to a porter bribed by Charles. It wasn't until three days later that the Prince owned up to the shoeless students.

His Naval career is dotted with similar schoolboy stunts and the Prince used to spend a fortune in joke shops buying exploding cigars, stinkbombs and imitation dog-pooh. So exasperated were his fellow officers at these childish displays that Charles was frequently 'debagged', exposing the royal rump.

Quite what such activities say for the mentality of this fully-grown Senior Serviceman is difficult to discern but it does hint at a need for escapism, if not a deep-seated desire to take less than seriously his role as a future monarch.

During this time in the Navy, Prince Charles also carried out his royal engagements. One such event again gave him the opportunity to exercise his juvenile wit. He was invited by the Master Tailors Benevolent Association to be their guest speaker. This was the same society that, earlier that year, had awarded Charles the dubious accolade of Worst Dressed Man. He turned up at the dinner dressed in a tatty old tweed jacket. Everyone else wore tail-coats. The Prince stayed in his jacket for more than five minutes until he pointedly removed it to replace it with a smart tail-coat.

Throughout his life, many people have been a great influence on the Prince, and none more so than his beloved uncle, Earl Mountbatten of Burma. Charles was so attached to his Uncle Dickie that he dubbed him 'Honorary Grandfather'. He enjoyed his company so much that, like his parents before him, he later chose to spend the first night of his honeymoon at Mountbatten's family home, Broadlands.

Lord Louis may have been a keystone within the Royal Family but he was no pillar of society. It is now generally recognised that he was a practising homosexual. Both he and his wife, Edwina, scandalised their close circle with their various affairs. The Royal Family has always turned a forgiving eye to homosexual practices among its members but it has often been marvelled at that Prince Charles was allowed to become so close to his adoring Uncle Dickie. Few fathers would have been as trusting and as understanding as

Prince Philip when his son spent so long in the company of a surrogate father-figure with such sexual predilections.

Mountbatten's proximity to the royals once prompted M15 to classify him as a security risk. He was known to have been consulted by press magnate Cecil King in his attempted coup against the Labour government of Harold Wilson in 1966. Such was Uncle Dickie's greed for unconstitutionally gained power.

It was with heart-stopping horror that Charles later learned that his uncle had been killed by an IRA bomb while holidaying at his Irish home, Classiebawn Castle, in August 1979. Charles was utterly devastated and wept openly. He could barely maintain his composure when he read the lesson at the Earl's funeral.

Following Mountbatten's death at the age of 79, the 31-year-old Prince turned to another man he had known since childhood, the gentle, softly spoken Laurens van der Post. It is through van der Post, the philosopher, that Charles has had his greatest life influences, providing the germ for many a disparaging headline as a result. For Sir Laurens's basic principle towards life is that man must live in harmony with himself, animals and the land. That is something that Charles strives to achieve in his solitary pastimes, but the result is that, like van der Post, he has come to be regarded as rather eccentric.

The pervading influence of Sir Laurens first became apparent when Charles addressed the British Medical Association in 1984. Then he stunned doctors when he suggested that they did not have the monopoly on healing. He attacked conventional medicine, with its dependence on drugs, and advocated that more 'alternative' holistic medicine should be employed.

The press pounced with glee on the news that Charles was trekking through the Kalahari Desert with Sir Laurens for four days. It was claimed the Prince was searching for the 'meaning of life'. When he returned, newsmen quickly realised that the nature of the trip had been less spiritual when the Prince went on to moan about his battery-powered razor failing!

Other spiritual and intellectual mentors of recent years have been architects Rod Hackney and Lady Wynn-Jones, art expert Marchesa Bona Frescobaldi, Tory MP Nicholas Soames, former Speaker of the House of Commons Lord Tonypandy, Canadian stores millionaire Galen Weston, Shakespearean actor Kenneth Branagh and outgoing comedy-actor Stephen Fry.

The major influences in his life have not always been male, of course. Even after marriage, Charles has enjoyed the company of female confidantes who share his interest in horses, hunting and the outdoor life. Apparently, they must also be good listeners! These female friends include women whose influence on the Prince has been considerable. Among them are Sarah Lindsay, widow of skiing victim Major Hugh Lindsay, Patti Palmer-Tomkinson, who was severely injured in the same accident, Lady 'Kanga' Tyron and Mrs Camilla Parker-Bowles.

Charles first met Camilla Shand in 1972 when they were both 23. He was shy and awkward; she was the blonde, vivacious daughter of a wealthy wine merchant, master of foxhounds and Deputy Lord Lieutenant of East

Sussex. She is also the great-grand-daughter of Mrs George Keppel, mistress of Edward VII during his reign.

Prince Charles was utterly smitten, despite the fact that Camilla was already being wooed by Charles's polo friend, Andrew Parker-Bowles, an officer in the Blues and Royals. For eight months she dated Charles before he went to sea with the Royal Navy. Early in 1973, they said their farewells in his palace rooms. Weeks later she announced her engagement to army officer Andrew. Yet they continued to see each other. In 1980 Camilla accompanied Charles as his official escort to Zimbabwe for the country's independence celebrations. She was a frequent guest at Birkhall, a secluded house on the Balmoral estate.

The friendship continued even after Prince Charles's own marriage. A year after their wedding, he confessed to Princess Diana in an angry scene at Highgrove that he remained friendly with a married woman and had 'no intention of giving her up – ever'. Not long after Prince William was born in 1982, Diana overheard her husband on the telephone saying: 'Whatever happens I will always love you.' A royal insider revealed to the authors that whenever Diana arrives at Highgrove she immediately presses the 'redial' button on the telephone ... far too often for her liking it is the Parker-Bowles house that answers.

Right through his ill-fated marriage, the Prince of Wales has continued to see Camilla. Her home is a 500-acre estate at Corsham, Wiltshire, only a 20-minute drive from Highgrove. They have spent days and nights at the Waleses' country home while Diana has been in London. She has supervised the domestic and kitchen staff, hosted dinners and sat next to him at table. She nursed him at Highgrove and at Balmoral when he broke his arm in his 1990 polo accident. A year later she accompanied him to Florence on a painting holiday. Camilla is the girl with whom Charles was passionately in love but to whom he never proposed. It is obvious to all that the old flame still burns bright.

However, if we go back to Charles's youth, we would find that although Camilla may have been the *real* love of the Prince's life, she has not been the *only* love.

Prince Charles may not be the most handsome man in the world but he has never had any trouble attracting beautiful women. Doubtless that may have something to do with his position. Over the years he has been linked to a string of society belles and European royals, none of whom he felt inclined to make the future queen.

In June 1977 the revelation that all of Britain had been awaiting hit the news-stands in big, bold type. The head-line read: 'Charles to marry Astrid – official'. The Astrid referred to was Princess Marie-Astrid of Luxembourg. However, it was not to be; the press had been the victim of a cruel political ploy to root out a suspected mole who was a member of the Privy Council. The story had been planted.

Charles's reaction at the time was one of incredulity. He had never even met his so-called bride-to-be. In an unprece-dented move, he issued a statement: 'There is no truth at all in the report that there is to be a formal announcement of an engagement to Princess Marie-Astrid of Luxembourg.'

The next day, when the press refused to let go of such sensational speculation, he issued another statement through the Queen's press secretary. This one was even more emphatic: 'They are not getting engaged this Monday, next Monday, the Monday after, or any other Monday, Tuesday, Wednesday or Thursday. They do not know each other and people who do not know each other do not get engaged.'

In the ensuing years gossip columnists were kept busy with their predictions as to his future bride. Charles gave them a run for their money. He dated a string of women, jokingly referred to as 'Charlie's Angels' after the American television series.

Among his escorts were Lady Jane Wellesley, Princess Caroline of Monaco, Maltese Governor General's daughter, Sybilla Dorman, Tricia Nixon and Sabrina Guinness of the wealthy brewing family. Charles again made headlines when he invited the latter to a ball at the Earl of Pembroke's house, along with her twin sister, Miranda – then left the two of them like Cinderellas at the end of the night's dancing.

Charles is the ultimate chauvinist and his many dates were expected to behave in an old-fashioned, subservient way. One who fell foul of his pig-headed attitude was Davina Sheffield, a beautiful 25-year-old blonde whom Charles met in 1976 at a dinner party in Fulham. Davina was invited to Balmoral to be put through the 'test' – one that was designed to see if the woman was suitable for a continuing relationship. Poor Davina failed to grasp the message that she was expected to stay at home with the ladies of the household while the Prince and the other men went stalking through the Scottish heather. She insisted on tagging along and the hard-hearted Prince ran her into the ground by walking her through the toughest terrain he could find. She left the next morning for London. When revelations of her past romance with another man hit the headlines, she was never seen with Charles again.

Another woman who failed to fit Charles's ideal was Lady Jane Wellesley, daughter of the eighth Duke of Wellington. A BBC researcher and representative of the National Union of Journalists, he found her a touch too radical and outspoken for his taste.

Anna Wallace, daughter of a Scottish landowner, was the only woman, apart from Lady Diana Spencer, to whom Charles ever proposed marriage. He was 32 and no nearer to finding a wife than when he made his first conquest (Lucia Santa Cruz) 13 years earlier. However, Anna was more spirited than most of his escorts and would not accept his cool, unromantic, passionless approach to the art of love, epitomised by the occasion on which he infuriated her by inviting her to a ball then ignoring her all evening. She was known as 'Whiplash Wallace', a testament to her hot temper, and she certainly cracked the whip that night at Windsor Castle during the Queen Mother's eightieth birthday celebrations when she stormed out at midnight – and out of his life.

Yet another seemingly serious contender for his hand shattered his male ego when she spoke frankly about her feelings for him to the press. Lady Sarah Spencer was on a skiing trip with the Prince in 1975 when she was asked where their relationship was going. She replied: 'Charles is a fabulous person but I am not in love with him. He is a romantic who falls in love easily. I would not marry a man I did not love, whether it was a dustman or the

King of England. If he asked me I would turn him down.'

By now the ageing Prince was getting quite worried about his failure to find a future queen. Then, quite by chance, he met up with Diana Spencer, younger sister of Sarah.

The romance progressed unnoticed by the press for the next two years until the summer of 1980. Lady Diana had decided to join her now-married sister, along with her husband, Robert Fellowes, assistant private secretary to the Queen, and their new baby at a holiday cottage at Balmoral. A sharp-eyed reporter peered through his binoculars and at last identified the pretty young woman he had seen at other functions yet never managed to put a name to. It was Diana. Fleet Street was ecstatic and spent the next six months following her everywhere she went.

The couple finally made the announcement on 24 February 1981, with Diana sporting a beautiful £28,000 diamond and sapphire engagement ring.

Until then and through the early years of his marriage, the Prince had had a good relationship with the press, their stories approvingly reporting a young man at first sowing his wild oats then settling down to family life. Bit by bit, however, his popularity waned. At times he became but a shadow in the glare of the spotlight on his beautiful wife, Princess Diana.

His love of painting, his quaint architectural vision, his devotion to the 'natural', his need for self-contemplation have lost him his earlier 'action-man' image. Indeed, far removed from the days when Charles was criticised for his macho pursuits as putting at risk the very life of the heir to the throne is his obsession with spiritual matters. Macho man has become mystic man. He has even appointed his own secret spiritual adviser for medical treatments. As well as his devotion to bringing harmony between humans and the planet, Charles has stepped back in time, calling on Mother Nature for healing.

He is a great believer in alternative medicine. So much so, that he is patron of a homoeopathic medicine group in London. Charles regularly and secretly attends meetings and he called on the group's doctors to help him with one particular problem.

A senior medical source has revealed that, despite reports that he would one day have to give up playing polo because of injuries caused to his arm after a fall, a far more serious ailment plagues him. The polo fall exacerbated an old back injury. The consequence is that the Prince will be in pain – not constantly but often enough to affect his sense of wellbeing – for the rest of his life. Sometimes his ailment is sheer agony for him and to those who know him closely, it shows.

Charles has begged his homoeopathic specialist friends to provide treatment for back pain. One said: 'Charles is often in agony with his back. Sometimes standing is excruciating for him. He's made it clear to us that's the most hindering health worry he has.'

Charles's back complaint may well have affected his outlook on life. Perhaps the physical pain, along with the mental anguish over his marital problems and the continuing controversy over whether he really is mentally fit to be king one day turned him into a solitary, inward-thinking and often selfish figure. He has wrapped a wall around himself, stubbornly ignoring advisers, believing he is on a far greater level of awareness.

Prince Charles considers himself to be the guru of the Royal Family. It has often led to rows with his down-to-earth, gritty father, when Prince Philip throws his hands up in despair. Despite his efforts to rear a tough, practical son able to reach his people, he has ended up instead with a remote loner living in a world of his own – a world that doesn't really exist.

Charles's plight has not escaped the attention of the press. He is seen as an inadequate, distant father. Unlike his child-adoring wife, Charles is never asked to fulfil engagements which involve small children. When did we ever see him cuddling a toddler or crouching down to talk to a sick youngster? It is something he simply cannot do. He sees his duties simply as obligations. His conversations with 'inner-city' teenagers – another of his causes – are well-meaning but awkward.

Never were his clumsy attempts at being 'one of us' more highlighted than in an embarrassing television programme shown in the summer of 1992. Accompanied by TV celebrity Selina Scott, the Prince visited the Scottish island of Berneray to meet people and bed down for a few days in the humble surrounds of a islander's cottage.

In one scene, Charles was seen almost squirming with discomfort in the home of an islander. He sat with a plate bearing a slice of cake on his lap and a whisky in his hand. He sang a few lines of a ditty that was politely acknowledged by his fellow guests. It made for excruciating viewing. Miss Scott subserviently followed him around, the dialogue was banal, and the British public watched in total bemusement as the couple strolled aimlessly along a wind-swept beach, the interviewer making all the right noises as Charles rambled on about being in tune with the elements. The aim of the visit was to publicise the necessity to retain the Gaelic language, a cause which even Charles himself admitted might not be seen as a priority by most of his subjects.

Princess Diana should have been warned what was to come when she married a bachelor of Charles's age and character. On the first morning of their honeymoon, he left his marital bed at the old home of his beloved Uncle Dickie to go fishing in the River Test.

It heralded a married life of loneliness and frustration for Charles's young bride. It was yet another sign of his total inadequacy to bond mentally and emotionally with another human being. Diana was already believing she might have made a terrible mistake; and as we follow Prince Charles's uncertain course through life it becomes increasingly obvious that the route will never lead to the throne.

CHAPTER FOURTEEN

Princess Diana

It was just a few days before the biggest fairytale royal wedding the world had ever seen. For the romance-loving British it was to be an occasion of pomp and pageantry that would lift the spirits of the nation and unite everyone in a heart-stirring day long to be remembered. It was natural that at times it all seemed too much for the bride-to-be. Lady Diana Spencer, a rosy-cheeked girl who blushed when she met the gaze of a stranger, was now having to suffer the eyes of the whole world upon her as she waited to take her place in history.

On one occcasion, Diana sat nervously adjusting her dress, picking her nails and desperately trying to cope with cameras trained at her as she watched her soon-to-be husband, Prince Charles, ride in a polo match. Despite an all-out effort to swallow the nausea she felt and to choke back the tears, the 20-year-old newest recruit to the Royal Family suddenly could cope with the ordeal no longer. The tears began to flow and, without giving a second thought to the loss of public image, she fled to the safety of a Range Rover where she could weep freely.

It was all put down to the stress of the monumental change that was to happen in Diana's life but close friends knew differently. Deep down, Diana was wondering if she hadn't made some terrible mistake. It wasn't that she didn't love Charles. Or that she was just having cold feet about coping as part of Britain's monarchy. Diana was in turmoil over her husband-to-be's flaunting of his relationship with another woman, a relationship that was to batter and bruise Diana and Charles's marriage and eventually tear it asunder.

None among an adoring public knew this, of course.

They knew nothing of Charles's insistence that Diana call him 'Sir' during the early days of their courtship, while his female confidante and long-term, married friend, Camilla Parker- Bowles, called him by his nickname of 'Fred'. Charles, in turn, nicknamed Camilla 'Gladys'. Only those well inside the Buckingham Palace circle were aware of the many telephone calls Charles made to Camilla on his private line, sometimes overheard by a distraught Diana. Only the closest of friends were told by a weeping Diana of how she had unwrapped a gift that arrived at the palace to discover that it wasn't a wedding present to them but a gold chain bracelet bearing the initials F and G which Charles was to give to Camilla.

When Diana fled crying from the polo field that day, all that onlookers saw was a frightened girl finding the glare of publicity before her marriage just too, too much. Eleven years later Diana was to break down in tears in full public focus again, amid an amazing private and royal turmoil. Diana has felt like running away again many, many times over.

For most of her married life since she walked down the aisle of St Paul's Cathedral on 29 July 1981, the Princess of Wales has been oppressed by stress, suffering and sickness. Most of her crying has been behind closed doors. Diana's brave face was the one she put on for her doting public and loyal supporters. She speaks gentle words to the little children she crouches down to meet during official engagements and to the elderly and the sick whose hands she shakes on visits. The real feelings of Lady Diana Spencer turned Princess of Wales are kept for the private turmoil she suffers as wife of a distant, totally unsuitable husband with whom she has nothing in common.

Very few know the real Diana and the extent of her misery, and that fiercely protective clique are too aware of the unique position they hold in Diana's life ever to tell the truth. Yet in 1992 the cracks in the wall of silence built around her began to show. Rumours about the intensity and enormity of her marital problems and her deep depression began to circulate. Diana, wife of Britain's heir to the throne, the woman who would one day take over from the Queen as the nation's female figurehead, had become so disturbed by living a royal lie that she had actually considered taking her own life. There was yet more than this chilling revelation to threaten the Royal Family's darkest secrets. For not only had the Princess of Wales's closest confidantes decided to bring to light the enormous and damaging strain she was under, but it appeared the Princess herself had co-operated over the release of explosive intimate details in a final bid to call attention to her loveless, lonely plight.

Diana had been married for nearly 11 years when her marriage sham was finally exposed. The revelations were a far cry from the gushing tributes that had poured out a year before when umpteen books and colour supplements marked her tenth wedding anniversary to Charles.

By this time, Diana was the mother of two sons, Prince Harry, aged seven, and Prince William, nine. She was the patron of nearly 40 charities and organisations. She was seen as the royal who, against adversity, composed herself at all times in a manner that was exemplary. She was held up as one of the hardest-working royals, fulfilling her duties without demur and always with a smile.

Where Prince Charles was never demonstrative towards his sons, Diana was the perfect, genuine mother, showing no restraint when it came to exhibiting the joy her children gave her. She had become a stunning ambassador for Britain. Her face had been seen on more magazine covers than anyone else in the world. When it came to style, everyone agreed that no one did it better. Unlike the devil-may-care Duchess of York, Diana's fashion flair was rarely criticised, but almost invariably copied and cooed over. In short, with her English-rose looks, willowy figure and impeccable demeanour, she was the perfect princess.

However, deep down, the little girl who was blessed enough to be born into the aristocracy wished she had not endeavoured to win the hand of a man whose character and family would force her into a cold-blooded, albeit very blue-blooded, existence. Her husband soon became jealous of the public adoration for Diana, which had once made him proud. He felt clumsy and ignored when he and his wife fulfilled official duties together. Once, a crowd even let their disappointment show when they were expecting Diana to make an appearance first but saw Charles instead step out of the car. There was an audible groan, followed by a jubilant cheer as they then set eyes on their beloved Princess. For photographers there was no comparison: pictures of Charles in his staid suits or Diana looking stunning whatever she wore, wherever she went.

Her first overseas tour to Australia and New Zealand, in April 1983, was a triumph. More than a million people turned out to see them during the visit. Charles could not help but be aware that the welcome was so warm because of his young, beautiful wife. Diana had decided to take her new-born son with her, a gesture that touched public hearts even more.

Eventually, Charles turned his resentment into anger aimed at his young wife. He tried to make her feel inadequate, with discussions he knew she would find too deep to share. He criticised her choice of friends, the way she spent her spare time and the way she looked. All the time he kept in regular contact with Camilla Parker-Bowles, the married woman who he felt understood him in a way his wife never could. All the time, Diana was sliding further and further down into a despair she felt she would never shake off.

No doubt, in her darkest hours, she recalled the legendary wooing and winning of her very own prince.

*　　*　　*

It is said that Diana fell in love with Charles after meeting up with him again when she was 16. She had been introduced to him at her home, Althorp, in Northamptonshire, which her father had inherited, along with the title Earl Spencer, upon the death of her grandfather two years before. Diana was home from school for half term when Charles arrived for a pheasant shoot. It was by no means a question of a member of royalty dropping by at the ordinary home of an ordinary girl. The Spencer family, by virtue of its aristocratic name and links, had always mingled closely and freely with the royals. Indeed, Diana was born at Park House, rented from the Royal Family on the Sandringham estate in Norfolk. It was inevitable that the Spencers and the Windsors would become friends. That is how Diana's elder sister, Sarah, first came to meet Charles and become his girlfriend.

That weekend pheasant shoot heralded another sport much loved by the upper classes: bagging a marriage partner to better oneself even further! No one would dare to suggest that Diana made the decision to steal Charles away from Sarah but steal him she did, by winning smiles, flirting and an unconscious determination to be noticed. Charles remarked later that he was absolutely enthralled by the gawky teenager. 'She was a jolly, amusing and attractive 16-year-old,' he said. Diana told friends her heart was lost on that very first introduction but she never dreamed that the Prince who impressed her with his man-of-the-world air and royal control would one day be her husband.

It was sad that neither ever sat down and evaluated what one partner could give the other. Charles was the product of a typical royal upbringing and schooling. He was well read, serious to the point of being stuffy, a maker of polite conversation, but totally detached from the every-day lives of everyday people. He hunted, rode, preferred intense debate to socialising with large groups of friends. No one could ever forget that here was a man groomed one day to be king.

Diana, on the other hand, was anything but an academic. She passed no exams at school, where her reports could do no better than say she was kind to animals and younger children (although she did win a prize at her West Heath private school in Kent for being enthusiastic and 'nice'). She later took several jobs, including cleaning, and she learned how to type and how to ski at a finishing school in Switzerland. Basically she was being groomed for nothing other than to marry well.

No one can guess what would have happened to Diana if Charles had not become a serious part of her life. What is certain is that she believed that, whomever she married, it should be for ever. One of the very first intimate conversations she had with Charles was about the divorce of her parents when she was six. It had had a profound effect on such a sensitive, sheltered girl. For Diana, divorce was a particularly heart-breaking word. Close friends believe that the bond Diana has with her own children has come about through a determination to shower as much love and security upon them as possible after her own unhappy childhood.

Diana's first memories are of her parents, the eighth Earl Spencer and Lady Frances Spencer, arguing as she and her two sisters, Lady Sarah and Lady Jane, covered their ears with their hands. Those years are still remembered by Diana. One private vow she made to herself was that her children would never hear harsh words between their parents, no matter how intolerable the relationship became.

Diana remained exceptionally close to her father, who was given custody of the children after the divorce. Her mother married Peter Shand-Kydd, heir to a wallpaper fortune. Earl Spencer married again just a year after moving to Althorp. His new wife was the Countess of Dartmouth, better known as Raine, daughter of romantic novelist Barbara Cartland.

Diana became a daughter torn. She worshipped her father but found it hard to accept her stepmother. She divided her time between Althorp and her mother's home in Scotland. Although Diana found it hard to love Raine, she was eternally grateful for the care the Earl's wife bestowed on him after he had a massive stroke when Diana was 18. It was that devoted care that enabled the proudest father in the world to walk down the aisle to see his daughter married to the Prince of Wales. Diana felt she would never recover from her grief when her beloved father died in March 1992.

It was a year after Charles and Diana's first meeting that their paths were to cross again. She was finding her independence in a London flat she shared with three friends. He occasionally asked her along to make up the numbers at private gatherings. Diana thought no further than getting closer to the Prince to discover the real man behind his detached, regal image. She certainly never envisaged becoming his wife, but she always kept her hopes up that she would become more than just 'Sarah's little sister' to him.

Charles was watching with sharpening interest as Diana blossomed from an awkward girl into an attractive young woman. By the time the Queen invited Diana and Sarah to Balmoral for a house party in 1979, the love match was taking shape. The invitation, Charles was to admit later, was a put-up job. He was no longer escorting Sarah; they had remained good friends, but inviting the two girls to the royal home was the only ruse he could think of to begin his courtship of Diana.

Royal courtships must be slow by ordinary standards, for it wasn't until early 1980 that Diana received another invitation, this time to join the Royal Family at Sandringham. A couple of months later Charles invited Diana to watch him play polo. Two weeks after that she joined him on the royal yacht at Cowes. As one wag remarked: 'The Di was now cast.'

Diana, although growing more deeply in love with the earnest Prince, was not prepared for the press interest that was growing too. From the moment, later that year, that she was spotted fishing at Balmoral with Charles, she became the target of intense media pressure. Her past was dug into, no one believing that there was such a thing as a virgin in these modern times. Her academic achievements (or lack of them) were commented upon. Diana was hounded wherever she went.

One incident particularly endeared her to the press, at the same time as filling many a newspaper page. She was pictured holding a small child at the London kindergarten where she worked, unwittingly wearing a cotton skirt that was virtually transparent when photographed against the sun! Everyone marvelled at the fine pair of legs belonging to Charles's likely wife-to-be.

Diana's flatmates, Anne Bolton, Carolyn Pride and Virginia Pitman, were all but bribed to discover exactly what Di got up to behind the doors of their Colherne

Court flat in London's upmarket Knightsbridge. In fact, the three girls were the first to know how serious Diana's relationship with Charles was. However, even they weren't prepared for the scene that greeted them one night when they got home. Diana had fled the bachelor girls' nest just before her engagement was officially announced. All that remained of her was a note saying: 'Please call me, I'm going to need you.'

The announcement of their engagement on 24 February 1981 was a merciful release for Diana but the intensity of press coverage did not let up. There were pictures of Diana as a child, pictures of Diana as a teenager, and even pictures showing what her wedding dress *might* look like. At least she now had the powerful protection of the Royal Family and a private apartment at Kensington Palace to shield her. A month after her engagement the Privy Council gave permission for the marriage; only then, because of protocol, could Diana be photographed with the Queen. Five gruelling months of pre-wedding royal tuition followed to prepare her as wife of the future King of England.

It was upon Diana's official acceptance into the Royal Family that Prince Charles gave his first comments about his feelings for her. He was asked if he was in love. The Prince replied: 'Yes, whatever that may mean.'

Diana's first public engagement with Charles was a recital in London. She wore a low-cut, black taffeta evening dress and got her first real taste of being the world's most photographed woman. There followed three state banquets, Trooping the Colour, the service of the Order of the Garter and a host of exhausting walkabouts which allowed the public to get to know their new princess.

Meanwhile Diana had to learn to adjust to royal life and all the restrictions it imposed and she had to learn quickly. The wedding was the grandest in memory, with 750 million television viewers world-wide watching her walk down the aisle wearing a dress created specially for a princess by designers David and Elizabeth Emanuel. Despite rehearsals, Diana still managed to get Prince Charles's four names in the wrong order when she repeated her marriage vows but all it did was to endear the Royal Family's newest princess to the nation even more.

Diana was looking forward to a dream of a honeymoon cruising around the Mediterranean, but it was far from the romantic, private interlude she envisaged. The newly-weds barely had a moment to themselves. What should have been intimate dinners were similar to official functions as officers on the royal yacht *Britannia* waited on them. Far from cuddling up to his new bride and planning their happy future, Charles read his heavyweight, thought-provoking tomes and discussed mysticism and the meaning of life.

On the surface, everything went well at the start of the 'radiant reign' of the new Princess of Wales. Her very first official engagement with Prince Charles had the Queen and royal advisers breathing a great sigh of relief. The couple went to Wales and, despite heavy rain that made the feather on Diana's green velvet hat go limp, their walk-about among the people of Carmarthen was an astounding success. The love she had for Charles positively glowed through. Her eyes sparkled. Her demure smile won people over wherever she went. Her way with children touched hearts. Slowly her confidence grew, together with the fashion style that brought praise throughout the world. They were heady days that now must be wistful memories as, with bitter challenges in her private life, 'Shy Di' has become 'Sad Di'.

Some say it is the 12-year age gap between her and Charles that made them grow apart. Upon marriage, she was a very young 20-year- old, while he had the attitudes of a man much older than his 32 years. She was the Pop Princess, he the Philosopher Prince. Tales were told of how Diana would dance her way through Kensington Palace listening to rock bands on her personal stereo, or exasperate her serious-minded, money-conscious husband with her love of shopping. 'On occasions, Charles was concerned that the earnestness and serious-mindedness built into him were not as strong in his beautiful young wife,' said one insider. 'But he would have had the same doubts about any woman he might have married. No woman ever born could have lived up to expectations as unrealistic as his.'

Charles himself gave a few clues as to whether married life was living up to his expectations when he said: 'I think an awful lot of people have got the wrong idea of what love is all about. It is rather more than just falling madly in love. It's basically a very strong friendship. I think you are very lucky if you find the right person attractive in the physical sense and the mental sense. If I am deciding whom I want to live with for 50 years, well that's the last decision on which I'd want my head to be ruled by my heart.'

One royal observer accurately described Charles as 'judging marriage as an additional burden in an already busy life'. His words were to ring true a few months after Diana gave birth to Prince William on 21 June 1982, when there arose the first of many clashes of private and public obligations.

Diana, suffering from depression and a feeling of being trapped, begged not to attend the annual Remembrance Day Service at London's Royal Albert Hall. She wanted to be at home with her new baby and she wanted her husband to stay with her. There was a violent row, over-heard by royal staff. Charles was stunned at the sudden change in his wife. It was her duty to attend the official function, he said, and duty always came first, she *had* to understand that.

There were anxious moments at the service when an obviously ruffled Prince Charles arrived without Diana. He whispered the official reason for her absence, pleading sickness on his wife's behalf. Five minutes later Diana turned up, confirming that Charles had left Kensington Palace not knowing exactly what she had decided to do. In fact, it was only the gentle cajoling of palace advisers that put Diana in her rightful place, at her husband's side on a royal engagement.

A year later, the couple gave an interview to television broadcaster Sir Alastair Burnet. It was extraordinary, in that Diana came across as totally articulate and utterly in control, while it was Prince Charles who looked uncomfort-able. There was reason for discomfort, for the couple had just suffered vitriolic revelations in the press. One bitter ex-valet had branded Diana a spoilt child who had got rid of many of Charles's loyal and trusted staff (indeed in the four years after their marriage, 40 staff members were to leave) and who had stopped her husband from enjoying his favourite pursuits of hunting and shooting. Reports said Charles was being 'pussy-whipped' by a petulant wife.

In a bid to correct much of what was being said in those early days, Diana and Charles invited Fleet Street editors to an informal lunch to discuss the situation. It was a wasted effort. The editors simply enjoyed their lunch and the chat, but gave no orders that coverage of the royal couple's marriage should be modified. The Prince and Princess made another mistake, too, in their bid to tell the world that all was well in their private lives. They invited television cameras to their Highgrove home in Gloucestershire to record scenes of domesticity and the quiet calm of a royal couple away from the public eye. Instead, viewers were irked at the glimpse into a privileged existence that allowed the Princess to spend time deciding which costly designer clothes she would add to her wardrobe. Instead of the public being endeared to a future King of England finding quietude among his herb gardens, they smirked at his confession of talking to his plants. That rare insight into the sensitive Prince's mind earned him the nickname the 'Loony Prince'. The couple felt hurt and cheated.

A little brother for Wills, Prince Harry, arrived on 15 September 1984. The Princess was a model mum but, in contrast to her new-found *joie de vivre*, her husband became noticeably stiff and formal in her presence. Trying to reach a compromise in marriage between a wife who revelled in parties and girlish chatter and a husband who worried about unsightly modern architecture and the royal obligations he was born into became impossible.

In public they mastered the art of putting on a united front. In private, things began to go badly awry. Diana felt a stranger in her own home. Her husband was cold and detached. He showed little interest in his sons. Worst of all, the bulimia nervosa that had taken a grip on her shortly after becoming engaged to Charles continued. Diana's self-esteem was low. The slimming disease of gorging and then making herself vomit had become a regular part of Diana's life. Her weight went up and down. Often Diana looked painfully thin, but she laughed off questions about her figure. 'I eat like a horse,' she told people, fooling them and herself. She sought medical and psychiatric help on occasions when she really felt she couldn't cope. She even made cries for help by cutting herself with a knife and hurling herself hysterically against a glass cabinet. Way back when Diana was three months pregnant with William, she was so insecure in her royal marriage that, after falling down a few stairs, she claimed she was being driven to suicide. It has even been alleged that some time later, in sheer desperation, she was to take an overdose.

Charles treated all the incidents as irritating dramas he hoped would never be known outside the tight palace circle; he feared the embarrassment they would cause. He turned more and more to Camilla Parker-Bowles, the 'safe' girlfriend whose relationship with him had the blessing of her husband.

Despite shining on every public appearance, Diana's smile hid feelings of despair that her life was a total sham, a mess, centred around a meaningless marriage. By 1986, Charles and Diana were both desperately unhappy and were drifting further and further apart. It was not just the stress of their relationship, but also the pressure put on them by a public forever looking for signs of those problems.

One particular incident made Diana realise that she would never be able to look to her husband for support. They were at the Expo World Fair in Vancouver, when Diana, whose dramatic weight loss had caused comment among her hosts, grabbed Charles's arm, muttered a few words and then collapsed in a heap. She had fainted through her erratic eating habits and the strain of trying to live a normal existence with such an abnormally inattentive husband as Charles. Far from receiving sympathy for her public faint, Diana received instead harsh words from her husband for not waiting until she was in private before making an exhibition of herself. At the end of that particular day's touring, Diana locked herself away in her room and sobbed.

It was becoming increasingly difficult for Diana to hide her frustration and feelings of isolation. She started to confide in close friends, despairing that her marriage had become one By Royal Appointment rather than one of passion. A telling remark came as Diana visited a hospital. She saw a romantic novel by a patient's bed and commented: 'I enjoyed that one, too, but my husband doesn't approve of the books I read.' That one comment hinted at the incompatibility between the couple and the kind of terse conversations that obviously took place between them behind the closed doors of their private apartments.

Later in the year, Diana's absence was noticeable when Charles attended a Mountbatten party, that of Timothy Knatchbull to celebrate his twenty- first birthday. The Princess, having had a run of arguments with Charles over his lack of interest in his family and herself, threw a typically female sulk. She turned down the joint invitation to the party in a fit of pique. The official reason was that Diana needed time with her children.

In August that year, Charles and Diana went on holiday to Majorca but the Prince flew home earlier than his wife. Despite the 'official smiles' the couple put on for the cameras during a tour of the Persian Gulf a few months later, the strain between them was obvious.

The next year began, doing little to improve the image of the Royal Family. The new Duchess of York, formerly Sarah Ferguson, and her husband, Prince Andrew, joined Charles and Diana on a ski trip to Klosters. Di was allowing herself to be influenced by her fiery, redheaded friend, and it caused many a royal eyebrow to be raised. On this skiing trip, as the four lined up for press photographs, the two young women playfully pushed each other on the slopes, laughing as they lost their balance. Charles was not amused at the unruly, unregal behaviour. There were reports from the same trip that Diana was forever teasing her husband and leaving him in their chalet alone while she went looking for nightlife. Eventually she left Klosters to return to London alone.

Gossip about the royal couple's marriage began to grow, especially when the beautiful Princess took to driving around London late at night on her own. She was also seen out and about enjoying herself at cinemas, pop concerts and restaurants.

It was at this time, too, that other men began to feature in Diana's life. In society circles, such male escorts are called 'walkers' – attractive men who escort wives on outings when the husband is absent. In the view of a distressed Charles, however, the likes of city banker Philip Dunne and cavalry officer David Waterhouse had absolutely no right to be photographed alongside his errant wife. Diana took exception to the press interest shown in her socialising. She snapped: 'Just because I go out without my husband doesn't mean that my marriage is on the rocks.'

Nevertheless, tongues wagged when the Princess was photographed with David Waterhouse at a David Bowie concert at Wembley. The couple whispered and giggled together in front of 72,000 witnesses! They were often spotted leaving the homes of friends together.

Philip Dunne was a regular member of house parties invited to stay at Windsor for Royal Ascot and he also joined Diana and Charles on a skiing trip to Klosters. Diana once spent a weekend at the country home of Philip's parents while Charles was out of the country and she was guest of honour in 1989 when Philip married Domenica Fraser, daughter of the former Rolls Royce chairman Sir Ian Fraser. Charles had declined his invitation in favour of a day's hunting.

Other close men friends include Nicholas Haslam, former equerry to Charles, Mervyn Chaplin, who runs an audio installation business, and Rory Scott, a young man for whom Diana sometimes did some ironing back in her single days.

Most of her male friends appreciate the privileged position they hold but one made an embarrassing faux pas over his closeness with the Princess. Sandy-haired army captain James Hewitt became devoted to Diana after he was chosen to teach Prince William to ride. His charm encouraged Diana to return to riding too. It was no mean feat; she had become terrified of horses after falling off one when she was a child. The friendship was to continue. Later, while he was serving in the Middle East during the 1991 Gulf War, Diana wrote regularly to the tank captain. Shortly after his return, Hewitt ended his relationship of five years with girlfriend Emma Stewardson, who claimed that James was totally smitten with Diana.

In April of 1987, Charles went off to the Kalahari Desert with Sir Laurens van der Post. Soon after arriving back in London he took off again, this time on a painting trip to Italy. Speculation over Charles and Diana's marriage problems grew stronger. That October, Charles travelled to Balmoral to see his sons. He stayed just one night, without even catching up with the wife he hadn't seen for a month. Much was made of the fact when the couple eventually spent a night under the same roof together. Even then, Diana was off 24 hours later. The next month she was absent from another private, family occasion: the marriage of Charles's old friend, Amanda Knatchbull, grand-daughter of his beloved Uncle Dickie, Earl Mountbatten.

Diana spent all night dancing with Philip Dunne at the wedding of the Marquess of Worcester. An incensed Charles stormed over to her in the early hours to say it was time to leave. Diana refused and once again a very public display of personal differences had Charles going home on his own.

The situation had got to the stage that at one point the couple had spent only one day together in six weeks. Even when they visited flood vicitims in Wales, the Prince and Princess made they way there separately. She arrived from Highgrove; he flew in from Aberdeen. They paid their condolences to the victims then left separately too.

Amid fierce speculation that the royal marriage really was on the rocks, Princess Diana and her Prince put on a brave front during their visit to Berlin, wearing determined smiles throughout. By this time, Charles was throwing himself into various 'causes' to take his mind off their marital problems but his sudden desire to become a high-profile prince did not fool the public.

The end of 1987 held a traumatic incident for Princess Diana. At the height of speculation over the couple's widening rift, she was spotted by a photographer giggling and acting playfully in a quiet Kensington mews in the early hours of the morning. She had just emerged from the home of her close friend, stores heiress Kate Menzies, whom the Princess had often visited to escape the rigours and formalities of life at Kensington Palace. Diana would hop into her car and quietly nip around the corner to nearby Queensgate Mews where friend Kate had a small maisonette. The immediate neighbours had often marvelled at the comings and goings there and at the many 'Sloane Ranger' girls and dashingly handsome young men who made up this exclusive circle. Neighbours were more than once tempted to complain about the late-night movements of motor cars in the narrow mews but the knowledge that the Princess of Wales was a friend and guest prevented them. Her solo visits were well known to them.

It was only when a keen-eyed photographer began to watch and follow Diana that her nocturnal escape route was revealed to a wider public. He waited outside and when Diana left Kate Menzies's home in the early hours he photographed her laughing and larking and acting altogether like a coquettish young girl alongside a particularly handsome young man. He was Household Cavalry officer David Waterhouse, who had long held a deep affection for the lonely Princess.

Diana spotted the photographer and immediately became distraught. Such pictures could not possibly be published. In tears, she begged the photographer not to use the pictures and to hand them over to her. It was the desperate act of a desperately unhappy woman. Some agreement was reached. The pictures did not appear but reports about the incident did. It was no wonder that the Queen finally summoned Charles and Diana to Buckingham Palace to order them to put right what had become a right royal farce of a marriage.

Another, more tragic event was to sour the image of the young royals just a few months later, in March 1988. Diana and Charles were on another Klosters ski trip, staying with close friends Patti and Charles Palmer-Tomkinson. Also in the skiing party were the Duchess of York and mutual friend Major Hugh Lindsay. On this particular occasion, not long after the obligatory photo call for the world's press, the Duchess and Princess decided not to continue their skiing fun. Instead, they stayed behind to relax indoors. That decision could have saved their lives.

Within hours, they learned that Major Lindsay was dead and Patti Palmer-Tomkinson was critically injured. A giant avalanche had swept over them as the ski party tore down a slope of deep virgin snow that was off the normal piste. Major Lindsay was killed outright. Mrs Palmer-Tomkinson was revived by mouth-to-mouth resuscitation. Her legs were horrifically crushed. The rest of the group, including alpine guide Bruno Sprecher and a Swiss policeman, had literally missed death by inches. They could only watch in horror as their friends were swept away.

It was a very humble and bowed group that returned immediately to London. Their tragedy was obviously treated with sympathy. Yet there was also public concern that the privileged royals had deliberately put themselves and their hapless companions at risk.

The tragedy was, however, a turning point in Diana's life. She had surprised herself at the practical way in which she had coped when faced with such a crisis. It was she who had organised the skiing party's return home, the packing of the dead man's belongings and the sensitive breaking of the news to Hugh's pregnant wife, Sarah, back home in London. Diana found a sudden maturity. She had been amazed at the way Charles let her take control of the situation and now, for the first time since meeting the Prince, she began to feel in control of her own life.

Diana returned from the trip a more confident woman. Yes, the obsessive slimmer's disease still regularly reared its ugly head and there were times when she shut herself away and wept, but she had discovered a new determination. She had also begun to despise the way her husband made her feel inadequate.

The Princess no longer felt embarrassed when well-meaning but unknowing members of the public asked her about having more children. Diana brushed aside their enquiries with a joke. She knew there was little likelihood of her becoming pregnant again. She and Charles had separate sleeping quarters. She could barely stand being in his presence.

Servants were more than once disturbed to observe Diana's manner when the couple were alone together. Said one: 'Her knuckles were white as she clenched them when he was talking to her. It was if she just wanted to scream.'

Another commented: 'There are rows, terrible rows. Anyone who has met the Princess in public would find it hard to believe how she is in private. You can feel the tension when you enter the room. Once, she walked along rows and rows of books, punching each one as she went, shouting, "No, No, No" as Charles tried to talk to her.'

It was at the end of that year that Diana chose to make her first major speech. It was on behalf of the children's charity Barnardo's and she spoke with feeling about children's needs within the family. Diana revelled in her newfound confidence and independence. She realised she was capable of a lot more than simply being a pretty patron of a charity or the perfect clothes-horse for the British fashion industry.

In a very telling move in 1989, Diana became patron

of the marriage-guidance group, Relate, and made it clear she wanted to be more than just a figurehead. During her official visits to Relate offices, Diana would listen intently as the counsellors described their work and how they encouraged partners to open up about the problems in relationships. On one particular Relate visit, Diana witnessed counsellors acting out different roles, pretending to be partners coming to them for advice. The Princess's attentiveness throughout was not overlooked and she was not slow in asking pertinent questions about marriage guidance.

The Princess of Wales was now paying more attention to her own health. She started having acupuncture sessions to help her relax. Then there were the visits to a chiropractor to iron out the nagging pains that had come with incessant standing and sitting for long periods at a time. Diana underwent reflexology, the theory of which is that certain parts of the feet are connected to vital organs in the body. She took up swimming regularly, something she had abandoned when she started to suffer depression. In an attempt to straighten out her mind, Diana called upon an astrologer and an interpreter of dreams.

She became obsessed with how astrology could determine one's fate. It was ironic that Diana should turn to things mystic, something for which she had always scorned her husband, to try to work through her failing marriage and desperate turmoil. She believed spirits were looking after her and guiding her. Diana no longer simply dressed to suit an occasion or win fashion acclaim. The colours she wore were carefully picked to help her inner karma.

It was an almost robotic princess who switched on the smiles for public appearances. However, she switched off in private, becoming disturbingly child-like and unsociable. Only her children and the support of a secret circle of friends allowed Diana to keep her grip on reality.

By now, the Princess and her husband were leading totally different lives, coming together only through necessity. Diana spent as little time as possible at Highgrove; Charles rarely stayed overnight in London. Whenever Princes Harry and Wills enjoyed a day out, it was always with their mother. Diana no longer had any qualms about going out on her own. She took to driving around London unescorted just for the sheer feeling of freedom it gave her.

Diana was also less cautious about her private life. She spent more time with old friend James Gilbey, a society car dealer. The dashing Gilbey, one of the famous gin family, first met Diana when she was in her teens and living in her bachelor-girl flat in London. James was the shoulder for Diana to cry on. He listened silently as she talked about her obsessive eating problems, her loneliness, the times she had threatened to kill herself just to get a spark of reaction from her husband. James had heard it all before but now he felt a growing unease. He sensed a more sinister mood in his old friend yet he knew that there was little he could do. Whom could he warn that the Princess of Wales might one day really attempt suicide?

As one of Diana's few and trusted *real* friends, James knew that the last thing he should do was to tell anyone what the Princess had revealed to him. However, he was later to be asked to speak out about the Princess's health and emotional troubles and would thereby become part of a group whose aim would be to raise Diana in the favour of the British public at the same time as alienating it from Charles.

Diana's closeness to James was first discovered when she was tailed by two journalists one evening in the autumn of 1989. The Princess drove to James's apartment in fashionable Lennox Gardens, Knightsbridge, accompanied by her private detective, Sergeant David Sharp. On arrival, she jumped out of the car at 8.20 p.m. and dismissed the policeman. She was in the apartment for a little over five hours. The reporters saw no one else arrive or leave.

Sergeant Sharp, obviously acting on instructions, returned to collect his charge at 11 p.m. but it was gone 1 a.m. when Diana made her exit. On leaving, she furtively looked up and down the street to make sure the coast was clear. Her face was hidden by a hat pulled firmly over her eyes. She was taken home by Sergeant Sharp, who had hung around for over two hours.

The reporters later questioned James Gilbey, who was at that time still the soul of discretion. He told them that the Princess had visited his home to make up a foursome at bridge. He was unable to comment when the newsmen pointed out that he had had no other visitors that night!

Prince Charles was well aware of the friendships that his wife was forging. What angered him and deeply offended his pride was that the public saw only one side of the picture. He was always portrayed in the press as the cold, unfeeling husband; she was always the mix of Madonna and Mother Teresa. It infuriated him but there was no way that he could change the impression given to the world.

The truth of the matter, as the authors can now reveal, is that Prince Charles has had many close females as confidantes but has had only one real love in his life, Camilla Parker-Bowles. She was equally firm in her regard for him, right up to his marriage to Diana. He has told his friends that from the moment of that fairytale wedding on 29 July 1981 he did his utmost to make his marriage work. He certainly saw Camilla (and Kanga and others) during the early years of his marriage but never once, he vows, did he imperil it.

It was five long years before he threw in the towel as a husband. Five years during which Diana grew apart from him just as obviously as he from her. Even dinner guests at Kensington Palace noted at the time just how difficult the Princess found it to be pleasant to her husband. One visitor noted how her knuckles were clenched and white whenever he passed an observation about her. 'I didn't then know whether it was nerves or fear or frustration at being talked down to,' said the visitor. 'I know now, however. It was hatred.'

Charles and Camilla only started meeting again after five years of his marriage. By then, Diana was also making friends outside the marital home. Charles knew about his wife's men friends just as she knew about Camilla. He felt that she was flouting her marriage vows in far too public a manner. It reinforced his view that he was entitled to make his own pleasures with his own friends.

Princess Diana is an emotional, impetuous, hot-blooded woman. There have been men friends in her life and

Charles has had to accept it. There must have been times when he wished for a reconciliation – perhaps only for the sake of their children – but only he and his wife know whether he ever attempted one. Although he once again stopped seeing Camilla Parker-Bowles in 1991, he knew by then that his marriage had, to all intents and purposes, ended. Yet the hypocritical pretence went on.

In public, the Princess of Wales was battling to adhere to what the Queen describes as 'the necessary training some of the younger members of the family find it hard to cope with'. In private, Diana was on the verge of a nervous breakdown. She often absented herself from Royal Family gatherings. She found excuses to break free, if only for a few hours, from a marriage that made her feel trapped.

As 1989 wore on, Diana threw herself more and more into work. She carried out official engagements for Turning Point, a group for those with drink, drug and mental problems, of which she had become patron in 1987. As patron of the Welsh National Opera, one of her major overseas visits was to watch them perform at New York's Brooklyn Academy of Music. Guests paid £500 each for the privilege of attending an after-concert party at which the Princess was present.

The rift between Diana and Charles was highlighted once more when the Prince took a tumble playing polo at Cirencester. The Princess was in London when news reached her that her husband had broken his arm in two places. Once again, the couple were spending their leisure time apart. On hearing of Charles's accident, Diana was put in a quandary over what she should do. For the sake of public appearances, she knew she should rush to his side but, quite frankly, she couldn't be bothered. She chose instead to keep a date with her lady-in-waiting, Anne Beckwith-Smith, who was holding a leaving party.

Later in the evening, the Princess had arranged to attend Puccini's *La Bohème* at Covent Garden with old friend Carolyn Bartholomew. It was only when warned that it wouldn't look good if she failed to visit Charles that night that she reluctantly drove down to Cirencester Hospital. Charles's injury was such that he later underwent a second operation and was out of action for several months. Diana's workload increased dramatically. Diana fulfilled not only her own scheduled duties but Charles's too, to avoid disappointing those who had long been on his itinerary of visits and engagements.

Diana also dutifully turned up to see her disgruntled husband at the Queen's Medical Centre in Nottingham, where he underwent his second operation. During her visits, Diana befriended the parents of a young man who was in a coma after a motorcycle accident. The Princess held his hand and helped bring him round. When the news leaked out, Diana's secret dedication, coupled with her gruelling round of extra royal engagements, made her shine like a saint in the eyes of her adoring public.

Tellingly, as soon as Charles was discharged from hospital, Diana once again went about her own independent life. The Prince flew off to France to recuperate, accompanied by his physiotherapist, Sarah Key. He then went to Balmoral to rest, where he was nursed by old flame Camilla Parker-Bowles while Diana remained in

London. Further restful days at Highgrove were also accompanied by Camilla. Royal lap dogs insisted the Waleses' separation simply reflected the Prince's need for time alone after his serious injury, and that he wanted to spend some weeks with the Queen Mother in Scotland, but they had no answer to the simple fact that a man who had suffered tremendous pain did not have his wife with him. It was the most natural thing for any married couple to be together when each most needed the other. Charles wasn't around either when William returned for his first weekend home after starting boarding school. It was Diana, as always, who was there for her children.

For the couple who had by now perfected living a lie, Charles's solitary recuperation was a welcome break for them both. Diana knew he was regularly in contact with Camilla and that he was visited by her but she was now past caring. Had they been an ordinary couple, she and Charles would have gone their own ways a long time before. However, there were the children. There was also, above all else, the fact that Diana was married to the man who could one day be king. Even though the chances of Charles ever making the throne were becoming more and more remote, Diana was nevertheless firmly ensconced as part of the higher echelons of the Royal Family. The charade she and Charles played out for the public seemed vital but in private life was a nightmare for them both.

It was only the privileged position they held that prevented many people, whom the Royal Family rightly considered totally trustworthy, from revealing exactly what was happening between Diana and Charles behind closed doors.

The effects of Princess Diana's bulimia nervosa were fairly clear for all to see. Not everyone knew of the clinical condition that was causing her such obvious distress but those around her became increasingly concerned for her wellbeing. Even workers at the Waleses' office at St James's Palace had noticed what one of them could only describe as 'irrational behaviour'. Staff there, as well as at Kensington Palace and Highgrove, generally found that dealing with Charles, crusty and formal though he could sometimes be, was preferable to answering to the Princess's whims. One worker who left their employ revealed that Diana's voice on the end of the phone made some of their hearts sink. Charles, it was said, might demand instant action in a polite but determined manner; Diana, on the other hand, might be chatty and charming at one moment then carping and critical the next.

Friends (though it must be said, principally friends of Charles) have spoken of their belief that Diana sometimes lacks touch with reality. She is rarely other than enchanting when in public, but in private her moods and sulks can be embarrassing. She has burst into tears in front of visitors. She has stormed out of rooms full of people. She has become hysterical in moments of upset, anger or frustration.

All this is perfectly symptomatic of bulimia. The Consumers Association issued a Drug and Therapeutic Bulletin on the disorder, which warned that sufferers:

indulge in episodes of massive overeating associated with a sense of loss of control. Between episodes of eating most sufferers fast or induce vomiting. Binges tend to be secret, sometimes pre-planned, and are often followed by strong mood swings expressed as guilt, depression, self-hate and even suicidal behaviour. Unlike anorexia nervosa, bulimia survives by disguise. It is a sophisticated illness in that sufferers do not admit they have a problem. They always appear to be happy and spend their lives trying to help others. Yet there is rage beneath the sunny smile, anger which sufferers are afraid to express.

They may, according to the bulletin, dislike their own bodies and feel guilty about caring for themselves. That disgust is translated into violent purging by vomiting or laxatives. Sufferers, it is said, 'have a sense of failure, low self-esteem and loss of control'.

Few knew of Princess Diana's traumas throughout the first decade of her marriage. However, the 'loss of control' was clear for all her household to see. Charles did his best to make himself scarce whenever the glint in his wife's eyes forewarned him of trouble, but there was one occasion at Highgrove, in the summer of 1990, when he could not escape in time.

Thoroughly embarrassed by his wife's voluble pursuit of some domestic row that no one can now recall, Charles tried to draw her away from the ears of the staff into a private room. Diana at first allowed herself to be led gently by the arm, then suddenly became animated. She began to rage at her husband and, according to one witness, was incoherent with anger at something he said to her in reply.

She wrested herself away from him, arms flailing. Charles ineffectually raised an arm as Diana's fists swung towards him. He blocked the blow but Diana appeared to hurt her wrist in the process. The fact that the incident was witnessed was excruciatingly embarrassing to Charles but seemed not to affect Diana one jot. She simply stormed upstairs.

Aides talked only in hushed whispers about such examples of Diana's hysterics. They were concerned at the regularity of their occurrence at a time when a public-relations exercise was being orchestrated to show their master and mistress in the best possible light.

Wholly unaware of the bubbling cauldron of domestic disharmony inside Highgrove at this time, a visitor turned up one day for a very special commission 'By Royal Appointment'. Accepted as the photographer who took 'nice' pictures of the royals, Tim Graham was invited to Highgrove for a session of at-home portraits. He arrived on a sunny day in 1990 to undertake the assignment any of the regular rat pack of royal paparazzi would have killed for. However, as soon as he set foot inside the door of the Prince and Princess of Wales's country mansion, an aide felt obliged to pull him aside and caution him that there was disharmony in this English idyll. Graham had arrived at a bad time. The photo session could not be cancelled but the photographer was told that he was likely to hear some raised voices. In an extraordinary briefing, servants were obliged to warn, effectively, that if the photographer heard the warring royals rowing, then he was to 'just ignore it'.

The glossy magazine photographs that emanated from this 'perfect' at-home session were all smiles, sweetness and light, but the fearsome rows that had been going on behind the scenes only got worse. Charles became increasingly frustrated at his inability to handle his wife's behaviour. Diana began to cut herself off in private life, not just from her husband, but from most of the Royal Family. It became a war of nerves as the Waleses organised separate schedules to ensure that they seldom met even on official duty. The Princess, drained and traumatised by more than a decade of bulimia nervosa – and blaming her husband for most of her misfortunes – was at the end of her tether.

During these times Diana sought solace from within her tiny circle of loyal friends... and it was to them she turned when her marriage hit the greatest crisis of all. But it was more than mere platonic comfort she was receiving. The Princess of Wales, it appeared, had been so in need of emotional support that she had encouraged the advances of admirers – and of one young man in particular. Indeed, Diana had been repaying her husband for his interest in other women – and repaying him in kind.

In truth, she had done no more than her husband had done. Like Charles, she had found more comfort outside her marriage. Like Charles with Camilla, she had found one special confidant to share the loneliness of her elevated station. Long after her husband had abandoned intimate love talk, that special person provided the warm words and support she so desperately craved, and only that special someone knew the real extent of her emotional turmoil. It was a disclosure of feelings Diana had never dared share with anyone else. The two came to rely on each other, meeting surreptitiously and sharing intimate secrets. Here at last was someone with whom she felt an equal. He did not sneer at her sometimes extraordinary naivety but found it endearing, just as Charles had once done. Here, too, was a man who brought out the 'daddy's girl' in Diana, gently chiding her when she showed self-doubt but firmly encouraging her when she felt able to fight back at the world.

The result of Diana finding new and stronger relationships outside her marriage was beneficial to her state of emotional health. She became more confident and better equipped to deal with the rigours of royal life. With her new-found feelings of self-worth, Diana was able to take on more duties. She at last felt a fully 'trained' member of 'the Firm'. She also felt strong enough to hit back when news of her secret friendship leaked out. And leak out it did, in the most extraordinary circumstances.

The Princess of Wales was warned of the existence of tape-recordings of her and her friend from teenage days: James Gilbey. Worse still, the tapes clearly illustrated that the relationship had gone far beyond the bounds of friendship. The tapes were of the two of them sharing not only small talk but love talk. They were circulated in Fleet Street and two newspapers acquired copies and put them 'on ice'. Several journalists on other newspapers, however, were also aware of the contents. It was a frightening new development that threatened to throw the entire royal machine into turmoil.

The tapes were of telephone calls dialled by the Princess

herself and recorded by a sophisticated monitoring device. The recordings were offered to journalists. Some information was taken from them but no deal was ever struck for their entire use. They 'vanished' for up to two years before resurfacing in the United States. Newspapers and magazines there and in Europe scrambled to be allowed to hear them. American voice analysts confirmed without equivocation that the female voice was that of the Princess of Wales.

The conversations between Diana and James Gilbey took place on New Year's Eve 1989 and the evening of 4 January 1990. He was apparently using a mobile phone in his car to speak to the Princess in her rooms at Sandringham, where she and her family were spending the holiday. He refers to her as 'Darling' and by the nicknames 'Squidge' and 'Squidgy'. They talk inconsequentially about the clothes they are wearing, and they mention several mutual friends, not always in flattering terms.

The Princess, at times sounding disturbed, reveals that TV host and charity fund-raiser Sir Jimmy Savile has been in touch with her, showing concern about her wellbeing. Diana and her man-friend joke about the star's reference to 'the redhead' (Fergie) as a 'lame duck', but the couple stop joking when Diana reveals that the showbusiness star had called her his 'number-one girl'. Gilbey insists that she is *his* number-one girl.

However, the most explosive part of the conversation comes when the couple talk about each other. The pair make plans for a meeting a couple of days later, 'Squidgy' getting a warning to be sure to cover her footsteps well.

'Jolly well do,' she says. Gilbey expresses impatience when he contemplates having to wait for the help of one of Diana's aides so that they can meet again. Gilbey is obviously ardently in love with the Princess and says so repeatedly. At one point he sighs simply: 'I love you, love you, love you, love you.'

The Princess uses intemperate language herself, but only when referring to the Royal Family. She reveals the difficulty she has in trying to grin and bear the 'confines' of her marriage. At one point she explodes: 'Bloody hell! What I've done for this f*****g family!'

Yet while the tapes expose Diana at her most vulnerable, they also reveal her genuinely caring nature. Her compassion, humanity, humour and endearingly coquettish appeal shine through. So does her courage and her frailty. Here is a woman crying out for the affection she fails to get from within her marriage and from within the Royal Family.

Diana speaks of a visit she had made that day to nearby Park House, the home on the Sandringham estate where she was born and spent her early years. Park House is now a rest home for the severely disabled and the compassionate Princess had considered entering quietly through a back door, but 'bugger it!', she tells Gilbey, why not walk straight in through the front door? This she did, and spent one and a half hours with the inmates, being photographed as they surrounded and hugged her. It must have been a most moving occasion.

Another example of Diana's sensitive nature is revealed when she speaks of an encounter with the Bishop of

Norwich, the Right Reverend Peter Knott, who was a guest of the Queen at Sandringham that Christmas. The Princess seems to have given the poor man something of a hard time. Diana told him she had lived before and that friends who had died still looked after her. The old cleric was apparently horrified, while the Princess was delighted in the way she had shocked him.

The Princess talks also of her puzzlement at the constant watch the Queen Mother keeps on her. Diana wonders wistfully why it is that, whenever she looks up, she catches 'his grandmother' staring at her with a strange look – a mixture of interest and pity.

At one stage, the taped conversation centres on a female friend, whose restaurant is closed over the New Year holiday. Mara Berni, a long-standing friend of Diana, is co-owner of her favourite restaurant, San Lorenzo in Beauchamp Place, near to Kensington Palace. San Lorenzo was indeed closed during that period.

Diana talks of going swimming near Sandringham with Fergie the following day. The two were pictured swimming together that week. She refers to a man called Ken taking her to London. At that time, Diana's Royal and Diplomatic Protection Squad bodyguard was Ken Wharfe, who took the wheel of her car on many occasions.

On the tapes, there is a reference to Diana having avoided the urge to 'binge' and she is asked about her weight – long before details of her desperate struggle against bulimia nervosa became public knowledge. Diana speaks of buying clothes for James Hewitt, the cavalry officer and Gulf War hero who became a close friend and was pictured alongside her at polo matches.

There is a reference to Nigel Havers, the dashing, 41-year-old movie star of whom Diana once said, prior to a royal premiere of one of his films: 'I don't care what it's about as long as Nigel Havers is there.' In the tapes, Diana says to Gilbey: 'Fergie said to me today that she had lunch with Nigel Havers and all he could talk about was you.' The fact is that Havers, famed for his smooth-talking role in the British television series *The Charmer*, had dined with Fergie only days earlier.

Diana also mentions Charlotte Hambro, 38, who had just become Countess Peel, second wife of landowner Earl Peel. Charlotte, from the wealthy Hambro merchant banking family, was a long-standing friend of Diana's and her daughter was a bridesmaid at her wedding to Charles. There is also a reference to Lady Lucy Manners, a 30-year-old former school chum of Diana's. She became Fergie's lady-in-waiting until she left the post in March 1992. She is a former girlfriend of Lord Linley.

Also among the *dramatis personae* in the world's most sensational phone calls are Diana's own children, William and Harry. At one stage, the Princess breaks off specifically to talk to Harry. Diana goes on to gossip in general terms about an afternoon out with her children and how much time her husband has spent with them. There is also a long discussion about astrology, which she follows so assiduously that she retains her own personal stargazer, Debbie Frank, whose predictions are referred to.

The deeply personal and obscure detail contained in the exchange leaves no doubt that the female voice on the tape is that of Princess Diana, but what confirms the identity of the man? Here are the clues from the tape.

He was 33 years old when the recordings were made, a Libran (born between 23 September and 22 October). At the time, he lived within 'knocking distance' of Diana's Kensington Palace home. He hunts and shoots, like his father, he has a car telephone, wears brown suede Gucci shoes and on the night of the call was dressed in denim jeans (a new pair which he said he'd bought the day before), green socks, a white and pink striped shirt topped with a dark, apple-green, V-neck pullover. He refers to a friend, City businessman Mark Davis, being a fellow guest at a recent tea party hosted by Simon Prior-Palmer and his wife Julia, adding that Davis hunts with the Belvoir and Quorn Hunts.

Only one man could fit – or have been privy to – all those facts: James Gilbey, a Libran born on 4 October 1956. At the time the tape was made, he lived at Lennox Gardens, not far from Kensington Palace. The handsome bachelor, a member of the wealthy Gilbey gin-distilling family, had been Diana's friend for 15 years. He has been quoted as saying: 'Diana is a private person who likes to keep her meetings with friends covered up. I am lucky to count her as a very good friend. We go back a long way. I knew her well before she got married.'

Dashing 6 ft 3 in Gilbey was first introduced to Diana by mutual friends when she was living, with three other girls, in a £50,000 London apartment bought for her as an eighteenth-birthday present by her father. Diana and Gilbey formed a deep friendship which lasted throughout her marriage. They regularly dined together at San Lorenzo, and Gilbey was on the exclusive list of close friends allowed easy access to the Princess at Kensington Palace and Highgrove.

At times, Gilbey needed Diana's shoulder to cry on as much as she needed his. After leaving Ampleforth, a leading Roman Catholic public school, he had headed for London to indulge his passion for cars at the upmarket end of the motor trade. His jobs included a brief spell with BMW, prior to joining Tom Dodd-Noble to set up the Holbein Motor Company, with franchises for Saab and Subaru. In 1991 the company fell victim to the economic recession and crashed, owing £500,000. Gilbey went on to work as a specialist marketing and sponsorship consultant for Lotus, driving a limited-edition Lotus Carlton. Former business associate Dodd-Noble said of him: 'He is a very good bloke. He's extremely nice to girls. He's understanding and a good listener. A problem can be talked over with James.'

Problems were presumably being talked over at length in October 1989 when they were caught out in their secret tryst at his Knightsbridge flat. Gilbey subsequently admitted: 'I suppose it wasn't that wise for Diana and myself to meet in those sort of circumstances. No doubt tongues will be wagging and there will be gossiping.'

His words were prophetic. Just a few weeks later, around New Year Eve 1989, they were caught out again. But this time it was *they* who were gossiping, and it was *their* tongues that wagged too freely.

Him: And so darling, what other lows today?

Her: **So that was it, I was very bad at lunch. And I nearly started blubbing. I just felt really sad and empty, and I thought: 'Bloody hell, after all I've done for this f******* family.'**

Him: You don't need to. Cos there are people out there – and I've said this before – who will replace emptiness. With all sorts of things.

Her: **I needn't ask horoscopes, but it is just so desperate. Always being innuendo, the fact that I'm going to do something dramatic because I can't stand the confines of this marriage.**

Him: I know.

Her: **But I know much more than they because . . .**

Him: Well, interestingly enough, that thing in *The People* didn't imply either one of you.

Her: **No.**

Him: So I wouldn't worry about that. I think it's common knowledge, darling, and amongst most people, that you obviously don't have . . .

Her: **A rapport?**

Him: Yeh, I think that comes through loud and clear. Darling, just forgetting that for a moment, how is Mara?

Her: **She's all right. No. She's fine. She can't wait to get back.**

Him: Can't she? When's she coming back?

Her: Saturday.

Him: Is she?

Her: Mmmm.

Him: I though it was next Saturday.

Her: No, Saturday.

Him: Not quite as soon as you thought it was.

Her: No.

Him: Is she having a nice time?

Her: Very nice.

Him: Is she?

Her: I think so. She's out of London. It gives her a bit of a rest.

Him: Yeh. Can't imagine what she does the whole time.

Her: No.

Him: The restaurant. If you have a restaurant, it's so much a part of your life, isn't it?

Her: I know, people around you all the time.

Him: That's right. The constant bossing and constant ordering and constant sort of fussing. And she hasn't got that. She's probably been twiddling her fingers wondering what to do.

Her: Hmmmm.

Him: Going to church every day.

Her: **I know.**

Him: Did you go to church today?

Her: **Yes I did.**

Him: Did you, Squidge?

Her: **Yes.**

Him: Did you say lots of prayers?

Her: **Of course.**

Him: Did you? Kiss me, darling *[sound of kisses being blown down the phone]*.

Her: *[sound of laughter and returns kiss]*.

Him: I can't tell what a smile that has put on my face. I can't tell you. I was like a sort of caged rat and Tony said: 'You are in a terrible hurry to go.' And I said: 'Well I've got things to do when I get there.'

Oh God *(sighs)*, I am not going to leave the phone in the car any more, darling.

Her: **No, please don't.**

Him: No, I won't. And if it rings and someone says: 'What on earth is your telephone ringing for?' I will say: 'Oh, someone's got a wrong number or something.'

Her: **No, say one of your relations is not very well and your mother is just ringing in to give you progress.**

Him: All right, so I will keep it near me, quite near to me tomorow, because father hates phones out shooting.

Her: **Oh, you are out shooting tomorrow, are you?**

Him: Yeh. And darling, I will be back in London tomorrow night.

Her: Good.

Him: All right?

Her: Yes.

Him: Back on home territory, so no more awful breaks.

Her: No.

Him: I don't know what I'd do. Do you know, darling, I couldn't sort of face the thought of not speaking to you every moment. It fills me with real horror, you know.

Her: It's purely mutual.

Him: Is it? I really hate the idea of it, you know. It makes me really sort of scared.

Her: There was something really strange. I was leaning over the fence yesterday, looking into Park House [the house on the Sandringham Royal estate where Diana was brought up, now a home for disabled people] and I thought: 'Oh, what shall I do?'
And I thought: 'Well, my friend would say go in and do it,' I thought: 'No, cos I am a bit shy' and there were hundreds of people in there.
So I thought: 'B***** that.' So I went round to the front door and walked straight in.

Him: Did you?

Her: It was just so exciting.

Him: How long were you there for?

Her: **An hour and a half.**

Him: Were you?

Her: **Mmm. And they were so sweet. They wanted their photographs taken with me and they kept hugging me. They were very ill, some of them. Some no legs and all sorts of things.**

Him: Amazing, Leonard Cheshire.

Her: **Isn't he.**

Him: Yeh, amazing – quite extraordinary. He devoted himself to setting up those homes. To achieve everything, I think it's amazing. Sort of devotion to a cause.

Her: **I know.**

Him: Darling, no sort of awful feelings of guilt or . . .

Her: **None at all.**

Him: Remorse?

Her: **None. None at all.**

Him: Good.

Her: **No, none at all. All's well.**

Him: OK then, Squidgy. I am sorry you have had low times . . . try, darling, when you get these urges – you just try to replace them with anger like you did on Friday night, you know.

Her: I know. But do you know what's really quite
un . . . . whatever the word is? His grandmother is
always looking at me with a strange look in her eyes.
It's not hatred, it's sort of interest and pity mixed
in one. I am not quite sure. I don't understand it.
Every time I look up, she's looking at me and then
looks away and smiles.

Him: Does she?

Her: Yes. I don't know what's going on.

Him: I should say to her one day: 'I can't help but ask
you. You are always looking at me. What is it? What
are you thinking?' You must, darling. And
interestingly enough, one of the things said to me
today is that you are going to start standing up for
yourself.

Her: Yes.

Him: Mmm. We all know that you are very capable of
that, old Bossy Boots.

Her: I know, yes.

Him: What have you had on today? What have you been
wearing?

Her: A pair of black jodhpur things on at the moment
and a pink polo neck.

Him: Really. Looking good?

Her: Yes.

Him: Are you?

Her: Yes.

Him: Dead good?

Her: I think it's good.

Him: You do?

Her: Yes.

Him: And what on your feet?

Her: A pair of flat black pumps.

Him: Very chic.

Her: Yes [pause in tape]. The redhead is being actually quite supportive.

Him: Is she?

Her: Yes, she has. I don't know why.

Him: Don't let the [?] down.

Her: No, I won't. I just talk to her about that side of things.

Him: You do? That's all I worry about. I just worry that you know she's sort of . . . she's desperately trying to get back in.

Her: She keeps telling me.

Him: She's trying to tag on to your [?]. She knows that your PR is so good, she's trying to tag on to that.

Her: Jimmy Savile rang me up yesterday and he said: 'I'm just ringing up, my girl, to tell you that His Nibs has asked me to come and help out the redhead, and I'm just letting you know so that you don't find out through her or him. And I hope it's all right by you.'

   And I said: 'Jimmy, you do what you like.'

Him: What do you mean, help out the redhead, darling?

Her: With her publicity.

Him: Oh, has he?

Her: Sort her out. He said: 'You can't change a lame duck, but I've got to talk to her, cos that's the boss's orders and I've got to carry them out. But I want you to know that you're my number-one girl and I'm not...'

Him: Oh darling, that's not fair, you're *my* number-one girl.

Her: *[voice much quieter in the background]* Harry, it might be in my bathroom. *[louder]* What did you say? You didn't say anything about babies, did you?

Him: No.

Her: No.

Him: Why darling?

Her: *[laughing]* I thought you did.

Him: Did you?

Her: Yes.

Him: Did you darling? You have got them on the brain.

Her: Well yeh, maybe I . . . well, actually, I don't think I am going to be able to for ages.

Him: I think you've got bored with the idea, actually.

Her: I'm going to . . .

Him: You are, aren't you? It was a sort of hot flush you went through.

Her: A very hot flush.

Him: Darling, when he says His Nibs rang him up, does he mean your other half or PA rang him up?

Her: Eh? My other half.

Him: Your other half.

Her: Yes.

Him: Does he get on well with him?

Her: Sort of mentor. Talk in the mouthpiece – you moved away.

Him: Sorry, darling, I'm resting it on my chin, on my chinless. Oh *[sighs]*, I get so sort of possessive when I see all those pictures of you. I get so possessive, that's the least attractive aspect of me really.
   I just see them and think: 'Oh God, if only . . .'

Her: There aren't that many pictures, are there? There haven't been that many.

Him: Four or five today.

Her: Oh.

Him: Various magazines. So darling, I . . .

Her: **I'm always smiling, aren't I?**

Him: Always.

Her: **I thought that today.**

Him: I always told you that. It's the old, what I call the PR package, isn't it? As soon as you sense a camera – I think you can sense a camera at a thousand yards.

Her: **Yes.**

Him: That smile comes on. And the charm comes out and it stays there all the time, and then it goes away again. But darling, tell me, how was your tea party?

Her: **It was all right. Nicholas was there and his girlfriend Charlotte Hambro. Do you know Charlotte?**

Him: Yes. She was there, was she? How was that?

Her: **It was all right. I went in in terrific form.**

Him: Where are they staying then? Nicholas's?

Her: **They are all staying with her sister down the other side of Fakenham.**

Him: Oh, Jeremy?

Her: **Yes.**

Him: Was he there?

Her: **Yes. Difficult man.**

Him: Very difficult man. Saw him at the ballet the other night.

Her: **Oh, he's always there.**

Him: Yes, always. So quite a long drive, then?

Her: Yes. But the great thing is, I went in and made a lot of noise and came out.

Him: Were they all very chatty?

Her: Yes. Very very very.

Him: Very kowtowing?

Her: Oh yes.

Him: Were they?

Her: Yes, all that.

Him: Darling, you said all your yesses and noes, pleases and thank-yous. You stared at the floor and there were moments of silence . . .

Her: No, no, no, no. I kept the conversation going.

Him: Did you.

Her: Yes.

Him: What about?

Her: Oh God, anything.

Him: What's she like? His wife looks quite tough.

Her: Suzanne? I think she's quite tough. I think she's given quite a tough time.

Him: Is she?

Her: Yes.

Him: So there with Charlotte and Willy Peel.

Her: **Yep.**

Him: I don't know him at all.

Her: **She's a very sexy number.**

Him: Quite. Bit worn out I reckon.

Her: ***[laughs]***

Him: Bit worn out, I reckon, darling. I wish we were going to be together tonight.

Her: **I know. I want you to think of me after midnight. Are you staying up to see the New Year in?**

Him: You don't need to encourage me to think about you. I have done nothing else for the last three months. Hello.

Her: **Debbie says you are going to go through a transformation soon.**

Him: I am?

Her: **Yes. She says you are going to go through bits and pieces and I've got to help you through them. All Libra men, yeh. I said: 'Great, I can do something back for him. He's done so much for me.'**

Him: Are you Squidgy, laugh some more. I love it when I hear you laughing. It makes me really happy when you laugh. Do you know I am happy when you are happy?

Her: **I know you are.**

Him: And I cry when you cry.

**Her: I know. So sweet. The rate we are going, we won't
need any dinner on Tuesday.**

Him: No, I won't need any dinner actually. Just seeing you
will be all I need. I can't wait for Ken to ring. And
I will be thinking of you after 12 o'clock.

  I don't need any reasons to even think about you.
Mark Davis kept saying to me yesterday: 'Of course
you haven't had a girlfriend for ages. What's the
transfer list looking like? What about that woman in
Berkshire.'

Her: Oh God.

Him: And I said: 'No Mark, I haven't been there for
months.' He said: 'Have you got any other transferees
in mind?' I said no. We then went off on a walk and
we started talking about Guy Morrison.

  He was telling me how extraordinarily Guy had
behaved towards me at Julia's party. And he said:
'Oh well, the only reason he probably didn't want
to speak to you was because you had been speaking
to you-know-who for a long time.'

  And so I just didn't sort of say anything. And I
said: 'I suppose that is my fatal mistake.' And Mark
said: 'You spend too much time with her' and that
was that.

  Then he said: 'I wonder whom she's going to end
up with?' And I said: 'What do you mean?' And he
said: 'Well, she must be long overdue for an affair.'

  And I said: 'I've no idea. I don't talk to her about
it. And I have only spoken to her twice since I saw

her.' And that was it – I just kill every conversation stone dead now. It's much the best way.

Darling, how did I get on to that? Oh, the transfer list. So I said no, there was no list drawn up at the moment. And even less likely there was anybody on it.

I tell you, darling, I couldn't. I was just thinking again about you going all jellybags, and you mustn't.

Her: I haven't for a day.

Him: You haven't?

Her: For a day.

Him: For a day. Why? Because you have no other people in the room. There were only three of us there last night. Four, actually. Mark, Antonia, their nanny and myself, and that was it.

And I definitely didn't fancy the nanny, who was a 23-year-old overweight German.

Her: Did you just get my hint about Tuesday night. I think you just missed it. Think what I said.

Him: No.

Her: I think you have missed it.

Him: No, you said: 'At this rate, we won't want anything to eat.'

Her: Yes.

Him: Yes I know. I got there.

Her: Oh well, you didn't exactly put the flag out.

Him: What, the surrender flag?

Her: **Oh.**

Him: Squidge, I was just going over it. I don't think I made too much reference to it.

Her: **Oh b*****.**

Him: I don't think I made too much reference to it. Because the more you think about it, the more you worry about it.

Her: **All right. I haven't been thinking a lot else.**

Him: Haven't you?

Her: **No.**

Him: Well I can tell you, that makes two ... I went to this agonising tea party last night. You know, all I want to do is to get in my car and drive around the country talking to you.

Her: **Thanks *[laughter]*.**

Him: That's all I want to do, darling. I just want to see you and be with you. That's what's going to be such bliss, being back in London.

Her: **I know.**

Him: I mean, it can't be a regular future, darling, and I understand that, but it would be nice if you are at least next door, within knocking distance.

Her: **Yes.**

Him: What's that noise?

Her: **The television, drowning my conversation.**

Him: Can you turn it down?

Her: **No.**

Him: Why?

Her: **Because it's covering my conversation.**

Him: All right . . . I got there Tuesday night, don't worry.
I got there. I can tell you the feeling's entirely
mutual.

　　　Ummmm, Squidgy . . . what else? It's just like
unwinding now. I am just letting my heartbeat come
down again now. I had the most amazing dream
about us last night. Not physical, nothing to do with
that.

Her: **That makes a change.**

Him: Darling, It's just that we were together an awful lot
of time and we were having dinner with some people.

　　　It was the most extraordinary dream, very vivid,
because I woke up in the morning and I remembered
all aspects of it. All bits of it.

　　　I remembered sort of what you were wearing and
what you had said. It was so strange, very strange
and very lovely too.

Her: **(unclear).**

Him: *[sighing]* Squidgy . . . kiss me *[sounds of kisses by him
and her]*. Oh God, it's wonderful, isn't it? This sort
of feeling. Don't you like it?

Her: **I love it.**

Him: Um.

Her: I love it.

Him: Isn't it absolutely wonderful? I haven't had it for years. I feel about 21 again.

Her: Well you're not. You're 33.

Him: I know.

Her: Pushing up the daisies soon, right?

Him: No more remarks like that. It was an agonising tea yesterday with, er, do you know Simon Prior-Palmer?

Her: I know who you mean, yes.

Him: And his wife Julia. Julia Lloyd-Jordan, you must remember her?

Her: Yes, I dooo.

Him: Do you?

Her: God, yes ... who was she after – Eddie?

Him: I can't remember. She lived in that flat in Cadogan Gardens, didn't she, with Lucy Manners?

Her: Yes, she did.

Him: She lost weight. You lived there for a while, didn't you?

Her: No, it's the wrong place *[could be saying an address like Feine or Alleyn Place]*.

Him: Oh! But the umm ... honestly, I loved going to [?]. I mean, they've got quite a nice house and things. And

I knew quite a nice Australian/Polish friend of theirs who was staying.

And God – Simon! He's 38 years old, but honestly he behaves older than my father. I cannot believe it. I find it so exhausting when there's peoplegthat age. They behave as if they're 50.

Her: **I know.**

Him: Anyway, we did time there. And that was it. We got back. A very quiet dinner. Mark was sort of exhausted from last night. And that was it really. He was talking about . . . hunting gets you gripped, doesn't it?

Her: **It does.**

Him: I mean, he drove six hours yesterday.

Her: ***[laughter]* My drive was two-and-a-half to three.**

Him: He's now talking about both ways. He drives three hours from Hungerford. He was hunting with – can't remember who he was with – oh yes, the Belvoir yesterday.

Her: **The Belvoir, umm.**

Him: That was three hours there and three hours back.

Her: **God.**

Him: And he'd done the same on Wednesday to the Quorn.

Her: **How wonderful.**

Him: Umm, tell me some more. How was your lunch?

Her: It wasn't great.

Him: Wasn't it? When are the Waterhouses turning up?

Her: Next Thursday, I think.

Him: Oh, I thought they were coming today.

Her: No, Thursday.

Him: To hold on to you, I've gone back to another point about your mother-in-law, no grand-mother-in-law, no, your grandmother-in-law.

I think next time, you just want to either outstare her and that's easy.

Her: No, no.

Him: It's not staring . . .

Her: No, no listen – wait a minute. It's affection, affection – it's definitely affection. It's sort of . . . it's not hostile anyway.

Him: Oh, isn't it?

Her: No. She's sort of fascinated by me, but doesn't quite know how to unravel it, no.

Him: How interesting. I'm sorry – I thought, darling, when you told me about her, you meant hostile.

Her: No, I'm all right.

Him: I miss you, Squidgy.

Her: So do I.

Him: I haven't spoken to you for 28 hours. I've thought of nothing else.

Her: **I know, I know.**

Him: Oh, that's all right. If it's friendly, then it doesn't matter.

Her: **It's all right, I can deal with that.**

Him: My stars said nothing about 1990 – it was all very sort of terribly general.

Her: **Fine, but it's definitely him WITHIN the marriage.**

Him: Right.

Her: **It's not ...**

Him: *[interrupting]* Did you see the *News of the World*?

Her: **No.**

Him: He's got to start loving you.

Her: **Yes, I saw that. Yeh. She ....**

Him: Did you? I thought: 'Well there's not much chance of that.'

Her: **No. I know. I know. But, um, definitely she said I am doing nothing. I am just having a wonderful, successful, well-awaiting year.**

Him: A sort of matriarchal figure.

Her: **I know. She said anything you want, you can get next year.**

Him: You should read *The People*, darling. There's a very good picture of you.

Her: **Arr.**

Him: Oh no, it's . . . where is there a good picture? In the *Express*, was there? I think there's a . . . wearing that pink, very smart pink top. That excellent pink top.

Her: Oh, I know, I know.

Him: Do you know the one I mean?

Her: I know.

Him: Very good. S∗∗t hot, actually.

Her: S∗∗t hot *[laughs]*.

Him: S∗∗t hot.

Her: Umm. Fergie said to me today that she had lunch with Nigel Havers the other day and all he could talk about was you.

And I said: 'Fergie, oh how awful for you.' And she said: 'Don't worry, it's the admiration club.' A lot of people talk to her about me, which she can't help.

Him: I tell you, darling, she is desperate to tag on to your coat tails.

Her: Well, she can't.

Him: No, she absolutely can't. Now you have to make that quite clear . . .

Her: If you want to be like me, you have got to suffer.

Him: Oh Squidgy!

Her: Yah. You have to. And then you get what you . . .

Him: Get what you want.

Her: No. Get what you deserve, perhaps.

Him: Yes. Such as a second-hand-car dealer *[laughs]*.

Her: Yes, I know *[laughs]*.

Him: *[laughs]* Do you know, as we go into 1990, honey, I can't imagine, you know, what it was that brought us two together on that night.

Her: No, I know.

Him: And let's make full use of it.

Her: I know.

Him: Full use of it. Funnily enough, it doesn't hold any sort of terror, any fright for me at all.

Her: *[sound of knock on door]* Hang on. It's OK – come in, please. Yes, it's OK – come in. What is it? Ah. I'd love some salad, just some salad with yoghurt, like when I was ill in bed. That would be wonderful. About 8 o'clock. Then everybody can go, can't they.**

Male voice: 'Bring it up on a tray?

Her: That would be great. Edward will come down and get it.**

Male voice: We'll bring it up.

Her: All right, bring it up. That'll be great, Paul. No, just salad will be great, Paul. Thanks, Paul.**

Him: How much weight have you lost?

Her: Why?**

Him: Darling, I am sure lettuce leaves aren't going to keep
 you strong. You'll run out of energy driving to
 London.

Her: **I am nine-and-a-half.**

Him: Are you? Are you? Nine-and-a-half. So are you
 staying in tonight?

Her: **I am, because I am babysitting. I don't want to go
 out.**

Him: Oh, I see. So is he going?

Her: **Yes. He doesn't know that I'm not yet. I haven't told
 him that yet.**

Him: I was going to say, darling. That was s***ty. You
 can't face another night like last Friday, absolutely
 right. But you are there, darling.

Her: **I know.**

Him: 1990 is going to be fine.

Her: **Yes, but isn't it exciting.**

Him: Really exciting.

Her: **Debbie said, I'm so excited for you. It's going to be
 lovely to watch...**

Him: I don't know, I've been feeling sick all day.

Her: **Why?**

Him: I don't know. I just feel sick about the whole thing.
 I mean wonderful. I mean straight-through real
 passion and love and all the good things.

Her: Becky said it would be all OK, didn't she? The most fulfilling year yet.

Him: You don't need to worry, do you?

Her: She's never questioned someone's mental state, or anything like that.

Him: What, his?

Her: Yes. Nobody has ever thought about his mind. They've always thought about other things.

Him: *[unclear]* . . . something very interesting which said that serious astrologers don't think that he will never make it.

Her: Yah.

Him: And becomes a [?].

Her: And Becky also said this person is married to someone in great power who will never make the ultima . . . or whatever the word is.

Him: Absolutely. Oh Squidgy, I love you, love you, love you.

Her: You are the nicest person in the whole wide world.

Him: Pardon?

Her: Nicest person in the whole wide world.

Him: Well darling, you are are to me too. Sometimes.

Her: *[laughs]* What do you mean, sometimes?

(Sections of the tape here, and elsewhere, are of such an intimate and sometimes explicit nature that they have been deleted.)

Him: I got up quite late, went for a walk this morning and this afternoon. Had lunch.

I only got angry because Mark gave the nanny too much wine and she was incapable of helping at lunch.

Her: I love it.

Him: He's a rogue, Mark David [?].

Her: Oh, Wills is coming. Sorry.

Him: Are you going?

Her: No, no.

Him: He's such a rogue, darling. He's the man you met.

Her: I remember. But I didn't recognise him.

Him: He's incorrigible.

Her: Would I like him?

Him: He's a sort of social gossiper in a way. He loves all that, Mark. He's got a very comfortable life, you know. He hunts a lot.

Her: He's got the pennies?

Him: He's got lots of pennies. He calls all his horses Business or The Office because when people ring up and he's hunting midweek, his secretary says: 'I'm sorry, he's away on Business.'

Her: *[laughs]* It's great to hear it.

Him: But, umm . . . an incredible, sort of argument last night about subservient women in marriage.

Her: Well, you're an expert.

Him: I kept very quiet actually. I could think, darling, of nothing but you. I thought: 'Well, I should be talking to her now.' You know, it's five past eleven.

Her: I know.

Him: You don't mind it, darling, when I want to talk to you so much?

Her: *[enthusiastically]* No. I LOVE it. Never had it before.

Him: Darling, it's so nice being able to help you.

Her: You do. You'll never know how much.

Him: Oh, I will darling. I just feel so close to you, so wrapped up in you. I'm wrapping you up, protecting.

Her: Yes please. Yes please. Do you know, that bloody bishop, I said to him . . .

Him: What's he called?

Her: The Bishop of Norwich. He said: 'I want you to tell me how you talk to people who are ill or dying. How do you cope?'

Him: He wanted to learn. He was so hopeless at it himself.

Her: I began to wonder after I'd spoken to him. I said: 'I'm just myself.'

Him: They can't get to grips that, underneath, there is such a beautiful person in you. They can't think that it isn't cluttered up by this idea of untold riches.

Her: **I know. He kept wittering about one must never think how good one is at one's job. There's always something you can learn around the next corner.**
      I said: 'Well, if people know me, they know I'm not like that.'

Him: Yes, absolutely right. So did you give him a hard time?

Her: **I did, actually. In the end I said: 'I know this sounds crazy, but I've lived before.' He said: 'How do you know?' I said: 'Because I'm a wise old thing.'**

Him: Oh, darling Squidge, did you? Very brave thing to say to him, actually. Very.

Her: **It was, wasn't it?**

Him: Very Full marks. Ninety-nine out of 100.

Her: **I said: 'Also I'm aware that people I have loved and have died and are in the spirit world look after me.'**
      He looked horrified. I thought: 'If he's the bishop, HE should say that sort of thing.'

Him: One of those horoscopes referred to you – to Cancerians turning to less materialistic and more spiritual things. Did you see that?

Her: **No I didn't. No.**

Him: That's rather sad, actually. Umm, I don't really like many of those bishops especially.

Her: Well, I felt very uncomfortable.

Him: They are a funny old lot.

Her: Well, I wore my heart on my sleeve.

Him: They are the ones, when they've got a five-year-old sitting between them, their hands meet. Don't you remember that wonderful story?

Her: Yes, yes.

Him: Gosh, it made my father laugh so much. Go on, darling. When you wear your heart on your sleeve . . .

Her: No, with that bishop, I said: 'I understand people's suffering, people's pain, more than you will ever know' and he said: 'That's obvious by what you are doing for the AIDS.'
  I said: 'It's not only AIDS, it's anyone who suffers. I can smell them a mile away.'

Him: What did he say?

Her: Nothing. He just went quiet. He changed the subject to toys. And I thought: 'Ah! Defeated you.'

Him: Did you? Marvellous, darling. Did you chalk up a little victory?

Her: Yes, I did.

Him: Did you, darling? Waving a little flag in your head.

Her: Yes.

Him: How marvellous. You ought to do that more often. That flag ought to get bigger.

Her: Yes, my surrender flag *[cackles]*.

Him: You haven't got one, have you?

Her: Yes.

Him: What, a big one?

Her: Well, medium.

Him: Is it? Well, don't wave it too much.

Her: No.

Him: Squidge, in this layby, you know, you understand how frightened people feel when they break down in the dark.

Her: I'm sure.

Him: I suddenly thought someone could have shot at me from the undergrowth.
Or someone suddenly tried to get into the car. I always lock the door for that reason.

Her: Gosh! That's very thoughtful. That's very good of you.

Him: I know. Darling, how are the boys?

Her: Very well.

Him: Are they having a good time?

Her: Yes, very happy. Yah. Seem to be.

Him: That's nice. Have you been looking after them today?

Her: Well, I've been with them a lot, yes.

Him: Has he been looking after them?

Her: Oh no, not really. My God, you know . . .

Him: Have you seen him at all today, apart from lunch?

Her: I have. We went out to tea. It's just so difficult, so complicated. He makes my life real, real torture, I've decided.

Him: Tell me more.

Her: But the distancing will be because I go out and – I hate the word – conquer the world.
  I don't mean that, I mean I'll go out and do my bit in the way I know how and I leave him behind. That's what I see happening.

Him: Did you talk in the car?

Her: Yes, but nothing in particular. He said he didn't want to go out tonight.

Him: Did you have the kids with you?

Her: No.

Him: What, you just went by yourselves?

Her: No, they were behind us.

Him: Oh, were they? How did he enjoy it?

Her: I don't know. He didn't really comment.

Him: No. Oh, Squidgy.

Her: Mmm.

Him: Kiss me please *[sound of kisses]*. Do you know what I'm going to be imagining I'm doing tonight, at about 12 o'clock. Just holding you so close to me. It'll have to be delayed action for 48 hours.

Her: **[giggles].**

Him: Fast forward.

Her: **Fast forward.**

Him: Gosh, I hope Ken doesn't say no.

Her: **I doubt he will.**

Him: Do you?

Her: **He's coming down on Tuesday and I'm going to tell him I've got to go back on Tuesday night. And I've got to leave and be back for lunch on Wednesday. But I can do that.**

Him: You can?

Her: **And I shall tell people I'm going for acupuncture and my back being done.**

Him: *[hysterical laugh]* Squidge, cover them footsteps.

Her: **I jolly well do.**

Him: I think it's all right. I think those footsteps are doing all right.

Her: **Well, I've got to kiss my small ones.**

Him: Oh no, darling.

Her: **I've got to.**

Him: No, Squidgy, I don't want you to go. Can you bear with me for five minutes more?

Her: Yes.

Him: Just five.

Her: What have you got on?

Him: I've got the new jeans I bought yesterday.

Her: Good.

Him: Green socks. White and pink shirt.

Her: How very nice.

Him: A dark apple-green V-neck jersey.

Her: Yes.

Him: I'm afraid I'm going to let you down by the shoes.

Her: Go on, then *[giggles]*.

Him: You can guess.

Her: Your brown ones *[shrieks]*. No, those black ones.

Him: No, I haven't got the black ones, darling. The black ones I would not be wearing. I only wear the black ones with my suit.

Her: Good. Well, get rid of them.

Him: I have got those brown suede ones on.

Her: Brown suede ones?

Him: Those brown suede Guccis *[laughs]*.

Her: I know, I know.

Him: The ones you hate.

Her: I just don't like the fact it's so obvious where they came from.

Him: Di, nobody wears them any more *[at this point, the conversation cuts off, then resumes]*.

Him: I like those ordinary Italian things that last a couple of years, then I chuck them out.

     It was a sort of devotion to duty. I was seeking an identity when I bought my first pair of Guccis 12 years ago.

Her: Golly.

Him: And I've still got them. Still doing me proud, like.

Her: Good.

Him: I'm going to take you up on that, darling. I will give you some money. You can go off and spend it for me.

Her: I WILL, yeh.

Him: Will you? *[laughs]*.

Her: I'm a connoisseur in that department.

Him: Are you?

Her: Yes.

Him: Well, you think you are.

Her: Well, I've decked people out in my time.

Him: Who did you deck out? Not too many, I hope.

Her: **James Hewitt. Entirely dressed him from head to foot, that man. Cost me quite a bit.**

Him: I bet he did. At your expense?

Her: **Yeh.**

Him: What, he didn't even pay you to do it?

Her: **No.**

Him: God! Very extravagant, darling.

Her: **Well, I am, aren't I? Anything that will make people happy.**

Him: No, you mustn't do it for that, darling, because *you* make people happy. It's what you give them . . . *[call breaks again, then resumes]*.

Her: **No, don't. You'll know, you'll know.**

Him: All right. But you always say that with an air of inevitability *[giggles]*. It will happen in six months' time. I'll suddenly get: 'Yes, James Who? *[giggles]* I don't think we've spoken before.'

Her: **No.**

Him: I hope not. Well, darling, you can't imagine what pleasures I've got in store this evening.

Her: **It's a big house, is it?**

Him: It's a nice house. Thirty people for dinner or something.

Her: **God.**

Him: I know. Do you want me to leave the phone on?

Her: No, better not.

Him: Why not?

Her: No, tomorrow morning.

Him: I can't, I can't . . . all right, tomorrow morning. Shall I give you a time to call?

Her: Yes, I won't be around from 9.30 to 11.

Him: Why not?

Her: I'm going swimming with Fergie.

Him: Are you? Are you taking the kiddies?

Her: Might well do.

Him: You should do. It's good for you. Get them out. It gives you enormous sort of strength, doesn't it? Have the lovebugs around you.

Her: I know, I know.

Him: Beautiful things pampering their mother.

Her: Quite right.

Him: That's what she wants. I think you should take them, darling. At least you are not battling with the rest.

Her: No, I'm not.

Him: Are you . . . *[call breaks again, then resumes]*.

Her: I'd better, I'd better. All the love in the world I'll speak to you tomorrow.

Him: All right. If you can't get me in the morning . . . you're impatient to go now.

Her: **Well, I just feel guilty because I haven't done my other business.**

Him: Don't feel guilty. They'll be quite all ... *[call breaks again, then resumes]*.

Him: Just that I'll have to wait till Tuesday. All right.

Her: **All right.**

Him: I'll buzz off and simply behave. I'll approach the evening with such enormous confidence now.

Her: **Good.**

Him: And you, darling. Don't let it get you down.

Her: **I won't, I won't.**

Him: All right.

* * *

Experts who first heard the conversation were straightaway convinced of the tape's authenticity. For it was not only the depth of feeling of Diana and her ardent lover that had been captured on the tape – the sheer minutiae of detail and the clarity of the recording were shattering. They immediately forced the question: Who made it and why?

1. Was the Diana love tape simply the result of radio hams scanning the airwaves and stumbling, by pure chance, across her intimate conversation?

2. Was the conversation monitored by a member of the household staff – perhaps a 'kiss and tell' merchant

anxious to elicit easy money from the tabloid press?

3. Or was this the work of a 'dirty tricks department', possibly operating on behalf of Britain's secret service or even at the behest of the palace?

At the time, questions were already being asked about Princess Diana's role in her uneasy marriage to Charles, though it was long before any public furore or suggestion that their differences were irreconcilable. Yet if Diana's telephone was officially tapped, the orders to bug the future Queen could only have come from the very highest level. It seemed beyond belief. The notion of a royal aide carrying out such a sophisticated operation was even less credible.

The story being examined by executives of the *Sun*, the newspaper that was first offered the tapes, was that two amateur radio hams had used a simple scanner, available at High Street radio stores, to 'capture' the conversation midway between James Gilbey's car and the nearest transmitter/receiver in the mobile phone network. These lucky enthusiasts, it was said, had recognised that they were indeed listening to the voice of Diana – and had the perspicacity to make a recording and to offer it to the newspaper.

The authors have investigated all theories. Every expert whose advice has been sought has found highly implausible the suggestion that a scanner was used randomly to pluck Princess Diana's conversation from the airwaves. British and American voice experts, security-service contacts, police and FBI – all veer towards the more controversial theory that the call was professionally monitored by a device targeted at Diana's end of the line.

Tom Owen is one of the United States' most experienced voice analysts. He was chief engineer of the Archives of Recorded Sound at the Lincoln Center and systems planning officer for the Performing Arts Research Center. Not only is he a certified voice-print examiner, he is in charge of vetting other experts on the Board of Certification of Voiceprint Licensing.

Owen says his test tape has been edited heavily and considerable time and trouble has been taken to 'clean it up'. An extremely powerful Digital Adaptor Filter has been utilised to eliminate background interference. It is an instrument that costs about $15,000 in the US and rather more in the UK. It is, says Tom Owen, 'restricted equipment, used by high-tech security organisations – such as MI5'.

Owen goes even further in his dismissal of the 'amateur' theory, thereby raising entirely fresh question marks over the manner in which the conversation was recorded. He says the tape shows no sign of the use of a mobile phone. There are no so-called 'drop-outs' (when sound is lost for microseconds) which are the trademarks of mobile phone tapes. There are no sounds of the phone handset even being HELD! The movement of a telephone receiver in a person's hand can normally be detected by Mr Owen's amazingly sophisticated equipment. There is not even the sound of a passing car (Owen's analysis would detect even the sound of the wind in the trees) which reinforces his view that the tape has been cleaned with a Digital Adaptor Filter.

Mr Owen says: 'I find no evidence of carrier noise, crosstalk or interference normally associated with mobile communications.' The whole scenario of the scanner is, in the verdict of Mr Owen, 'not a very credible story'.

An FBI expert on the tapping of mobile phones also gave his verdict on the possibility of such a conversation being recorded with a scanner. The FBI man has been involved in more than one 'sting' in conjunction with British law-enforcement agencies. He found that when working in the UK it was 'impossible to pick up cross talk . . . the conversations were always interrupted'.

The FBI man says that in Britain the mobile phone calls are 'bounced around' the frequencies to a far greater degree than in the US. This is simply because the cellnet receivers (aerials) are far closer together and they constantly 'fish out' the best frequencies and change them in a microsecond, without the users knowing. A scanner could not follow such changes. Indeed, says the FBI expert, when working in Britain he was forced to use not one but two scanners even to have a chance of keeping tabs on a conversation.

One of the most respected British experts on voice authentication is Derek Faraday, for more than 40 years vice-president of the Association of Professional Recording Studios. Mr Faraday, who spent World War Two serving in His Majesty's Radio Security Service, regularly appears as an expert witness in cases involving magnetic tape-recording in both civil and criminal courts, and before disciplinary tribunals and courts martial. He has been retained as consultant by the regional police authorities, the investigative branch of Her Majesty's Customs and Excise, the General Medical Council and by industrial security organisations. He is officially recognised by the Law Society as an expert witness. What then is his verdict on what became known as the 'Dianagate' tape?

According to Derek Faraday, the chances of such a recording being made by chance are 'infinitesimal'. Observing Tom Owen's tests in the United States, the English expert concurred with his American counterpart's findings. Mr Faraday points to the lack of background noise on the Dianagate tape. He says: 'A mobile phone conversation has an immediate "trademark", obvious to an expert. Whenever a person stops talking, if only for a second, the receiver tries to pick up any other sound and amplify it during the gap in the conversation. The background would rise and fall. But in the Dianagate tape, the background noise is level.'

Mr Faraday says that 'the most plausible theory is an in-house recording because the voices, especially the Princess's, are so clear and there are no radio noises on the tape'. He adds: 'This is a very professional recording which has none of the trademarks of a radio link. It was obviously made by someone who was ready and waiting, with all the apparatus ready for a recording, probably taken off a hard-wire line. This is the one conclusion that fits all the known parameters – except for the theory of the random scanner.'

Checks with Britain's two major mobile-phone services, Vodaphone and Cellnet, confirm that there would 'inevitably be some such electronic background or associated radio noise. Using a scanner, an even higher level of background noise – on *both* voices – would be clearly detectable on the tape.' It is not, and the only explanation for this is the use of one of the top-range Digital Adaptor Filter units.

An expert who was involved in selling surveillance equipment in the United Kingdom has confirmed that the purchase of such a piece of equipment by an ordinary member of the public would immediately set alarm bells ringing. Security clearance is required before the sale of these devices is allowed, because the customers for such DAFs are generally the military or MI5 and MI6. The Special Branch also uses them.

Contacts in the British security services are naturally reluctant to discuss the analysis of the tape. But an MI5 source who is a specialist in this field has told the authors that a 'security and protection unit' within one of the official security services would be the most likely users of the equipment required for such an operation.

So what of the various theories – all extraordinary, to say the least? Was the recording of Diana's phone conversation a million-to-one chance? Was it beamed to amateur scanner-users having previously been recorded by a professional? And if it was the work of professionals, who were they and why were they bugging the Princess of Wales's line?

The answer might, of course, be the Royal Protection Squad, who regularly make official security checks on the various royal households. But the organisation most likely to be interested in the relationships between senior royals and 'outsiders' would be a section of the Special Branch.

It would not be surprising to learn that the Special Branch make regular checks on the activities of the Royal Protection Squad, so would know of any covert phone-tapping operation in which they were engaged. Their inside knowledge of the Royal Family's private activities would be enhanced by the fact that they operate a hush-hush liaison group which links the operations of the Metropolitan Police and St James's Palace. The liaison group spends much time monitoring official royal movements – foreign tours and so forth – but its security checks run a great deal deeper. The Special Branch also have ready access to the experts of the Met's little-known and extremely well-equipped 'tape laboratory'.

The Special Branch are, of course, in constant communication with MI5 and MI6. There is a kind of Eton-and-Guards 'mafia' of senior officers who have worked in Military Intelligence. Anyone from a senior courtier to Prince Charles himself would have had little difficulty in recruiting the services of one of these experts to 'screen' in secrecy the telephone traffic at Sandringham.

The reaction of Princess Diana when she was first tipped off about the existence of the tape is hard to imagine. She would instantly have known it was genuine – and she would have known the effect its publication would have on her 'fairytale princess' image. The senior royals have always been aware that sensitive stories about them are kept 'on ice' in newspaper offices (Andrew Knight, chairman of News International, announced as much in relation to *Sunday Times* revelations about the Princess in 1992). Diana could have panicked. Instead she moved surely but swiftly. She accused royal aides of monitoring her phones and she ordered a debugging of her private apartments. Then she set about organising a 'damage limitation exercise' . . .

Diana promptly consulted with close friends over what action she should take to counter the crisis. Cold-shouldered by royal advisers, she felt that drastic and unprecedented measures were warranted. But most of all she needed a shoulder to lean on. Naturally, that was James Gilbey's. He gathered round her five others, who constituted the Princess's 'war cabinet'. They were her brother Charles Althorp and friends Carolyn Bartholomew, Rory Scott, Angela Serota and Adam Russell. None had to be sworn to secrecy; they were all so close, and they all knew the burden the Princess was bearing. Yet they could barely believe her bizarre plan of campaign.

Diana was so determined to reveal her desperation over her marriage to Charles that she was willing to sacrifice her public esteem by exposing her own mental and health problems to tarnish her husband. Diana's 'own story' would be told to the world and the chosen mouthpiece was the former Fleet Street royal-watcher, author Andrew Morton.

Said a friend: 'Diana was determined to settle what she sees as old scores with an awful lot of people. She had been pushed into the incredible position of wanting intimate facts made public. Most of us thought it was an astonishingly brave thing to do, but there was this tremendous feeling of unease – or of fear, if we were honest.'

Diana felt she really had nothing to lose. Her marriage

could not suffer any more than it had done already. Her relationship with the inner royal circle was already strained. She also believed that, with Charles being increasingly seen as no more than a mild but ineffectual eccentric, some of the pressure had been taken off just what the nation expected of *her*. She felt it was doubtful her husband would ever become King of England. She realised she would never be Queen. Her dreams and those of her bedazzled public would never come true.

So she allowed the reports of her private traumas to filter out, fuelled by her ever 'helpful' friends. When the stories began to circulate about her slimming sickness and her suicide attempts – including the occasion when she was said to have taken an overdose of painkillers before sounding the alarm – it all came as a relief both to the Princess and to those who had spent the years since her marriage desperately trying to shield her from any hint of scandal.

The Queen viewed it all with horror. She had already seen her only daughter's marriage fall apart, then that of her middle son, all in the most spectacularly headline-making fashion. Now she felt the latest revelations were potentially the most damaging of all.

The Queen had already suffered anguish over the way Charles had been pilloried by the pro-Diana faction. She angrily refuted accusations that rows with Charles had made Diana suffer from bulimia nervosa. The Queen told a friend: 'It was not the unhappy state of Diana's marriage that caused her bulimia – it was the bulimia that wrecked my son's marriage.'

If Princess Diana felt she had passed through the saddest, most challenging time in her life, she was wrong. Shortly before the shock revelations were unleashed on the world, Diana was on a skiing trip when Earl Spencer died in hospital. Returning to Britain as soon as was humanly possible, she was nevertheless wracked with guilt that she had not been with the father she worshipped in his final hours. She felt alone in her grief. Charles, as usual, was unable to provide the emotional crutch she so desperately needed.

The shock revelations of Diana's personal problems came out that summer in a book entitled *Diana, Her True Story* by the former Fleet Street journalist Andrew Morton. The book, seen by many as Diana firing the first broadside at the Royal Family and her husband, sparked an all-out war. Friends of Charles hit back, claiming Diana had continually gone out of her way to stage public appearances that ensured herself good publicity. They alleged that she deliberately organised engagements on the same day as Charles was due to make personally important speeches or visits, knowing she would steal his thunder. In short, it was suggested, far from being the sweet-natured wife, Diana was really a vixen.

Another book, serialised in newspapers the same year, was even more sensational. The author was quite a story in her own right, being a beautiful, titled socialite who had been brought up as a boy. However, the allegations of Lady Colin Campbell (one being that Diana had a 'string of lovers', including her ex-detective) were considered so outrageous that the Princess was little affected by them.

However, there was another woman for whom all the adverse publicity was exceptionally embarrassing. Diana's older sister, Jane, was torn between supporting the emotionally weakened Princess and sticking with the Royal Family's stiff-upper-lip party line. Jane is married to the Queen's private secretary, Sir Robert Fellowes. Jane could not condone the unofficial publicity campaign Diana had started for herself, yet at the same time she also felt desperately sad for her sister. The two women found themselves in a very strained situation.

Matters were brought to a head when Diana tackled Sir Robert Fellowes over the supposed bugging of her private phone calls at both Kensington Palace and Highgrove. The Princess said certain conversations with close friends had filtered back to her. She claimed it was all a palace ploy to provide proof that she had masterminded the leaking of revelations in Andrew Morton's book. Courtiers dismissed her allegations as paranoia.

How cruelly wrong they were! The truth about the bugging was bound one day to emerge. Charles's friends would take comfort from the tape-recording of Diana and her admirer. It does, after all, redress the balance of public opinion in his favour. The Prince had long been cast solely in the role of marriage-wrecker. The existence of the tape was to change all that — and make many people believe that Diana must share the blame.

Throughout all the private traumas, the Princess of Wales had always managed to keep her emotions under control when she ventured out in public. It was no easy task. The eyes of the whole world were upon her. It took

Diana back to those weeks before her marriage to Charles, and to that day when she fled weeping from the polo field. In amazing, unprecedented scenes, the Princess of Wales again found herself sobbing in full public view. Desperately trying to carry out her official duties as normally as possible in the midst of all the dramatic newspaper coverage, Diana visited a hospice on 11 June 1992 to cheer up the terminally ill patients. A crowd of hundreds welcomed her as if greeting a saint. 'We love you,' they told her. It was all too much for Diana. Despite biting her bottom lip and trying to carry on with the visit, she was overcome. The Princess of Wales broke down and had to flee. Some of the most startling royal pictures ever seen hit the front pages the next day – Diana, her face creased with sadness, weeping pitifully.

Were those tears for the patients? For her marriage? For her family? For herself? Or were they the most honest, humble reaction to the words of Bill Davidson, Chairman of the Queenscourt Cancer Hospice at Southport, Merseyside, who had just told her: 'By your example, you have won the admiration and devotion of caring people worldwide. God bless you and may you always remain, Ma'am, just you.'

Conclusion

Is there any future for the monarchy in Britain? That question, once unthinkable outside downright republican circles, is now being asked by the growing number of previously loyal subjects who have lost their respect for the institution. In the preceding chapters, we believe we have shown why that respect was never merited – and why the House of Windsor rests on shaky foundations.

There can be no doubt that there has been a remarkable sea-change in the British public's opinion of, and attitude to, the Royal Family. This has mainly been caused by the enormous upheavals in our society that have occurred during the Queen's reign.

When Elizabeth II ascended the throne, Britain was still a deeply conservative country and our sense of national indentity was rooted in its past. 'Duty' and 'Service' were the paramount virtues instilled into most children by schools which still taught respect, even reverence, for authority. The ruling class ruled; the masses were expected to toil without complaint and tug their forelocks to their betters. The aristocracy flourished, and at its head, given almost mystical qualities by the sycophantic media, was the Royal Family.

Times have changed so radically that the Britain of then and now often seems like two different countries. People are far more self-assertive and far less in awe of public figures or national institutions. They also have different idols; nowadays, pop stars are as famous as princes and receive as much, if not more, attention.

In 1992 Britain, the expectation of selfless service and duty rarely exists outside the staff quarters of Buckingham

Palace, where attitudes formed when Britain ran a mighty empire still hold sway. The Queen certainly believes she is serving her country selflessly and dutifully and therefore expects her family's hundreds of servants to do the same for the royals.

In these new, brasher, 'Jack's as good as his master' days, there can surely be little rational argument for continuing with a hereditary monarchy. After all, most countries manage quite happily without one and citizens in democracies like the United States of America relish the chance of being able to choose the head of state. It must be said that few countries have been as fortunate with their head of state as Britain has with Elizabeth II, but that does not alter the fact that a growing number of people have come to view her role as an irrelevance.

It is also sadly the case that the Queen has become less sure-footed in her understanding of these feelings. A popular monarch, in tune with the people and their changing tastes, can forge a sense of nationhood to the benefit of the state more successfully than any president. The monarch's job is to harness that national pride to the authority of government. However, if the monarchy loses touch with the nation, as Louis XVI did in 1789 and Tsar Nicholas II did in 1917, then not only the monarch but the state itself is in danger.

There is no danger, of course, of Queen Elizabeth ever having to mount a scaffold in the Mall. She is still widely admired as a person, even by many who have no love for the monarchy itself. However, there are pointers that Her Majesty would be wise to heed.

Her refusal to pay taxes, for instance, causes widespread anger and annoyance throughout the realm. Only the Queen and her courtiers seem to think it is acceptable that she should be free of a burden common to all her subjects. The liberal sexual attitudes of many members of her clan, especially the younger ones, are another source of irritation to a public brought up to believe that the Royal Family's prime role is as a moral model for the masses.

These fears have already been voiced by historian Dr Martin McCauley of London University, who said: 'The Queen has been attacked for not paying tax and the Duchess of York's acrimonious marriage split did the monarchy lasting damage. There is a growing movement in both Australia and Canada to break away as republics. The Queen sees both her empire and her family breaking up. The fact is that the Royal Family and what it stands for is disintegrating before our eyes.' The famous journalist Sir John Junor added his concern. Talking of the Queen and her Church, he noted: 'Isn't it the unhappy truth that both institutions are pretty close to being in terminal decline?' When a journalist on *The Guardian* tried to find a single courtier who could explain the constitutional reason for monarchy in a straightforward way, he had to report failure.

Pro-royalists, of course, dismiss the fears and criticisms as alarmist propaganda. The Queen has no more eloquent defender than Lord St John of Fawsley, a constitutional expert and former Tory cabinet minister. He points out: 'In a country where divorce is widespread one cannot expect the Royal Family to be immune. The appeal of a monarchy is precisely that these are ordinary people with ordinary problems, with whom others can identify. It is the combination of their humanity and their extraordinary lifestyles which makes for our fascination with the monarchy.'

Ivor Stanbrook, a pro-royalist Tory MP for more than 20 years, confirms that the Andy–Fergie marriage crisis was discussed by the cabinet which, under some strange rule of etiquette, then sent its good wishes to the couple and expressed the hope that things could be 'patched up'. Stanbrook declares that the monarchy is not in danger 'so long as the Queen and Prince and Princess of Wales are its main figures. The monarchy has been strengthened by the addition of Princess Diana and is more popular than ever. She has a sense of duty which the Duchess of York unfortunately does not. But the antics of the lesser royals do not matter so much. They just add to the institution of monarchy by showing a human face.'

However, these sentiments, though reassuring to those who cling to the belief that the monarchy can do no wrong, cannot disguise the harsh fact that the majority of British people now think most of the royals are doing great harm to the very institution they seek to preserve. The change in attitudes was perhaps most clearly shown in January 1992, when the *Daily Express* conducted a survey asking people to vote on which members of the Royal Family were setting a good example.

Only the Queen and the Queen Mother could take much satisfaction from the result. The Queen topped the poll with 54 per cent approval, one point ahead of her mother. Superstar Diana came third with 38 per cent. The rest of the royals took a pasting. Anne, on 30, was one point in front of her brother, Charles, who got little reward for his efforts to improve the environment. Philip got 16 per cent, Andrew 9, Princess Michael of Kent got 5 and Edward 3. Unsurprisingly, poor old Fergie was rock bottom with just 2 per cent.

Sobering reading, but did the Royal Family read it? Sadly, they seldom bother to scan public prints, thereby increasing their appalling lack of appreciation of what the people think and do. This lack of awareness highlights yet another threat to the Windsors' future existence. In common with other aspects of our society, the media have changed beyond recognition from the days in the 1940s when, as the young Princess Elizabeth, the Queen learned (or failed to learn!) the essential art of coping with the problems of publicity under the tuition of her private secretary, Richard Colville.

To the modern reader, what happened in those far-off days – probably fondly regarded as golden by the older royals – is highly amusing. Colville, an ultra-stuffy courtier of the old school, would simply summon a couple of well-vetted, accredited court correspondents to hear the royal 'news'. These 'trusties', suitably dressed in black jackets and striped trousers and wearing solemn, respectful expressions befitting their station, turned up to be told, again with due solemnity, that the Princess would soon be visiting a hospital or a flower show or going on holiday to Balmoral. Questions were actively discouraged and it was unthinkable that the newsmen would embellish the terse details given to them.

These briefings, if they could be so described, were non-events of stupefying, stultifying tediousness. They did little of real value for the Royal Family and even less for the newspapers and broadcasting organisations. More importantly, they did nothing to provide the young Princess with the proper understanding of the importance of the media which might have helped her to be better prepared for the days when the newspapers, especially the mass-selling tabloid ones, became very different animals indeed.

However, as Elizabeth inherited a court where little had changed since the thirties, she failed to realise just how outdated and patronising the palace seemed to both press and public. Although the royal publicity machine has, grudgingly, changed for the better, the senior royals still find the whole idea of communicating with the people highly distasteful. The Queen herself is not a great news-paper reader, although *Sporting Life* is a must, especially when her horses are running in big races. She relies on the brief digest of the morning papers prepared for her every day by the small Buckingham Palace press team which scans the prints for every mention of the royals. This digest is presented to her along with her governmental papers. 'She often glances through them,' said one palace adviser.

This lack of awareness might explain why, when the royals have tried to use publicity to their own benefit, they have failed to grasp what a two-edged sword it can be. Although the royals use the printed media badly, and have a highly uneasy relationship with them, they have been more successful with TV. The Queen proved herself to be an astute operator when she first decided to allow the cameras to reveal the inner workings of 'the Firm'.

Encouraged by the huge success of a TV documentary entitled *Royal Family* in 1969, she followed up with *Elizabeth R* to mark her 40 years on the throne. Both programmes revealed her warmth as a person without reducing her 'separateness'. The monarchy, once deified, was brought into every sitting room. *Elizabeth R* broke records without losing any respect in the process. The Queen could afford to pat herself on the back.

Unfortunately, other royals were not so successful when they ventured before the cameras. The Duchess of York was interviewed by Sue Lawley, Prince Andrew by Selina Scott, Anne went on Terry Wogan's chat show and Charles on Michael Aspel's. The blunt truth is that they managed only to make unwitting laughing stocks of themselves.

'The Firm' seems at last to have realised that publicity is an important weapon in the royal armoury, perhaps the most important of all in a world of wall-to-wall communication, but this particular weapon is now backfiring more than it is hitting the target. In his book *Elizabeth R: The Role of the Monarchy*, analyst Anthony Jay wrote: 'In many ways the Royal Family are bestowing the gift of publicity. But you cannot bestow it unless you have it. Publicity is a two-edged sword. You can, of course, shun all publicity, but once you accept it you cannot restrict it to favourable publicity. You have to take what you get.'

Undoubtedly, the royals have had much to take as the press has clinically dissected their lifestyles. There is no question that the Windsors have retained their interest for the public. Every major royal story sells thousands more papers, and international magazines know that a cover picture of Diana is a godsend to the circulation department.

If familiarity breeds contempt, then publicity must surely speed the process. Especially the relentless, pitiless publicity the royals now receive. This must be even more stressful to the Windsors because familiarity is not what they really crave or expect. They still want, above all else, respect, dignity and privacy. Overstep the line with them and their wrath is ill-concealed. Every so often the mask slips and we are allowed to see a glimpse of their *real* opinions of themselves and us. Princess Margaret was once laughing and joking with a group of old friends, a glass of whisky in one hand and a cigarette holder to her lips. Forgetfully, one of the friends addressed her as 'Margaret'. The room froze as the Princess, with withering Windsor contempt, icily informed the red-faced culprit: 'The proper way to address me is "Ma'am".'

This incident neatly illustrates the very real danger now facing the House of Windsor. Too much daylight has been allowed to rush in at once on a family which, by any standards, is clearly flawed. They have been shown too often to have feet of clay, and every fresh exposure adds to the groundswell of contempt and ridicule in which they are now held throughout every section of British society. These days a duke can, in private at least, be just as disdainful of them as any dustman.

We believe the Windsors have fallen badly between two stools. On the one hand, they were desperate to appear to be a modern, ordinary family whose problems should be forgotten and forgiven, but it is clear the royals still hanker wistfully for the old days when they were above criticism and allowed to glide through a privileged world set apart from mere mortals.

Philip Ziegler, author of *Crown and People*, pointed out that it was by keeping aloof from ordinary people, by surrounding themselves with a glittering court of aristocrats, with castles, jewels and lands, that monarchs preserved their mystique. There is little mystique left about the Windsors. The Queen and members of her family are now constantly revealed as being only too vulnerable human beings. Divorce, separation, scandal and greed tear apart their dynasty. Its members are depicted 'warts and all' in the press. They are openly attacked and ridiculed, often with telling accuracy. Can they now possibly survive, having been brought so suddenly and so cruelly down to earth? Our conclusion, reached with genuine regret, is that it is too late. Too much damage has been done and there is now too deep a well of resentment against them among their paymasters, the public.

Prince Philip once told the Canadian people during a state visit: 'The answer to this question of the monarchy is very simple: if people don't like it they should change it. The monarchy exists not for its own benefit, but for that of the country.' It was typical plain speaking from the straightest-talking member of the illustrious clan, and he was right.

The people *are* forcing change on the Royal Family, who have previously resisted any attempt to make them face up to the facts of life as it is lived now. The crucial question is whether the changes will be enough to satisfy the public that the monarchy is worth keeping and can play a vibrant role in the coming century. We fear they won't and that the institution that has, until now, seemed such an enduring fixture of British life is doomed to wither and die. It will finally be destroyed by the Windsors' own efforts at making it too ordinary, with power and influence weakened to the level of the Grimaldis of Monaco. It will limp along as a virtual circus act for tourists until the people tire of the distressing spectacle and simply say: 'No more'.

There is still hope while Elizabeth is on the throne, deftly trying to walk the tightrope between royal grandeur and being one of the folks, but it is not Elizabeth herself who will seal the fate of the House of Windsor. It is *all* of 'the Firm'. As with any other firm, survival depends on whether anyone wants to purchase the goods.

The rot **has** long set in and the customers are growing increasingly hesitant about buying the damaged goods. Only the Queen, with her dignity still intact despite all her tribulations, retains her value. After her, the writing is on the wall for the dishonourable House of Windsor and they will have only themselves to blame.